HOW CHINESE MANAGERS LEARN

STUDIES ON THE CHINESE ECONOMY

General Editors: Peter Nolan, Lecturer in Economics and Politics, University of Cambridge and Fellow and Director of Studies in Economics, Jesus College, Cambridge, England, and Dong Fureng, Professor, Chinese Academy of Social Sciences, Beijing, China

For a long period in history China's economy was the most advanced in the world. In the twenty-first century China may well be at the centre of world economic development. This series will analyse issues in the China's current economic development, and shed light upon that process by examining China's economic history. It will contain a wide range of books on the Chinese economy past and present. The series will include not only studies written by leading Western authorities, but will publish translations of the most important works on the Chinese economy produced within China. It intends to make a major contribution towards understanding this immensely important part of the world economy.

Published

J.J. Guo
PRICE REFORM IN CHINA, 1979–86

Zhu Ling
RURAL REFORM AND PEASANT INCOME IN CHINA: The Impact of China's Post-Mao Rural Reforms in Selected Regions

Michael Korzec
LABOUR AND THE FAILURE OF REFORM IN CHINA

Malcolm Warner
HOW CHINESE MANAGERS LEARN

Gordon White (*editor*)
THE CHINESE STATE IN THE ERA OF ECONOMIC REFORM

Wang Xiaoqiang and Bai Nanfeng (*translated by Angela Knox*)
THE POVERTY OF PLENTY

Xun-Hai Zhang
ENTERPRISE REFORMS IN A CENTRALLY PLANNED ECONOMY

Forthcoming

Li Bozhong
THE ECONOMY OF JIANGNAN IN LATE MING AND EARLY QUING

Wu Cheng-Ming and Xu Dixin
CHINA'S CAPITALIST SPROUTS, Vols 1–3

Hua Sheng
THEORETICAL DEBATES IN CHINESE ECONOMIC REFORM

Hua Sheng, Zhang Xie Jung and Luo Xiao Pong
CHINESE REFORM AND STATE SOCIALISM

Akio Takahara
POLITICS OF WAGE REFORM IN POST-REVOLUTIONARY CHINA

I-Chaun Wu-Beyens
FERTILITY CONTROL 1949–86: Politics in the People's Republic of China

Lin Zili
CHINA'S SOCIALIST ECONOMY

How Chinese Managers Learn

Management and Industrial Training in China

Malcolm Warner
Fellow of Wolfson College, Cambridge

Foreword by
John Child
Guinness Professor of Management Studies
University of Cambridge

First published 1992

Published by
MACMILLAN ACADEMIC AND PROFESSIONAL LTD
Houndmills, Basingstoke, Hampshire RG21 2XS
and London
Companies and representatives
throughout the world

Printed in Great Britain by Billing and Sons Ltd, Worcester

ISBN 0–333–52707–0

A catalogue record for this book is
available from the British Library

Series Standing Order

If you would like to receive future titles in this series as they are
published, you can make use of our standing order facility. To place a
standing order please contact your bookseller or, in case of difficulty,
write to us at the address below with your name and address and the
name of the series. Please state with which title you wish to begin your
standing order. (If you live outside the United Kingdom we may not
have the rights for your area, in which case we will forward your order
to the publisher concerned.)

Customer Services Department, Macmillan Distribution Ltd
Houndmills, Basingstoke, Hampshire, RG21 2XS, England.

To the memory of
Professor Oiva Laaksonen,
(1924–1989), of
The Helsinki School of Economics

Contents

List of Tables

List of Illustrations

Acknowledgements

I should like to thank the following publications for permission to quote from or reproduce sections of previous papers: *The China Quarterly, International Journal of Human Resource Management, Journal of Industrial Relations, Journal of General Management, Journal of Management Studies, New Technology, Work & Employment, Organization Studies* and the *University of Wales Business & Economics Review*, as well as Pinter Publishers Ltd.

Foreword

The mobilisation of an effective workforce at all levels is an essential requirement for any successful economy. It presents a particular challenge for a country like China which has adopted an ambitious programme of economic development based on modernisation and the achievement of substantial increases in productivity. The training of large numbers of managers and technical personnel in modern methods has become a necessary condition for these intentions to be realised.

The need was clearly recognised in the policy document on economic reform issued by the Central Committee of the Communist Party of China in October 1984, which stated that:

> Reform of our economic structure and the development of our national economy badly need a large contingent of managerial and administrative personnel, and especially managers, who are both knowledgeable in modern economics and technology and imbued with a creative, innovative spirit . . . a mighty contingent of managerial and technical cadres for the socialist economy. This contingent should consist of qualified personnel in all trades and occupations for the whole chain of enterprise management.

While the Chinese have professed their desire to learn advanced methods from 'Western' sources, they seek at the same time to adapt these to a context which is both Chinese and socialist. As the economic editor of the official *Beijing Review* put it in 1985, 'We must absorb and learn advanced management methods which reflect modern socialised production law from various countries, including the developed capitalist countries.' From this perspective, there are two aspects to the training process – the mastery of modern methods and then their adaptation.

During the ten grim years of the Cultural Revolution education and training came to a virtual halt. The providers of education were relegated to the lowest rank of society and reviled for their 'intellectualism'. This was an aberration from the long-standing respect given to qualifications in China. The economic reform programme, initiated in late 1978, gave rise to a decentralisation of initiative (though not necessarily final authority) to the managers of factories who took on wider business responsibilities. Many enterprises, as they have become, were also given greater scope to engage in international economic relations through exporting and establishing joint-ventures with foreign partners. For these reasons, a major effort was launched to provide training in business management, including a number of schemes to bring in foreign experts for this purpose.

Professor Malcolm Warner, (who is a Fellow of Wolfson College, Cambridge), ably traces the background to management and industrial training in China today in this book. He considers the infrastructure of Chinese management training and then goes on to analyse in detail the various forms and levels of training available. On the basis of evidence which he has gathered first-hand over the past decade, Professor Warner provides a unique insight into both the achievements of management training in China and its present shortcomings. This analysis is enhanced by an instructive comparison with the experience of other countries. There is to my knowledge no other source on this topic which provides anywhere near the same up-to-date coverage or conveys the same informed insight.

Important as the subject of management training is to the Chinese authorities, it is also of vital concern to the many foreign companies which either already operate in China or are seriously thinking of so doing. Plans for staffing and systems in joint-ventures depend upon the assumptions that can be made about the training of Chinese managers – the technical content of that training, the attitudes it has encouraged and the extent to which managers have had the opportunity to undertake responsibilities which build upon the training.

Management development in China still faces many problems, many of which are addressed in this book. As has been found time and again in the West, the benefits of even the best training can be nullified if the management philosophy and climate of the enterprise is not receptive to personal development and initiative. Despite the considerable progress made towards realising the goals of economic reform, many vestiges of the old command system remain and continue to impose constraints on the exercise of managerial judgement and responsibility. Effective mechanisms for the transfer of modern management knowledge from either the classroom or the practical laboratory of the foreign joint-venture to the Chinese enterprise still do not exist. Some management training schemes, such as that run by the China–European Community Management Institute in Beijing (of which I was until recently Dean and Director), are making progress towards bridging this gap through linking the content of management education with carefully designed in-company project work, but this is a relatively small-scale programme and much remains to be done.

China is still very short of personnel who can manage modern competitive enterprises and run sophisticated technologies. This book looks at the efforts to make up the deficiency and should be read by anyone with an interest in Chinese industry.

JOHN CHILD
Guinness Professor of Management Studies
University of Cambridge

List of Abbreviations

ACFTU	All-China Federation of Trade Unions
CAIME	Chinese Association of Industrial Enterprise Management Education
CEDA	Chinese Enterprise Directors' Association
CEMA	Chinese Enterprise Management Association
CEMI	China–European Community Management Institute
CIDA	Canadian International Development Agency
CQ	*China Quarterly*
ECAM	Europe–China Association of Management
EC	European Community
FEC	Foreign Exchange Certificate
GMP	Gross Material Product
GNP	Gross National Product
HEC	Higher Education Commission
JTU	Jiaotong University
MBA	Master of Business Administration
NI	National income
PC	Personal computer
PRC	People's Republic of China
R&D	Research and development
SCRE	State Commission for Restructuring the Economy
SEC	State Economic Commission
SEDC	State Educational Commission
SEMA	Shanghai Enterprise Management Association
SEZ	Special Economic Zone
SUFE	Shanghai University of Finance and Economics
SWB	Summary of World Broadcasts (BBC)
UMS	University management schools
VEC	Vocational Educational Commission
YEMA	Young Enterprise Manager's Association

Preface

This book attempts to place the role of management education and training in the People's Republic of China in the context of the 'Four Modernisations' and 'Open Door' policies over the decade 1979 to 1989.

The research on which the study is based was only possible with the support of several funding agencies which I would like to thank, namely the British Academy, the Chinese Academy of Social Sciences and the Economic and Social Research Council, as well as the numerous Chinese enterprises and universities which many times offered their hospitality and time. I should particularly like to thank the China–EC Management Institute, the Chinese Enterprise Management Association and the European Commission for their invaluable assistance and cooperation. I should single out the following individuals for their kind encouragement and/or generous help: Peter Abell, Jan Borgonjon, Max Boisot, William Brown, John Child, Alison Cooper, Chen Derong, Steve Frenkel, Colin Gill, Wang Hao, John S. Henley, Frank Heller, Y. S. Hu, Brian Hook, Peter Nolan, Stuart R. Schram, Eduard B. Vermeer, Ding Yi, Jiang Yiwei, Bernard Wilpert, and Wang Wei. Last, I must thank Stephen Watson and colleagues at the Judge Institute of Management Studies, University of Cambridge (and especially Jo Grantham for administrative and secretarial back-up) as well as the President, Vice President, and Fellows of Wolfson College for their invaluable support in enabling me to finish this book.

Cambridge   MALCOLM WARNER

Part One
Introduction and Background

1 Introduction: Setting the Scene

INTRODUCTION

This book is intended to illustrate several general themes. First, it tries to shed light on the *modernisation* process and its implications for human resource development. Second, it addresses itself to the 'softer' aspects of *technology/knowledge transfer*, of which management training is one facet. Third, it seeks to examine the role of the *foreign expert* as an agent of organisational change. Whilst the focus of the study is primarily on management education and industrial training in the PRC, the treatment of the material is also intended to contribute to the comparative and cross-cultural study of human resource management and organisation behaviour. The collection of first-hand data has been informed throughout by such concerns from the inception of this research on Chinese management in the early 1980s, up to the present time.

The events in Tiananmen Square in June 1989 have, however, significantly changed the critical observer's perspective on the significance and direction of what had been achieved in a decade of reform. It may no longer be possible to extrapolate confidently the trends which appeared plausible between 1979 and at least mid-1989. Nonetheless, this account of how Chinese managers learn to manage must be seen as an attempt to place the developments between these two dates in context, and offer a balanced interpretation.

THE BASIC ISSUES

The first question we should ask is whether the idea of 'business schools' can be transplanted from the West to the East. It is difficult to say: perhaps 'yes', perhaps 'no'. China has introduced many Western management training practices as part of the 'Four Modernisations' policy. Given that the number of industrial managers who need to undergo training exceeds the current total populations of Switzerland and Norway added together, the size of the problem is

1

daunting. China's economic growth over the decade will be dealt with shortly: suffice it to note that China needs to feed and clothe adequately over one billion citizens. With around 7 per cent of the globe's cultivable land, China has to sustain 22 per cent of its people.

Since 1979, China has experienced a period of economic transformation as it opened its doors to the outside world. The 'Cultural Revolution' had earlier caused dislocation and imbalance in the period 1966–76. Afterwards, targets were set too high in 1977 and 1978, as official sources now readily admit. Agriculture was duly given greater priority (1979–84), together with small firms. The 'Responsibility System' was brought in, first in the rural and then the urban sectors, in order to decentralise management decision-making in industry (1984–88). The Sixth and Seventh Five-Year Plans, which ran from 1981–85, and 1986–90, set out technological and organisational changes, including an all-round reform of how managers were to be trained (see Table 1.1).

It is said that Confucius, praising a prosperous province he visited, commented: 'What a flourishing population!' A Disciple asked: 'When the population is flourishing, what further benefit can one add?' The Master replied: 'Make the people rich.' To which the acolyte responded: 'When the people have become rich, what further benefit can one add?' Said Confucius: 'Train them.' (Confucius, *The Analects*, translation D. C. Lau, 1979, p. 120.) Perhaps the Master's logic can be turned on its head. After the death of Mao Zedong, training became a vital precondition for achieving prosperity.

China had many 'bottlenecks' in its economy: the lack of adequately trained human resources notwithstanding. The educational fall-out of the 'Cultural Revolution' still bedevilled attempts to raise production, although as we shall soon see a number of reforms in education and training have been attempted. A major restraint on organisational change was the shortage of professional managers, especially in market-related disciplines. In the context of the 'Four Modernisations' (of Agriculture, Industry, Science and Technology, and lastly Defence) can we not see attempts to alleviate the shortage of professional managers, as a vital necessity?

Thus, since the death of Mao Zedong, China has embarked on a period of economic development. The Party Central Committee had stressed the urgency of restructuring the economy underlining the need for trained, competent people at all levels, capable of coping with innovation and new technology. In 1983, the government empowered the State Economic Commission to implement appropriate

Table 1.1   Chronology of background events

1911	Outbreak of the Nationalist Revolution
1921	Chinese Communist Party has its first Congress in Shanghai
1924	First National Congress of the Kuomintang (Nationalist) party
1925	Foundation of the All-China Federation of Trade Unions (ACFTU)
1934–35	The 'Long-March'
1945	End of the Second World War: the Japanese surrender
1949	The 'Liberation': the Communists take power
1951	Outbreak of the Korean War
1953	First Five-Year Plan announced
1958	The 'Great Leap Forward'
1960	Sino–Soviet Split: Moscow recalls technicians
1966	The Cultural Revolution: years of strife follow
1976	Deaths of Premier Zhou En-Lai and then later Chairman Mao Zedong
1978	Start of the new Economic Reforms in Sichuan Province
1979	Enterprise reforms extended to other areas
1980	Trial of the 'Gang of Four'
1981	Sixth Five-Year Plan (1981–85)
1982	Workers' Congresses set up in 95 per cent of large firms
1983	Substitution of taxation for profit remittance in state enterprises
1984	New Law in enterprise management in urban factories
1985	Enterprise Responsibility Contract System approved
1986	Seventh Five–Year Plan (1986–90)
1987	Food prices increase substantially
1988	Zhao Ziyang approved as Party General Secretary: Li Peng as Premier
1989	Tiananmen Square student demonstrations. Imposition of Martial Law, and fall of Zhao Ziyang
2000	Target year of 'Four Modernisations' goal for gross GNP to reach $1,000 per capita (at current prices)

training programmes. Since then, official policy has pressed 'economic cadres' at all levels to receive some form of training.

China was set to become a 'commodity economy', ostensibly not only to build socialism, but to ensure basic survival for its burgeoning population. Its leaders faced the awesome responsibility of feeding, clothing and housing over a billion people, around a quarter of mankind, the majority of whom still cultivate the land. A new set of economic rules was therefore introduced in order to move the PRC from a 'command economy' to one more responsive to 'market' signals. China embarked on a series of industrial reforms thought by many in the late 1980s to be more far-reaching in being market-oriented than anything attempted in, say, the Soviet economy at the time, although inflationary pressures have now led to a call for firmer direction from the central authorities.

Developments in training must here be seen against the background of the 'Four Modernisations' mentioned above, otherwise it is not easy to understand the logic of the reform policies. Formerly, a planned economy was regarded as the best way to achieve rapid industrialisation; for many years, the Soviet model was followed with substantial aid from that source, at least until the Sino–Soviet split in 1960. In the early days, cadre training courses were taught by Soviet advisors and technicians. There were over 10,000 Soviet 'experts' in China up to that time. An emphasis on production management teaching characterised this period for example (Chen, 1988). Later, cadre training continued but was geared to the economic strategies of the 1960s (1988, pp. 38–40).

Manpower and vocational training

Any discussion of management education in China will be more meaningful if placed in the context of manpower and vocational training generally. The system overall was still very short of skilled people, partly due to the depredations of the Cultural Revolution in the mid-1960s and early 1970s when more formal education was greatly disrupted. The worst shortfall has been of personnel who were capable of managing modern enterprises and running sophisticated technology. The electronics industry, employing about one and a half million people and constituting over 3,000 firms, was a case in point. There was a shortage of managers and technical specialists. There were too few applications engineers, for example, in the manufacturing sector, as well as general in-house engineering skills. Electronic engineers and computer specialists were scarce, as well as those trained to manage them (Khanna, 1986). Indeed, the production of managers, as well as scientists and technologists, remained a major priority.

The number of graduates produced by the system was clearly insufficient to keep pace with the requirements of the economy. China had critical shortages of key specialists in management (see Table 1.2), as well as languages, science and technology. Since 1978, over 2.8 million students graduated from Chinese universities and colleges, which partly remedied the adverse effects of the Cultural

Table 1.2   Comparison of graduates specialising in economics, finance and management

	Graduates 1928–47 (19 years)	Graduates 1949–85			
		1949–56 (17 years)	1966–76 (11 years)	1977–85 (9 years)	Total (37 years)
Total number of graduates in 10,000	18.5	155.44	103.29	242.62	471.35
Graduates of economics, finance and management in 10,000	1.9	7.13	2.17	7.68	16.98
Percentage of economics, finance and management graduates of total (%)	10.3	4.6	2.1	3.6	3.6
Average number of graduates per annum	950	4,194	1,972	8,533	14,589

Source: Qiu *et al.* (1988), p. 121.

Revolution, but it has not been enough. Education has also been encouraged to have greater relevance. By the mid-1980s, all graduates had to have at least one year of work experience as part of their educational programme. Restructuring of state firms and government bureaux had at the same time attempted to cut down overmanning but also revealed shortages of key personnel. Major problems arose in the output of graduates in foreign languages, especially English, computing and accounting, where only 10 per cent of those needed were forthcoming from the system. This insufficiency represented a major headache for those estimating future training needs.

Deng Xiaoping, it seemed, wanted rapid results: 'If the cat catches mice, it doesn't matter if it's black or white,' he once remarked. Managers could catch their requisite quota of mice, without their factory party-committee amateurs looking over their shoulders. In the mid-1980s, Zhao Ziyang, the Prime Minister at the time, added his authority to the reforms and demanded that:

cadres engaged in economic work [must]. . . . conscientiously learn economic management and modern science and technology. . . .

[and] all enterprises and institutions should train their employees in a planned way. To obtain practical results the content and requirements of such training should vary with the posts and ages of employees. From now on, in recruiting workers and staff members, the enterprises must provide pre-job training for candidates and enlist those who have done well in examination. This is to ensure the quality of workers and staff, labour-discipline, production-safety and good condition of equipment in factories and mines.

(*Beijing Review*, 11 June 1984, p. x)

A major problem of technology transfer, whether 'hard' or 'soft', was whether to choose an external model, or at least one or more of its parts, at all. If a country chose to 'import' an institution, practice or behaviour, it has to choose one appropriate to its level of economic development. Moreover, this import had to fit its cultural norms. If a country sought to change its economy, it had to look elsewhere for ideas as to how to train its managers to use the new 'rules of the game' and provide them with techniques to manage the new technology it imported. The managers had to learn how to respond to the market signals which characterised the more open economy at hand.

As the Chinese moved away from a command-style economy, they looked elsewhere for training models, turning to North America, Western Europe and South-East Asia. Chinese training experts often pointed to a variety of influences, from the 'capitalist' as well as the 'socialist' societies when interviewed in the mid-1980s. Of the latter, no single Eastern European country was particularly favoured, least of all the Soviet Union. Yugoslavia was rarely referred to without criticism: it was felt, for example, that the State there did not enjoy sufficient control over that economy. The success of the decentralised Hungarian economic model was, however, noted favourably. The influence of the Soviet model was clearly tempered by the negative experience of the period after the break with the USSR in 1960. Yet, there appeared to be no strong desire to learn from Soviet example amongst Chinese management educators, even if they were willing to look at other countries' experience.

MANAGEMENT 'WITH CHINESE CHARACTERISTICS'

Taking a broad view of the Chinese organisation, it has been noted that:

> Chinese organizational behaviour is a field of immense variety, as its context ranges from the politically dominated organizations of the People's Republic of China (PRC) to the extremely *laissez-faire* capitalist institutions of Hong Kong, with all varieties of organizational purpose, forms of ownership, technologies, products and services represented.
>
> (Redding and Wong, 1986, p. 267)

There has been a broad cultural base to economic behaviour, although it would be premature to see it as the only cause of economic success. It has been argued that there were core values 'which underlie social interaction among Chinese people' (Lockett, 1988, p. 486). Mainland China undoubtedly has shared many of these values with overseas Chinese, in Hongkong, Singapore, Taiwan and so on.

The interaction between culture and management has clearly affected the effectiveness of training in Chinese organisations, we would argue. But it has worked in a double direction, for it may not only have inhibited improvement when formal 'Western' management techniques have been adopted, but it may also have mitigated the impact of reversions to more ideologically explicit 'political' models.

Chinese culture, through the reliance of personal connections (*guanxi*), may have led to informal solutions to problems, irrespective of the formal bureaucratic rules. It was beneficial when it overcame planning rigidities, such as the case of materials allocation, but less so when it undermined managerial legitimacy, or led to possibilities of corruption. Lockett (1988) argued that there was a built-in contradiction between 'modern' – say, Western – management methods as promoted by the economic reformers and their impact in practice because of the cultural intervening variables involved. Group norms, respect for age and hierarchy, and so on may have undermined attempts to change managerial structure and behaviour, as we shall for example see in Chapter 8. The historical traditions of Chinese management have often weighed upon its recent features and policy innovations (see Table 1.3).

Table 1.3   Chinese management: historical background, recent features and policy innovations since 1979

Historical background	Recent features	Policy innovations
Tradition	Rapid change	Four Modernisations
Hierarchy	Formalisation	Enterprise reform
Confucianism	Marxist pragmatism	Market socialism
Centralisation	Decentralisation	Responsibility system
Classical bureaucracy	Maritocracy	Management training

Because of the need for cultural adaptation, the Chinese therefore wanted to develop a model of management 'with Chinese characteristics', as one of their experts noted:

While seeking for a management style with Chinese features, we must adhere to the principle of relying mainly on ourselves, proceed from the reality of the Chinese society, sum up our own practice and experience, follow the basic policies and development direction of our country, and extensively and selectively learn from the strong points of other countries worldwide. In addition, we must carefully study the unique culture, tradition and special features of the Chinese society with 5,000 year-old civilisation which still has pervasive influence in very diversified fields in the nation's activities and development. Such old culture and tradition of China does not exist in other younger countries like the United States. We are against inheriting everything ancient without analysis, hold to it and even 'swallow' ancient learning without digesting it. We are also opposed to either the adoption of a national nihilist attitude towards our nation's past or undervalue the wisdom of our ancestors. In general, by summing up and abstracting from our rich practical experience in the present and past, as well as by making foreign things serve China and ancient things serve the present, we can gradually create a specific management style of our own.

(Pan, 1988, p. 2)

Have China's top and middle managers basically sought *general management* skills more than anything else? Given that policy changes seem to occur more frequently than in other economic systems, was a degree of flexibility needed? Most of these managers had already received a specialised education, often in a technical, engineering or scientific subject. The problem did, however, arise of whether their training in a specialism was up to date. Another important consideration was whether the general management skills acquired on a course were too geared to, on the one hand, a Western-oriented business education, or on the other one with 'Chinese characteristics', and indeed whether the latter fitted the ideological flavour of the times.

If the manager concerned had acquired skills to deal with the economic reforms, how was he or she be able to deal with 'old style' planning? How was such a manager able to be an 'economic management cadre' again?

These questions did not yield ready answers. One thing was clear, that 'political' responses have produced less organisational effectiveness than 'pragmatic' ones in the past. But the dilemma for managers is that they wanted to 'survive' in the system, many wanted a 'quiet life' and strayed on the side of caution. What saved the manager's self-interest might well have been 'a strategy of maximising intra-firm resources of which he or she has exclusive control' (Krug, cited in Henley, 1990, p. 8). What was rational might depend on the rules of the game in the system or organisations concerned.

What the Chinese manager may have tried to aim for was not necessarily diametrically opposite from what a Western manager might have looked for in that the latter may also not necessarily be a profit maximiser or cost minimiser in neoclassical economic theory terms. Western managers have also sought 'political' goals within their own organisations, but it was probably a matter of degree. Western managers may be said to have sought to pursue greater business efficiency in approximate terms *vis-à-vis* Chinese managers. It was hard to compare the two approaches given differences in the cultural contexts, bureaucratic backgrounds, accounting conventions and so on. For example, as Henley pointed out, 'without an effective market mechanism to equilibrate supply and demand no rationalization of production occurs' (Henley, 1990, p. 9).

It was therefore difficult to define what is 'rational' and 'calculative' in the Chinese economic system, and at what time. It was also not easy for outsiders to decide where power and influence lay in Chinese organisations: a debate as to whether the Party secretary retained power in the factory after the reforms might have yielded different results depending on how closely one looked, and when (see Figure 1.1).

Deciding whether a management training programme would help Chinese managers was no easy task, for it depended upon *who, what, where, when, how, why* and *to whom. Who* was going to sponsor and teach the course? *What* was to be taught? *Where* was the course being held? *When* did the course take place? *How* would it be taught? *Why* was the course designed? *To whom* was the course directed?

PLAN OF THE BOOK

In trying to understand how Chinese managers learn to be more effective in their jobs, we have to see what they studied, where they were trained and how their training was linked to the industrial context in which they work. Chinese cadre training has evolved from the earliest days of the Revolution and has more recently become relatively professionalised. University level management education also has roots in the recent past, especially the inter-war period. Such developments will be looked at *vis-à-vis* the problems of the last decade, to ask if the degree of managerial effectiveness has risen as a result of the recent training inputs. This introduction sets the scene for what follows in subsequent chapters.

In Chapter 2 we shall examine the economic reform programme itself. Since 1979, China has introduced a set of economic policies designed to bring about a greater measure of economic decentralisation and delegation of decision-making.

In Chapter 3, the implications for management training of the fast rate of industrial growth are then discussed, and we move on to survey the main national institutions China has developed in the field of management education. Here we shall discuss the setting up of the Chinese Enterprise Management Association and its related bodies, as well as the nationwide system of examinations for managers.

In Chapter 4, the establishment of post-experience, executive training centres will be described and analysed. We will look at these institutions in some detail *vis-à-vis* their provincial settings in six major cities, their curricula, teaching facilities and so on. The specific 'foreign expert' assistance they receive will also be discussed here.

In the next chapter we shall examine university-level management education programmes. In this section we first look at the broad range of such training, then concentrate on six specific examples in major cities such as Beijing, Shanghai and Tianjin. Several of the University Departments of Management established in the last decade have their roots in pre-Liberation days, but their major growth has been since the early 1980s.

After this, in Chapter 6, we shall look at industrial training in

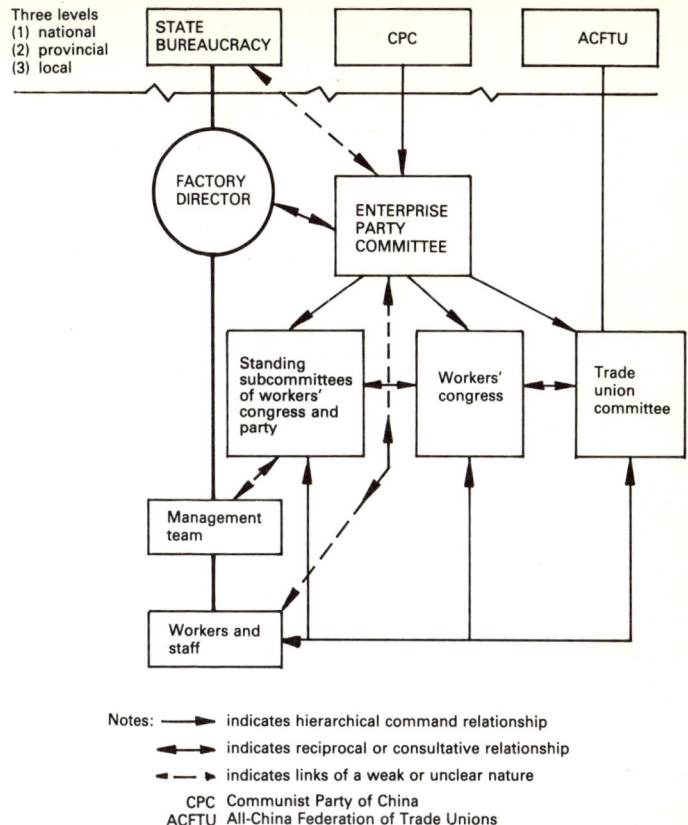

Figure 1.1 A simplified diagram of the decision-making structure of a Chinese state enterprise.
Source: Henley and Nyaw (1986), p. 642.

Chinese industry, as well as seeing how the more technologically advanced firms are coping.

In Chapter 7 we shall then compare management and industrial training in China with what happens in other countries.

In Chapter 8 we shall discuss, evaluate and sum up the importance of the training policies between 1979 and 1989.

2 The Economic Background of Chinese Management

INTRODUCTION

In this chapter, we examine the economic changes which have shaped the development of management and its training in China over the last decade. First, we briefly look at the demographic changes in the PRC; then second, we discuss the main economic trends over the period, highlighting the economic reforms taking place in the industrial sector. Last, we draw some conclusions *vis-à-vis* the managerial training needs of the economy. Providing for China's burgeoning numbers has become increasingly problematic. If in 1980 four out of five people had been country-folk, by 1986 over one in three were described as 'urbanised', according to the State Statistical Bureau (cited in Gittings, 1989, p. 4), although this may have been an overstatement. Out of a total population of over one billion, nearly 400 million people lived in or near townships and cities nonetheless, with food consumers growing at the expense of food producers. If the Party ideology had originally reflected the peasant character of the revolution, it later had to balance this with concern for the urban industrial worker, the vanguard of which was concentrated in state-owned enterprises.

The pressure of people upon resources continued throughout the decade. The total population for year end 1988 (see Table 2.1) was 1,096,140,000 (15,410,000 over 1987) with birth-rates during 1988 falling slightly. The number of Chinese in 1978 had, however, been 958,090,000 with a birth-rate of 18.2 per thousand (having been 541,670,000 in 1949, with an equivalent birth-rate of 36 per thousand). There has also been in the last few years the well-publicised 'one child family' campaign.

Table 2.1   Total population in millions

1978	963	1984	1,039
1979	975	1985	1,050
1980	987	1986	1,065
1981	1,001	1987	1,081
1982	1,016	1988	1,096
1983	1,028		

Source: 'Statistical Outline of China' (1989), p. 14.

THE ECONOMIC REFORMS

At least five phases have characterised the Chinese economy since the death of Mao Zedong. The first extended from late 1976 to late 1978. This period saw an attempt to achieve fast growth but without institutional change. A second phase of 'readjustment, reform, consolidation and improvement' lasted from late 1979 to early 1981, featuring rural reform and experiments with greater enterprise. Autonomy in decision-making started in Sichuan province, and was later extended to other parts of the country. The third phase from mid-1981 to mid-1984 saw urban and industrial reform slowed down, with an emphasis on greater managerial efficiency, but still extending rural reform. The fourth phase began in late 1984 with the implementation of the 'Factory Director Responsibility System'. A fifth phase from 1988 onwards brought in a period of 'stagflation'. China had embarked on a new policy broadly encompassing the 'Four Modernisations' which would extend from 1977 to the end of the present century, it was hoped (see Riskin, 1987). However, both political and economic set-backs were to dim this early optimism.

Deng Xiaoping had initially called for an 'Open Door' to the West to bring about technology transfer from the Western economies and Japan. The establishment of 'Special Economic Zones' along the coastal regions of China was to be a priority. Agriculture and light industry were to be emphasised rather than heavy industry (see *China Quarterly*, 1984). According to one view, China was embarking on the crucial first stage of economic modernisation with policies similar to those which had transformed the South Korean and Taiwanese economies and had allowed Japan to catch up with the West (*The Economist*, 1987, p. 1).

As Henley and Nyaw (1986) pointed out:

Table 2.2   Gross value of industrial output[1]

	Gross value of industrial output	Of which: Light industry	Heavy industry
1978	100.0	100.0	100.0
1979	108.8	109.9	108.0
1980	118.9	130.8	110.1
1981	124.3	149.4	105.0
1982	134.0	158.1	115.5
1983	149.0	172.9	130.6
1984	173.3	200.7	152.0
1985	210.3	246.2	182.7
1986	234.8	276.3	203.0
1987	276.4	327.8	236.9
1988	332.6	401.9	281.4

1. An index in real terms with price increases abstracted out.

Source: 'Statistical Outline of China' (1989), p. 10.

Coupled with this strategic shift have been a series of reforms introduced in various sectors. These included the greater use of material rather than moral incentives, greater emphasis on the efficiency of production, freeing of centrally set prices, reducing subsidies and giving more freedom to factory directors.

(1986, p. 636)

The consolidation of these policies was to be contained the Decision of the Third Plenary Session of the Twelfth Central Committee of the CPC on 20 October 1984.

Economic development had previously been decidedly fast (see Tables 2.2 and 2.3). The first *World Bank Report* on the PRC concluded that GNP per capital had expanded at between 2 and 2.5 per cent a year between 1957 and 1977, (faster than the 2 per cent growth of the population), *vis-à-vis* the average 1.6 per cent economic growth rate of other developing countries (cited in Gittings, 1989, pp. 105–6). All this had been achieved under a command economy, but one which exercised much less detailed control than its Soviet counterpart (*The Economist*, 1987, p. 11). As far as the trade union members were concerned, industrial growth permitted the enhancement of their welfare, as well as the growth of employment at enterprise level. As one observer noted:

Table 2.3 Indices of Gross Material Product[1] and National Income[2]

	GMP	NI
1978	100.0	100.0
1979	108.5	107.0
1980	117.6	113.9
1981	123.1	119.4
1982	134.7	139.2
1983	148.6	142.0
1984	170.3	161.4
1985	199.7	182.3
1986	222.0	197.3
1987	251.1	217.4
1988	289.6	242.3

1. Excludes non-material production as normally defined in accounting procedures in Communist economies.
2. Net Material Product.

Source: 'Statistical Survey of China' (1989), p. 8.

Between 1952 and 1978, China's urban economy expanded rapidly. Industry's gross output in 1978 was sixteen times that of 1952. Heavy industry had grown some twenty-seven times, light industry almost ten times.

(Lockett, 1988, p. 111)

By the mid-1980s, China was *seventh* from the top, in terms of absolute level of GNP, in the world 'league table', *sixth* in industrial output. She was *top* producer in power generation, *sixth* in crude oil, *fifth* in chemical fibres, *fourth* in steel output, *third* in chemical fertilisers, *second* in coal and cement, and *top* in terms of clothing production. The PRC was thus in 'the front rank of world economic powers' (Kueh, 1989, p. 421). In technological development, this was accompanied by a certain 'dualism', for together with backward factories in many sectors, China was well ahead in inter-ballistic missile and satellite production. Productivity was relatively high in the industrial sector *vis-à-vis* agriculture. In 1987, industrial workers who were only a quarter of the total workforce added just over a half to national income. Large and medium sized industrial plants employed only 2 per cent of all workers, but contributed half of industrial output in gross value, and through taxation 65 per cent of all state revenues (Kueh, 1989, p. 431).

Table 2.4   Inflation: data for 1987

	1978 = 100	1980 = 100	1985 = 100	1986 = 100
Staff and workers' cost of living index	188.5	172.2	140.5	120.7
Of which:				
Consumption goods	191.7	174.2	141.6	121.3
Services	156.9	155.7	129.2	113.8

Source: 'Statistical Outline of China' (1989), p. 89.

Between 1953 and 1978, industrial output grew at an annual rate of 11.3 per cent by value, with this rising to 11.8 per cent per year after 1978 up until recently. Between 1978 and 1988, industrial growth rose from 423 million yuan per year to 1,378 million yuan per year. Between 1979 and 1987, Gross National Product also rose rapidly, at an annual rate of 9.3 per cent per annum. However, by late 1989, the economy was entering a period of stagnation, partly due to the 'overheating', and partly due to the 'uncertainty' generated by the Tiananmen Square massacre, which affected prospects of foreign credit and trade (*Financial Times*, 8 November 1989).

Inflation had greatly increased over the period of introducing a socialist market economy (see Table 2.4). Whereas prices were more or less stable in 1978, by 1988 urban inflation was officially admitted as over 18.5 per cent, in 1989 over 25.8 per cent, and probably in reality much higher. By March 1989, 11,000 worker price-supervision stations had been set up by the trade unions in 40 provinces (Xinhua News Agency, in *SWB*, 17 March 1989). Official estimates recorded inflation as falling to around 4 per cent by spring 1990, however.

Urban unemployment had risen over the decade from a couple of per cent to much higher levels. By 1989, there were over 10 million officially unemployed, with another 7.5 million entering the work-force each year. Estimates of 100 million workers to be displaced from the land circulated, with some accounts envisaging a labour surplus of as many as 250 million. Official sources estimated that there were 'at least 15 million unneeded workers in China's state-owned enterprises' (Xinhua News Agency, in *SWB*, 24 August 1988). In the 1980s, for example, in my own empirical investigations in Chinese factories, several directors stated that no new apprentices were being hired (Warner, 1986a and b). Temporary labourers would

Table 2.5   Index of output per worker in industrial enterprises (publicly owned units with independent accounting, at 1980 prices)

1978	100	1984	126.4
1979	106.4	1985	135.5
1980	108.5	1986	142.0
1981	106.6	1987	151.7
1982	109.0	1988	n.a.
1983	117.2		

Source: Statistical Outline of China' (1989), p. 48.

Table 2.6:   Index of average real wages of staff and workers in publicly owned units

1978	100	1984	133.9
1979	107.5	1985	140.4
1980	113.8	1986	153.0
1981	112.4	1987	153.7
1982	113.5	1988	152.6
1983	115.1		

Source: 'Statistical Outline of China' (1989), p. 95.

also be released, and older workers retired early as the drive for higher productivity put pressure on factory directors. Wage increases averaged 18.8 per cent in 1989, but this represented a fall in real wages (*China Now*, Autumn 1989, p. 4), although they had been on a rising trend in the 1980s (see Tables 2.5 and 2.6).

Reliable statistics concerning labour disputes in China were not available for 1978, anymore than for 1988. Even so, miscellaneous sources suggest that a wave of strikes has hit the Chinese economy in the late 1980s. Accounts of disputes in the Shenzen SEZ were described by the Hong Kong-based Asia Labour Monitor Group. Out of 4,000 foreign-funded enterprises, only 1,000 were unionised (Xinhua News Agency, in *SWB*, 22 October 1988). Altogether, there were over 8,000 joint-venture businesses in China set up over the decade, constituting 2.7 per cent of the total industrial output by 1988 (*Beijing Review*, 2–8 October 1988, p. 20). Managers in such enterprises had stronger powers to 'hire and fire' than in state-owned firms (see Yue, 1987; Henley and Nyaw, 1990).

The pace of change was stretching the economic system to its limits (see Table 2.7). As Fairbank summed up:

Table 2.7: Summary of percentage increases in main indicators of the national economy

Item	Increase of 1988 over the years below					Average annual increase		
	1952	1965	1978	1980	1985	1953–88	1953–78	1979–88
I Population								
Year-end population	190.7	151.1	113.9	111.1	104.4	1.8	2.0	1.3
II Wage and labour force								
1. Labour force (year-end)	262.1	189.5	135.3	128.3	108.9	2.7	2.6	3.1
Of which staff and workers	848.9	274.1	143.3	130.3	110.1	6.1	7.1	3.7
2. Total wages	3,405.9	821.3	407.0	300.0	167.5	10.3	8.5	15.1
III Gross National Product			250.2	215.7	133.2			9.6
IV National Income	1,095.1	554.8	241.5	212.1	131.8	6.9	6.0	9.2
V Total social product	2,105.3	815.4	289.9	246.6	145.6	8.8	7.9	11.2
Of which total output value of agriculture and industry	2,261.8	843.0	290.5	249.0	147.9	9.0	8.2	11.3
VI Prices indexes								
General retail price indexes	210.0	174.1	172.7	159.7	134.7	2.1	0.8	5.6
General indexes of cost-of-living prices of staff and workers	236.3	196.5	188.5	172.2	140.5	2.4	1.0	6.5
VII Agricultural production								
Total agricultural output value	346.9	266.2	182.6	167.5	113.7	3.7	2.7	6.2
VIII Industrial production								
Total industrial output value	5,525.4	1,220.8	333.1	280.2	158.7	11.8	11.4	12.8

Source: Beijing Review, 2–8 October 1989, p. 32.

19

By the Spring of 1989 the reform program of the Four Modernizations under the aegis of Deng Xiaoping had been ten years underway. Problems were accumulating. Current trends if continued would risk disaster. Population growth was not being held in check. Enterprise in agriculture was bringing material prosperity in some areas but not in others. The reform of industry was stymied and getting mixed result . . . Corruption spread like a cancer . . . Finally, inflation was running at 30 per cent or more a year with no reduction in sight.

(Fairbank, 1989, p. 32)

Whilst we cannot speak of a complete reversal of the economic reforms, it is clear that a number of shifts in policy have occurred since mid-1989, accompanying the political changes along less 'liberal' lines subsequent to the Tiananmen 'events', as they were euphemistically referred to in China. It is, of course, moot as to how far the earlier 'liberalisation' extended. One view pointed to the 'Maoist legacy' of China's industrialisation strategy in the 1980s (Kueh, 1989). It noted how 'any policy initiatives after 1978 were bound to be influenced by Mao's industrial heritage' (1989, pp. 433 ff.), and the imbalances which have not yet been corrected. Heavy industry had relatively held its own *vis-à-vis* light industry and agriculture, and, in this view, was likely to expand again.

There had always been the possibility of a partial reversion to older macroeconomic policies albeit on a limited scale. The economic conservatives favoured a re-emphasis on central planning and tighter control by government. The roots of this shift in policy were not entirely clear, but the 'old guard' wanted to rectify the policy they believe had led to 'undesirable' economic and political consequences. They believed liberalisation led to 'disorder', be it further inflation or greater dissent. Above all, the older leadership wanted to re-assert *control* over enterprise managers and private entrepreneurs. They thought that the centralised control of raw material supplies and the restriction of imports were essential to putting China's house in order. (See *Financial Times* (Supplement) 24 April 1991.)

In such circumstances, it was likely that the role of the large enterprises which dominated the Chinese economy (and management training) would be re-emphasised. In late 1989, state enterprises were given priority; amongst other reasons, they could be more easily controlled by the centre.

Again, if the economy was suffering from 'stagflation', they were surer levers of maintaining output, especially of essential production, than the proliferation of small firms held responsible for the economic ills of the last couple of years. Non-state sector firms had grown from zero to about a third of national production since 1978. But resource bottlenecks and imbalances have been an increasing problem for such companies. By contrast, large state enterprises were to receive further subsidies to shield them from the consequences of the economic chill. It was precisely such firms which required more effective management and supplied the bulk of the senior executives sent for training.

The role of small businesses and private entrepreneurs was now given less prominence. They had risen over the 1980s to supply 4 per cent of GDP from an initial 1 per cent. The total number of individually owned enterprises had fallen from around 14.5 million in 1988 to about 12.3 million according to official estimates. Similarly, the numbers employed in such firms fell from 23 million to just over 19 million over the same period (*Financial Times*, 5 January 1990). Such businesses would not now be allowed to compete for scarce raw materials and energy with state enterprises. Private firms could previously outbid the state companies as they could raise their prices to carry such cost increases. A reduction in their rate of expansion would not in any event affect the activities of management training centres, for us we shall see later, they did not constitute any substantial part of their clientele.

The economic challenge was not recentralisation versus free markets, according to one view (Jin, 1989, p. 20): the correct approach to the challenge was to lie between the two extremes (1989, p. 20). The State would have to continue to play a leading role in modernisation, but encourage economic decentralisation, changing the forms of industrial organisation with some deregulation.

As the 1980s came to a close, a senior Chinese economist (Liu Guoguang) presented a more conservative view. He argued that:

> A certain degree of centralization of the economy will be stressed; administrative means will be used to restrict enterprises, such as a limit to credit and control of off-budget investment through bank-grants. Even these measures, however, are far from enough. China should also establish such economic regulations as are necessary to achieve sustained, stable and coordinated growth in the economy while avoiding sharp economic fluctuations.
>
> (*Beijing Review*, 15–21 January 1990, p. 16)

It can be seen from the above description of economic options that there was a good case for continuing the management training policies of the 1980s into the next decade, if only to counter the effects of such regulative activities. Even so, a mix of policies would probably persist, with the 'Open Door' in its place and the 'Four Modernisations' tempered by the 'Four Cardinal Principles' (namely, the socialist road, the dictatorship of the proletariat, the leading role of the Communist Party and *Marxism-Leninism-Mao Zedong* thought).

CONCLUDING REMARKS

Not only the rapid growth of the economy, but the problems of 'stagflation with Chinese characteristics' (Prybyla, 1990, p. 116) brought pressure to bear on the trained managerial resources available. The expansion of the late 1970s and early 1980s had highlighted the relative dearth of trained management and it was to eliminate this bottleneck that a nationwide infrastructure of management education and training was to be set up. In the next chapter, we shall look in greater detail at this attempt to establish an institutional framework to train more and better managers.

3 The Infrastructure of Chinese Management Training

INTRODUCTION

Any discussion of China's training infrastructure must be placed against the backdrop of its educational system (see Hayhoe, 1989). To compensate for the years of the Cultural Revolution, there has been a period of growth in student numbers since 1976. The number of higher educational institutions had grown from 200 in the early 1950s to over 1,000 in 1988 (see Table 3.1). Student enrolment came to over two million, of whom over 120,000 were postgraduates. But China had a low percentage of graduates *vis-à-vis* Third World states, let alone advanced economies. Only 1 per cent of young people of the same age group were admitted to higher education compared with 9 per cent in India, 30 per cent in Japan and 57 per cent in the USA (see *Times Higher Education Supplement*, 11 November 1988). China had only six million university graduates for a population of over a billion people. If China had the European equivalent percentage of graduates, this would run to 100 million or more.

The shortage of trained manpower not only led to the Chinese authorities expanding management studies at university level as we shall subsequently see, but also to the development of an infrastructure of training for practising managers. In this chapter, we shall examine the evolution of such a framework after 1979.

COORDINATION OF MANAGEMENT TRAINING AT NATIONAL LEVEL

After the economic reforms were initiated, the Education Bureau of the State Economic Commission (SEC) was given the responsibility for coordinating training in heavy industry and associated sectors (see Appendix 1). The Bureau itself was based in Beijing the capital, with national responsibilities, employing over forty officials. First, it dealt

Table 3.1: Education statistics (1952–88)

	1952	1965	1978	1980	1985	1988
Number of institutions of higher learning	201	434	598	675	1,016	1,075
Students enrolled in institutions of higher learning (000)	191	674	856	114	1,703	2,066
Students enrolled in secondary specialised schools (000)	636	547	889	1,243	1,571	2,052
Students enrolled in regular secondary schools (000)	2,490	9,338	65,483	55,081	47,060	47,615
Students enrolled in primary schools (000)	51,100	116,240	146,240	146,270	133,700	125,360

Source: 'Statistical Survey of China', cited in Beijing Review, 2–8 October 1989, p. 32.

with courses for the senior managers of large factories, such as chief engineers, accountants, economists and so on. In China's 8,000 large and medium sized firms, there were about 70,000 of these senior cadres. Second, it initiated training for top technologists. Third, it ran programmes to update technical middle managers. It can be seen that it restricted its activities to the management training system for the industrial sector. After the end of 1987, training activities were transferred to other bodies, such as the State Commission for the Restructuring of the Economy (SCRE) which was to oversee management training.

The standardisation of qualifications was seen as an essential part of the new managerial reform policy as rewards are to be more closely linked to grading, as well as performance. There was a general shift in the systems of rewards in Chinese industry, with the attempts at phasing out the former 'iron rice bowl' policy of equal benefits for all, indeed 'everyone eating out of one big pot'. The new employment policy established 'labour contracts', and was intended to end the 'jobs-for-life' system.

A nationwide examination scheme for top managers was introduced. The examination depends on different requirements for each sector in the economy. The content is based on the management knowledge and background of economic policy an enterprise director was thought to need. A National Guiding Committee for Examinations, responsible to the State Council, the equivalent of the Cabinet in the British system, supervised the scheme, with its members being drawn from various Ministries. There was also a parallel system at provincial level. The initial wave of examinations concerned the managers of large factories, but later attention has turned to those running smaller firms. By mid-1987, many top managers had taken the examinations. The exam was spread over two half-days. The level was difficult to compare with that of university courses, but as many managers were already graduates in other subjects it was claimed that the standard was exacting, yet at the same time, as many had technology degrees, their detailed knowledge of management was not very deep. The pass rate appeared to be on the high side, with over 95 per cent getting through: a sharp contrast with Japanese practice. Either Chinese managers were particularly studious, or the exams were not demanding enough. It was said that it was relatively difficult to fail candidates particularly in examinations in Chinese management training institutions. Perhaps there was the problem of 'losing face', or perhaps the egalitarian habits of past days died hard (see Lockett, 1988). There was also great pressure from the enterprises sponsoring the students for a respectable pass mark. In addition, with the negligible level of job mobility, it was hard for candidates to find posts elsewhere if they failed the exam, and they would have to face colleagues as well as their superiors on returning to their post.

A comprehensive network of Economic Management Cadre Training Institutes was set up, both in the provinces as well as in Beijing (see Appendix 1). These totalled over 100 altogether by 1988. There were around 7,500 full-time and 2,000 part-time teachers in these institutions. Every department of the State Council had its own training institute amongst this number. Half of them depended financially on the Central Government and half on the major cities. There were in addition altogether over 3,000 cadre training colleges and schools, dealing with both industrial and governmental personnel, of which about 170 were specialised in training administrative personnel. In addition, there were ten Senior Economic Cadre Training Centres (as we shall see in Chapter 4) mainly dealing with short-course training, with the Institutes offering Diploma courses of longer duration. In addition, managers were sent to university departments to study for Diplomas.

The SEC Education Bureau also dealt with a selected number of postgraduate courses for a period of time. First, it looked after the

Dalian Training Centre situated in a large sea-port in North-East China, which ran programmes in collaboration with the State University of New York at Buffalo, as will be described in Chapter 5. This Centre was one of the 'show-pieces' of management education in China, and was aided by the US Department of Commerce. Its MBA (which started in 1984) was that of the American university, not a local award. Second, the Bureau had responsibility for Masters courses in management through five selected institutions in other major cities, namely Fudan, Jiaotong, Qinghua, Xian, as well as Harbin Industrial, and the People's Universities. Apart from these centres, however, there were over 300 higher education bodies and over 1,000 polytechnic schools currently offering cadre management training courses.

Given the human resources shortfall, the allocation of managers or potential managers to training courses for most of the 1980s worked as follows: first, the enterprise estimated how many of its employees needed training, and second, this was then matched against the plan of the SEC of how many were to be trained at particular levels of qualifications, such as diploma or degree standard. The enterprise had to provide the funds for such training, whether in management studies or in other fields.

Managers in the system did not normally carry the financial costs of their own training, and normally received their full salaries while on courses. Many were reluctant, however, to be absent from work and home for long periods, as in other countries. There are further reasons why Chinese managers resisted training, such as innate conservatism, and fear of changing long-standing habits and attitudes.

Normally, training costs generally amounted to around one and a half per cent of the wage bill of the enterprise (see Warner, 1986b). The real cost to the enterprise was higher, given the penalty of covering for absent employees and candidates' salaries. If the factory was using new technology, the cost of the training ended up at a higher level. Additional costs were also incurred if the trainee had to be sent abroad to learn how to use new and sophisticated equipment.

CHINESE ENTERPRISE MANAGEMENT ASSOCIATION

We shall now examine how China has tackled the problem of developing institutions to prepare professionally a generation of better trained managers. To oversee the new policy, a coordinating body for management education in China was set up in the late 1970s by the State Economic Commission, namely the Chinese Enterprise Management Association (CEMA).

It is understandable that in order to diffuse new management ideas and create a forum at both national and local levels for managers, a national association had to be established. Like the British Institute of Management (BIM) and similar bodies in other countries, it would play an important role in not only promoting 'management', but *legitimising* its function in a society where until recently the very word itself was ideological anathema. The Chinese Enterprise Management Association was therefore a vital step in both creating a new status for managers as well as stimulating a climate in which 'management' as a set of ideas could flourish. Its main goals were described as:

> The modernisation of production technology and that of management (as) . . . indispensable and mutually promoting parts for modern industrial development. Modern industry needs a scientific management system. The declared purpose of Chinese Enterprise Management Association (CEMA) was to study and deal with problems in the system and methods of management and the related economic policies.
>
> (CEMA, 1983, p. 1)

It aimed to improve enterprise management, enhance management capability and serve socialist modernisation and construction through its activities (1983, p. 1). Management was to be seen as 'a branch of science, governed by its own laws'. Only by 'running the enterprise in a scientific way would it be possible to bring into full play the potentialities of the manpower and material resources, and to gain greater economic results' (1983, p. 1). As part of its activities, CEMA ran lecture courses, such as 'How To Be a Good Factory Director' to promote its aims (examples of its meetings can be seen in Table 3.2).

Founded in March 1979, CEMA brought together leading officials and experts in industry, government and research as well as universities (Warner, 1986a). It was set up as a non-profit-making entity, but its funds inevitably involve a government subsidy. The Association clearly had high status and was usually the first stop for VIP delegations of foreign businessmen visiting Beijing. The organisation of CEMA was based on its central headquarters in Beijing, with local associations around the country. It had over 2,000 group associates, over 4,000 individual members and over 3,000 enterprise-associated

Table 3.2   Examples of meetings sponsored and organised by CEMA

Topics	Participants	Papers
Experiences and Lessons of China's Enterprise Management in the Past 30 Years	156	50
Behavioural Science and Enterprise	110	32
Tasks of Enterprise Management in the Readjustment Period	180	60
Raising the Productivity and Economic Results of Enterprises	130	40
Rationalisation of Industrial Structure	75	53
How To Be a Good Factory Director	144	40

Source: CEMA (1983).

members. CEMA's governing board is serviced by sixty staff of the central Secretariat in six main departments.

A major problem *vis-à-vis* management reforms in China was that up to the recent past all too few people, even experts, spoke English (or indeed any other foreign language) very well, although some of the older scholars and practitioners spoke Russian, which they had studied in the 1950s. However, an increasing number of young professionals had mastered English either at interpreters' school, or by study abroad, and were given additional training in the management field to enable them to act as intermediaries and help contacts with foreigners.

DIFFUSION OF MANAGEMENT KNOWLEDGE

It was clear that an expansion of training for managers was vital once the economic reforms were introduced. Because the close linking of theory and practice has been a Chinese educational practice pre-dating the 'Liberation' in 1949, on-the-job training had also been part of this strategy. There was considerable motivation for self-study, and this was channelled into distance-learning and adult educational channels (see St John Hunter, and McKee Keehn, 1985; McCormick, 1986; Vermeer, 1988).

Thus far, the Chinese Enterprise Management Association set up a network of training activities involving:

- institutes/universities
- institutes with specialised courses
- state-owned industrial enterprises
- TV/correspondence schools/Periodical University and self-study courses
- MBA courses in selected training centres.

The aims of the policy outlined above were threefold: first, to build a top team of management educators, and to raise the standard of the training nationally; second, to avoid simply copying the North American model and take advantage of the experience with the 'Second World', rather than relying on links with either superpower; third, to create graduates versed in the practice and language of international business, with English as the *lingua franca* to work with Western European and (through the language link) with North American multinational corporations in joint-ventures. There were probably not enough graduates at this high level to go round and there was therefore a conflict between the needs of the business and teaching sectors. Even if the entire output of MBA graduates went into teaching, however, it would only amount to very limited numbers over the next decade. The number of PhD graduates in management would be smaller, even in several years' time.

Training management teachers became a top priority in the 1980s. The MBA programmes at Beijing, Dalian and elsewhere were designed to help produce teachers of management who in some cases have already replaced foreign professors brought in to set up the programmes. There were other programmes, as we shall later see, such as the Tianjin Enterprise Management Training Centre's programme for teachers which had sent teacher-trainees to Japan in rotation. There was also a similar programme in Shanghai, collaborating with the Federal Republic of Germany. Nonetheless, the total potential output of teachers was low, no greater than the low thousands in the period up to 1990. Bringing in foreign experts was expensive, and few spoke Chinese. Most were therefore brought in as a stop-gap solution.

How then to reach the 'mass' of managers at low cost? In order to implement the distance-learning strategy mentioned earlier, a new institution was set up in 1983, popularly known as the 'Periodical University', or to give it its full name the Economic Management Periodical (Joint) University (see Warner, 1986a). It worked in a similar way to the British Open University, although with less reliance on audio-visual materials than other media-based courses in China. It set out to enrol 10,000 managers a year, for the three-year course. Of these about seven out of ten were middle managers.

As it was very short of experienced management teachers, China planned to use recent graduates of its distance-learning experiments as much as possible. A major iron and steel corporation, for example, enrolled 100 students in the Periodical University, many of whom later became instructors 'in-house'. The company initially bought 2,000 sets of teaching material from the Periodical University, for the three years and eight courses. In addition to buying the monthly 'periodical', each person participating paid 50 yuan to enrol. This was not an inconsiderable sum, as it was not far short of an average monthly industrial wage for a trainee, and about £8 sterling at the time of writing. In addition, the student's employing enterprise paid a similar amount.

Against this background, the British Open University and CEMA discussed a joint-venture to produce distance-learning material for Chinese managers in both Mandarin and English (see Warner, 1987a). The scale of China's problem in training its vast number of managers underlay the attempt to bypass traditional 'chalk and talk' methods by using a 'high-tech' approach by which a few highly skilled faculties could diffuse case-material via distance-learning media, backed up by in-house support at factory level. It was early days however, as China had not yet entered the era of widely owned video-recorders.

Not only did large-scale state enterprises have their own educational programmes, but trade unions also had them. These were training institutions under the All-China Federation of Trade Unions (ACFTU) known as 'Workers' and Staff Universities'. The latter were collectively supervised by the Labour Union, the Labour Bureau and the State Educational Commission at different levels of validation (see Vermeer, 1988, p. 60).

It is hard to evaluate the work of CEMA but its national scope, its professional goals and the breadth of its interests were initially ambitious. Nonetheless, as an umbrella organisation for improved management education in such a vast country, it clearly had an uphill struggle, given the magnitude of its task.

Nonetheless, new managers' clubs have proliferated. Linked with CEMA, for example, was the Young Enterprise Managers' Association (YEMA) which started to run local training programmes, and the China Enterprise Directors' Association (CEDA) which held its first national conference in the winter of 1984.

In order to diffuse and popularise new business ideas in China, CEMA published many books for managers, for example: *Management Teachers' Reference* in seven volumes, *Teaching Material of Dalian Management Training Centre* in eight volumes, *Special Edition on Practical Management Techniques of Japan*, as well as an *ABC for a Team-Leader* and so on.

Each month, CEMA published a more accessible review called *Qiye Guanli* (that is *Enterprise Management*), which claimed a national circulation of over 200,000 copies per issue. In order to supply articles, the *Harvard Business Review* signed an agreement with CEMA's journal to allow it to feature translations of any HBR papers, past or present. The HBR was already published in six languages, and would now have an edition in Mandarin. CEMA also published the *Chinese Enterprise Management Encyclopaedia*, the first ever to appear in the People's Republic of China. Work on the encyclopaedia started in the early 1980s, and CEMA was made responsible for its editing and publishing by the State Economic Commission. The editing committee comprised senior officials and specialists from all over China, with 12 subcommittees in Beijing and other main cities.

The purpose of publishing the encyclopaedia was 'to systematise the evolution of enterprise management in China, sum up experience and introduce management concepts and techniques developed both in China and abroad, thus providing a comparatively comprehensive and appropriate reference book to managers, management teachers and researchers' (CEMA, 1985, p. 4). An initial print-run of a quarter of a million copies of the two-volume encyclopaedia was decided by its promoters.

Another new CEMA-sponsored development was the China Enterprise Management Consulting Company which was ratified by State Economic Commission, and based in Beijing. Professor Pan Cheng-lieh, Deputy Secretary-General of CEMA, and a leading Chinese management educator, became its General Manager. Under the leadership of CEMA, the company set out to provide consulting service to both foreign and Chinese organisations and train managers and consultants for those enterprises.

PROBLEMS TO BE FACED

The main problems facing Chinese management education in the mid-1980s were described by CEMA spokespersons as follows:

- The academic infrastructure was still not yet able to cope with the training implications of the economic reforms.
- The managers on courses, it was suggested, liked everything too formally structured and 'on the blackboard'.
- Active interaction needed greater emphasis, although it was resisted by many participants on courses.

Chinese enterprises also began to expand on-the-job training for middle and senior management. For example, CEMA sponsored seminars taught by foreign experts; the Japanese particularly offered training of consultants at factory level. Several European countries, such as France, West Germany, Italy and Sweden also provided help.

Chinese management teachers, in turn, were exhorted to learn from Western capitalist practice and, noting the good points (so the official-line goes), match these with their own to create a specifically *Chinese* model of management education. The priority-areas involved were mostly specialist, such as:

- enterprise management
- finance and accounting
- management information
- managerial economics.

Foreign advisors suggested that 'organisational behaviour' ought to be included, but this was controversial. A number of university centres eventually set up departments in this area of study. Previously, courses dealing with behavioural science had been mostly taught in sociology and psychology departments, as opposed to management faculties. There has also been the same rivalry as in the West between 'hard' and 'soft' subjects in management studies.

To encourage the development of a corporate identity, a professional body for teachers of management in China was set up in 1980, known as the 'Chinese Association of Industrial Enterprise Management Education' (CAIEME). Professor Liu Chunqin, based at the Institute of Industrial Economics, was its first Permanent Secretary. With over 75 universities and institutes associated nationwide, it had three categories of membership: first, general universities (for example, Beijing, Fudan and Qinghua); second, specialised universities (which focused on technology and engineering, for example Harbin Industrial and Jiaotong); third, financial institutes (for example, the Beijing Monetary Institute).

How then to compare the challenges the Chinese faced *vis-à-vis* British ways of training managers? First, and most obviously, there was the 'dual' nature of the system in each country, namely the split between university and post-experience sectors (as we shall see in subsequent chapters), although both overlapped to some degree. Second, the length of courses in the respective sectors was broadly comparable here and there. Third, the size and organisation of training institutions, at least of the elite ones, was broadly similar. Fourth, the curricular headings were broadly the same, at least in terms of the type of topics studied.

The Chinese system, on the other hand, faced problems different from both the British (and American) models both in terms of *quantity* and *quality*. On the basis of negligible previous experience, it was to try, albeit with insufficient experience, to build in *indigenous* elements in order to better cater for local needs. Given the very large numbers of managers to be trained, and given the lack of an initial infrastructure of management education, the problems were to be considerable, as will be seen in the next two chapters. In starting to move towards a 'mass' system of management and industrial training (see Chapter 7), they had to train their very top economic cadres first, to improve enterprise performance, but at the same time desperately needed many others as the 'trainers' of tomorrow: a difficult problem to resolve, as we shall shortly see.

CONCLUDING REMARKS

From this overview of Chinese management training bodies, it is clear that they had a long way to go to remedy the educational 'fall-out' of the Cultural Revolution. Far too many Chinese managers lacked formal qualifications commensurate with their responsibilities, and this was a major constraint. Indeed in the broadest sense, China lagged behind its neighbours, like South Korea, in industrial training. Economic reform required that managers be trained to cope with the enterprise-level decision-making, yet major discrepancies still separated the explicit aims of the reforms and the quality of management at factory level. Whilst considerable priority was given to management education, it still only affected relatively limited numbers of

China's vast cohorts of managers and we must remain cautious about its effectiveness. During the Seventh Five-Year Plan (1986–90), it was hoped that managers would receive training. Many of them were to obtain some training, but how systematic was it to be? Could the government achieve its ultimate economic goals by 1995 or 2000?

In the next two chapters, we shall see how China's management training strategy has been implemented in detail, at both post-experience and university levels.

Part Two
Management, Education and Training in China

4 Senior Executive Training in China

INTRODUCTION

We hope in this chapter to outline the development of senior executive training in China: a great deal has been accomplished since the economic reforms began in 1979 (see Warner, 1986c).

In order to do this we must look at the developments not only in terms of broad trends, but also in detail at the provincial level. The chapter will therefore cover senior management training institutions in six major cities in their respective provinces. These densely populated centres are all vital for China's future prosperity, namely (1) Beijing, (2) Chengdu, (3) Fuzhou, (4) Shanghai, (5) Tianjin and (6) Wuhan (see map in Figure 4.1).

Over the last decade, many changes have taken place, not only in agriculture, but also in industry (see Warner, 1987a). The reformers wanted decision-making to be increasingly decentralised to the enterprise level, in the context of a growing reliance on market socialism, albeit 'with Chinese characteristics'. The separation of the managerial and the party functions in the enterprise became a major goal of the economic reformers, although this met with varying degrees of success, and has remained fundamentally untested. In order to prepare China's managers for these changes, an extensive training programme was launched (see Appendix 1). Most top executives in the industrial enterprises which were run by the State Economic Commission (SEC) had been sent for training from 1979 onwards, especially from the larger factories under the SEC. Out of 450,000 production units, however, only a fraction were relatively important. The managers from these enterprises, in turn, constituted only a small minority of the potential training pool.

As we have already pointed out, enterprises had to think about their training needs in the context of the post-1979 economic reforms rather than the old way. Firms had to consider how many managers they needed to train, and to see how this matched the number the government had envisaged in the overall policy framework. Greater flexibility in the managerial, as well as other, labour markets was

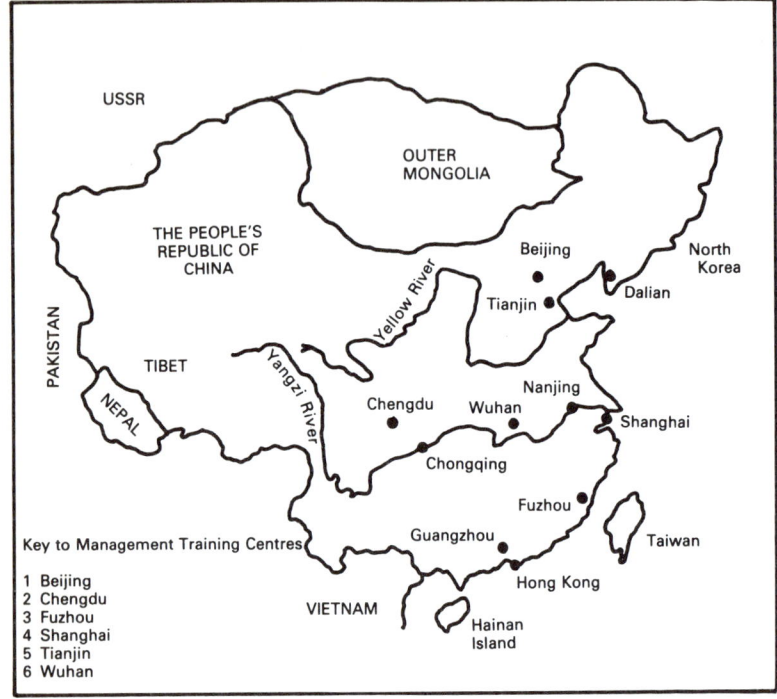

Figure 4.1   Map of the People's Republic of China.
Source: Adapted from Warner (ed.) (1987), p. xii.

envisaged, although this was not yet a reality. There was no substantial labour mobility in the PRC as, for example, there appeared to be in the Soviet Union. Companies hoarded skilled labour and, more importantly, graduates. There were, however, signs of a shift in policy and in future those graduating will have more say as to where they want to work.

Up to early 1988, the SEC had played a major role in providing support for management education for the section for which it is responsible. However, the responsibility for their training activities is to be taken away from the SEC and given to the State Commission for the Restructuring of the Economy (SCRE). This body from this date was to oversee the main organ coordinating management education in China, namely the Chinese Enterprise Management Association (CEMA) set up in 1979, as described in the previous chapter. This institution was partly funded by central government and partly by individual enterprises and covered a variety of activities, such as training, publishing, consultancy and so on (see Warner, 1986a).

To recapitulate, the major role of CEMA had been to encourage and promote management training. It mainly helped train economic cadres from the SEC, including chairmen at the provincial and municipal levels; it also provided courses for managers of large and medium sized enterprises. In addition, it selected managers for study abroad over the period in order to improve China's management knowledge (much of which is at a low level, or lacking – see Table 4.1), some on short courses and some on longer study-visits.

Taking the system as a whole, Chinese management had several, although limited, strategic options. First, it could better exploit the existing system, and make it more efficient. Second, it could return to 'traditional' ways of managing. Third, it could import foreign and especially Western-style management methods. Fourth, it could evolve a specifically new style of management, with 'Chinese characteristics'. The basic strategic choice was therefore between indigenous and exogenous management models, although it could try to combine these in varying mixes. There are clearly constraints on either of these routes. Given the weakness of many aspects of the status quo of both strategy and structure, it did not seem feasible to rely entirely on purely internal models. Conversely, whilst importing foreign notions and expertise was nothing new, it would not have been politically possible to rely entirely on external models either.

In order to introduce change, and as part of the 'Four Modernisations' and 'Open Door' policies, China tried to operationalise general ideas of technology transfer via the development of 'Special Economic Zones' and 'joint-venture' companies (Henley and Nyaw, 1990). Part and parcel of the above endeavours had been the importing of non-Chinese 'scientific management' methods. If earlier Soviet Taylorist efforts were included, as well as current Japanese practices, the term 'Western' management may have been a misnomer. It might have been better simply to label such influences as *foreign* 'scientific management' notions, although even the term 'scientific' might possibly have been misleading. We may end up with something called *modern* management methods, which Chinese management lecturers believed they were teaching, often with overseas academic assistance usually from advanced economies.

Broadly speaking, cadre training, especially at the senior level, had a long tradition in China, going back at least to the mid-1920s. Before that, China enjoyed an even longer tradition going back millenia in

Table 4.1:   Assessment of functional management knowledge lacking in
the Chinese economy

Marketing:
   Market research
   Advertising
   Product design
   Industrial marketing
   Consumer marketing

Manufacturing:
   Total quality control
   Managing high-volume/high-variety operations
   Value analysis
   Inventory management
   Manufacturing information systems
   Distribution systems

Ethics and comparative management

Contract law

Human resources:
   Motivation and incentives
   The concept of directorship
   The role of the manager
   Executive compensation
   Organisational design
   Leadership styles

Finance:
   Investment analysis
   Methods of financing
   International finance

Accounting:
   Establishment of control systems
   Auditing
   Public accounting

Management of science and technology:
   Anticipating technology change
   Managing innovation and creative groups

Source: US Congress, Office of Technology Assessment (Washington DC,
1987).

the training of its traditional scholar bureaucracy. The Whampoa Military Academy, before the break with the Kuomintang, served as a training-ground for a number of key Chinese leaders and administrators. During the Yanan period, the CCP had set up its own cadre training centres in its mountain retreats. The Communists developed their own governmental and industrial infrastructure during the years of Civil War and Opposition to the Japanese invasion. The training for such cadres was Marxist-inspired in form and content, was institutionalised after the 'Liberation' in 1949, and was standard right up to the Cultural Revolution.

Economic cadre training, however, became, after 1979, the principal vehicle for the diffusion of what CEMA called 'scientific' management ideas (see Chapter 3), which were taught in addition to the compulsory courses which characterise all Chinese further and higher education curricula. The institutions devoted to economic cadre (we would call management executive) training became the focus for such diffusion (see Appendix 1). Some of these centres were based on older, existing cadre training institutes; others were created *de novo*.

Initial questions to be kept in mind when examining training include some of the following:

- What did China need in terms of improving the management of its industry?
- How could this best be taught to her managers?
- To what degree did external training models have a relevance to Chinese economic circumstances?
- In what ways could external and internal models be blended?
- Which levels of managers should have more external and less internal model inspired training?
- How could such training be evaluated in terms of its impact?

SELECTED SENIOR MANAGEMENT TRAINING CENTRES

In this section, we shall look at the detailed responses of the six selected senior management training centres out of the ten in existence nationally, all of which were located in major centres of population and economic importance, which were investigated by the present author (interviews with faculty at six centres in summer 1987 and spring 1988). These centres were located outside the university system, which encompassed its own management schools. Indeed, there were over 1,000 universities and colleges which offered management courses, concentrating on pre-entry training, either undergraduate or postgraduate, by the late 1980s. The training centres principally offered courses for top-level practising executives (as well as some middle-level and other upcoming younger managers). Several centres were set up with overseas assistance: the examples to be cited have been aided by Canada, Japan, Norway and West Germany, as well as the EC. (The US Department of Commerce also provided support for a training institution at Dalian, as noted earlier.)

Usually, the researcher and colleagues/interpreters were welcomed to the Training Centre by a group from the faculty led by the Director, the latter speaking most of the time either in his introductory remarks and subsequently in response to questions. Later in the session, the rest of the senior faculty were asked to respond to questions.

Interviews invariably took place in the reception lounge of the Centre, a common practice in most Chinese institutions, be they educational, bureaucratic or economic. Tea and soft drinks were served during the discussions and sometimes cake or fruit. There was always a ceremonial as well as a utilitarian aspect to the proceedings, as we were 'honoured foreign guests'. There was on all occasions a two-way exchange of views, as the Chinese teachers were very keen to hear about Western business schools.

The Training Centres were, on the whole, rather austere places, with spartan classrooms. The equipment was mostly elementary, with a blackboard rather than flip-chart or overhead projector. Computer equipment, often Chinese-built or assembled PCs, was confined to a special part of the building. Accommodation was clean and adequate, although Western managers would have found it rudimentary.

Beijing

A Training Centre for Economic Cadres was first set up in Beijing, in 1979. Its basic goal was to train senior economic cadres in modern management methods. There were over 12 full-time faculty and numerous part-time professors who were in high government posts, enterprise positions, or in Chinese universities. The teachers for the collaborative programmes with Norway and the EC came from overseas for short periods.

The Basic Management Programme of the Centre spanned two months, during which time both theory and applications were taught. It was targeted at economic directors and deputy directors of enterprises as well as section heads. The course covered management, economic and leadership topics, for example. There was also a Senior Executive Programme, as well as one for factory directors. The main subjects studied were Economic Theory, Economic Policy, Management Knowledge and Modern Management Practice. There was, in addition, a Computer Application Programme with participants from different enterprises of the SEC and was a joint programme run in collaboration with the Norwegian government.

From 1979 to 1986, nearly 2,000 executives had been through the Basic Management Course, over 800 through the Senior Executive Programme and nearly 150 through the factory director one. If the 36 and 66 candidates of the first two China–EC Collaborative MBA Programmes based at the Training Centre (see Chapter 5) are included, this added up to a total of almost 3,000 managers over those eight years, although this constituted a heterogeneous group. A more detailed description of China–EC postgraduate collaboration will be provided in the next chapter. (See also Appendixes 3 and 4.)

The Centre was well-endowed by Chinese standards with an air-conditioned teaching block, computer facilities (including several microcomputers) and an audio-visual studio. The largest lecture room accommodated 120 students, with many seminar rooms close by. The library mainly consisted of Chinese publications (around 10,000) and the Collaborative MBA Programme had a limited stock of books in English, plus journals and magazines also in that language.

The Centre occupied a prominent place in the field of training, mostly by dint of its location in Beijing and its physical proximity to the CEMA headquarters office which was in the same building. It had been since its inception a *national* training centre, drawing on course participants from 29 provinces, municipalities and autonomous regions. Furthermore, its alumni played an increasingly important role as leaders in local industrial, commercial and governmental activity, and were considered an 'elite group', having been trained in the capital.

Provincial management training: the case of Sichuan

Focusing on the *provincial* level, as opposed to the *national*, we now turn our attention to a good example of a 'go-ahead' provincial training centre, namely the one at Chengdu, in Sichuan, a part of South-West China.

The province has a population of over 100 million people; if it were a nation-state, it would be the *eighth* biggest in the world. It is the country's largest province in terms of head-count, with the highest rural population density. It is also the granary of China, with its most substantial production of rice. Chengdu is its administrative capital, a city over 2,000 years old and itself with over four million citizens. The first enterprise reforms were reputedly piloted in Sichuan in 1979 (as we shall shortly see) so one would expect it to be in the vanguard of management training (see Special Issue of the *China Quarterly*, 1984). Chongqing, its business centre, has an even larger population of over six million and is a bustling, smoggy 'powerhouse' of industry. Formerly the wartime capital, it is an important inland port on the Yangzi River.

With its large population, Sichuan offers cheaper labour than the coastal areas. It is rich in resources, with natural gas, minerals and water. With industrial fixed assets at over 200 billion yuan, it holds the second ranking in China. Most of China's export products are made from the province's raw materials. Chemical, nuclear, military and machine-building industries have been developed there. However, its geographical isolation remains a problem in spite of the Yangzi River's potential. By 1988, 55 Sino-foreign joint ventures and 18 cooperative enterprises had been established in Sichuan, with an investment value of US$ 140 million. The low cost of labour and raw material inputs perhaps persuaded foreign investors that the high cost of shipping could be offset. Sichuan increased its programme for power generation and tried to improve its infrastructure to compete with the coastal provinces (Yue, 1987).

An important fact, which helped Sichuan's cause no little way, was that Deng Xiaoping, China's leader, was himself born in that province. Zhao Ziyang, the former Party General-Secretary, was coincidentally local Party boss there from 1975 to 1980, and was seen as an energetic administrator 'who got things done'. Production in both agriculture and industry rose rapidly due to his organisational vigour, and he soon moved onto the national stage, taking on former Premier Zhou Enlai's mantle as the 'arch-moderniser'. Whether or not Zhao Ziyang personally 'masterminded' the enterprise autonomy reforms is moot, and whether or not Sichuan's party leaders took the lead is debatable. It is even claimed that the autonomy policy had its roots in the 1950s in the 'Great Leap Forward' and that the Sichuan pilot schemes in 1978 were authorised from a higher level, namely the SEC. It also might be argued that Sichuan was not the only locality chosen for the experiments (Lee, 1986).

Even so, Sichuan's experiments became forerunners for versions elsewhere in China. Unlike Sichuan, other provinces tried out pilot schemes with less flexibility. For example, Guangdong province did not get started until late August 1979. In Shanghai municipality, pilot schemes were a response to central directives in the second half of 1979. Beijing experimented about this time. It seems that localities mainly provided the sites for experiments for policies authorised by central government. Sichuan province produced three versions of enterprise autonomy, which became the forerunners of similar experiments elsewhere in China. In Sichuan, they were respectively called 'small expansion', 'medium expansion' and 'big expansion' in terms of the autonomy given to enterprises. The 'small expansion' version came in from October 1978 to January 1979, before the July 1979 enterprise autonomy policy at national level was promulgated by the State Council. It allowed participating units to use 'enterprise funds', 'bonus funds' and 'retained profits' based on fulfilment and overfulfilment of annual plans. It adopted the 'circular comparison method' in profit calculation, taking the achievement in the year previous as a baseline. The 'medium expansion' version was introduced in December 1979. Where profit retention was concerned, this version used a 'fixed comparison method'. The 'big expansion' kind was one of the early versions of 'substitution of taxation for profit remittance' carried out in the Sichuan province in February 1980, half a year before the SEC announced its formal policy in August 1980 (Lee, 1986, p. 58).

In October 1978, six enterprises in Sichuan became the first to implement the new reforms. Eight special rights were given to such enterprises (see Laaksonen, 1988). These were formulated as follows:

1. The right to keep part of their profits. This could be spent in developing production, or on bonuses, or for the welfare of employees.
2. The right to expand production with funds accumulated, with the possibility to keep the surplus for the first two years.
3. The right to retain 60 per cent of the depreciation fund, *vis-à-vis* 40 per cent previously.
4. The right to engage in production outside the state plan.

5. The right to market part of their products.
6. The right to apply to export their products.
7. The right to issue bonuses at the firm's discretion.
8. The right to penalise those responsible for heavy losses, be they managers, party secretaries or workers.

(1988, pp. 234 ff.)

From the limited Sichuan experiments, the State Council then expanded the scale of the reforms to over 6,000 enterprises across the PRC by 1980, which accounted for about one in six of the very largest state-owned firms. Of the total, nearly 200 contributed to the state-only income tax, industrial and commercial taxes and a tax on fixed assets, while keeping the rest of their profits, with responsibility for surpluses or losses subsequently.

Chengdu Management Training Centre

In light of the province's economic initiatives, we would expect Sichuan to have offered something 'special' in management education provision. There was, in fact, no shortage of such activities, and we will now note a number of illustrative cases. The programme at the Chengdu Management Training Centre, assisted by the Canadian International Development Agency (CIDA), a body very active in China, has been pre-eminent. In fact, Canada contributed eight times as much as the USA to management training in the PRC by the late 1980s. The Centre had a faculty of 220 and over 1,200 students at any one time, in a purpose-built building. Its activities were divided into sub-degree diploma work, a BA in management studies, an eight-month managers' course and consultancy. It had not yet developed its own MBA scheme (although some of the faculty teach Master's courses for other universities), nor did it offer a PhD degree. It taught a diploma course under what were previously State Educational Commission regulations and ran other training courses for the SEC (with fees running to 2,000 yuan for each half-year courses – about £300 sterling at the time of writing). Under the latter, it had been responsible for seven South-Western provinces including the Tibet Autonomous Region. This Centre had a wider ambit than others because of the lower level of development of its surrounding provinces. Students came from Tibet for example, and teachers also went there to run courses, having set up a three-month training programme for local managers.

Several local enterprises in Sichuan sent their managers abroad for training. First, however, they went to the Centre for preparatory work and, above all, for language training, for example if they were to study in North America. Thirty managers were sent to Canada each year to Montreal for training, and to York University if they attempted the MBA. All fees and expenses, including travel, were paid by the Canadian International Development Agency (CIDA). Several Canadian universities such as Dalhousie, McGill and Waterloo for example participated in such projects, which of course were not restricted to Sichuan province but were also available on a national basis. The Centre built up several new ventures (in such collaborative schemes). There was, first, a centre of microeconomic management; second, an information centre to exchange information between Chinese and Canadian enterprises; third, a management consultancy centre; and fourth, a specialised training centre for information and behavioural sciences, planning economics and related research.

Chengdu Science and Technology Cadres College

Several other institutions in Chengdu promoted management studies. For example, the Science and Technology Cadres College dealt with technology-oriented managers. They had over 30 faculty and guest lecturers, offering courses to undergraduate engineers and part-time students and short-courses for enterprises, but with no postgraduate work as yet. Their fees were cheaper than the Training Centre, about 1,000 yuan per student per year.

Technology cadre education carried out through the College in Chengdu had four streams of activity. First, management training was a major activity. It was divided into two kinds, namely work directed to production bureaux and production companies, as well as technologists in the rural sector. Next, the College developed human resources for technology and management teachers in their respective branches. This work was divided amongst different departments such as industrial, chemical, transportation, etc. It in addition worked with the Science Association in Chengdu and numerous R&D units locally. It also assisted with the various bodies involved in 'technology transfer', namely five universities and six training centres. Last, it developed a management information systems office to offer advice to technology managers and to provide consultancy services.

Sichuan Academy's Institute of Industrial Economics

Another important management training activity was undertaken by the Institute of Industrial Economics of the Sichuan Academy of Social Sciences, in Chengdu, which organised courses as well as carrying out research on enterprise behaviour. It was said to have pioneered ideas as to how China's economic and industrial strategy might be transformed, as described in Professor Ma Hong's (1983) influential book *New Strategy for China's Economy*. The work in the Institute centred on four areas of concern, namely Industrial Economics, Business Management, Energy Studies and Technological applications. There were 17 faculty members, of whom five did advanced research.

In the business management field, the Institute dealt with the development of enterprise systems and structures. It concentrated on the reforms of management systems and ways to increase profit and efficiency. The Centre was set up in 1981, mostly doing surveys for the Sichuan provincial government, on the enterprise reforms. The Institute tried to help enterprises by carrying out studies of top managers and decision-making in firms. They also organised research on management training to help them run their own courses better. They published details of courses and sent them to enterprises, who if they saw what they wanted, proposed managers for training.

The Training Centre in the Academy has trained top managers in a relatively non-specialised fashion. The programme lasted two months, with 80 students on each programme, with 400 managers a year in total completing. The courses covered include the usual mix of Macro- and Microeconomics, Business Administration, Marketing and so on. In addition, there were courses on the Management of Western enterprises, Eastern European Economies and new Chinese Management Methods.

Chengdu's programme in Shenzen SEZ

One of management programme activities run by the above Institute had been a specific innovation which merits special mention here. It was called the 'Hong Kong Macro-Economic Management Course' and took place in the Shenzen Special Economic Zone (SEZ), rather than in Chengdu. This exercise was run by the Institute to make managers more aware of the 'Open Door' policy. (The Shenzen SEZ, which has greater economic latitude in order to help exports, is adjacent to Guangzhou and Hong Kong, in the South-East.) The managers on this course spent three hours a day on lectures, and the rest of the time in special-topic seminars and on factory visits. This endeavour exemplified the enterprise of those running the Institute and it was most unusual to see an initiative of this kind in such institutions, although a course on parallel lines was found at Jiaotong University (see Chapter 5). The goal was to 'open up the minds' of the Sichuan managers. The course cost 2,000 yuan, (over £350 sterling at the time of writing) paid by the enterprise.

The Chengdu-SEZ programme tried to lead the managers taking part to have a more receptive approach and hence enable them to do their job more effectively later. There was a feedback seminar at the end of the programme. Professors came from Hong Kong to lecture on the course in Chinese. Most of the participants did not speak English, which was fairly common with practising managers in China. After the lectures and the visits, they held seminar-discussions on the differences between the management methods they have been told about and seen in visits in the SEZ, and their own experiences in Sichuan. On each course, the 80 managers were split into groups of 12 for discussion purposes. It was in all one of the more interesting experiments in management training encountered in the PRC.

Fuzhou

The Fujian Province Institute of Economic Management at Fuzhou in south-eastern China was founded in 1983. There were over 400 students, excluding those on short-term courses, over 70 faculty members and as many again administrative staff by the late 1980s.

The Institute offered courses for the province and the cities within it at diploma, sub-degree, university and postgraduate levels. Many post-experience courses were available. Three levels of diploma work were taught. Sub-degree courses took two or three years, with a certificate of study at the end. University level work required a college level qualification for entry, but no degree was offered. Postgraduate work also carried no degree award. There were also short-term training courses and open-learning facilities.

In the higher level courses, there were several specialist subjects, such as Commercial Organisation, Financial Analysis, Industrial Enterprise Management and so on. Two groups have graduated from the college-level courses up to now. As far as short-term courses were concerned, 2,300 managers had been trained to date. These included top directors, as well as staff specialists, for whom tailor-made courses had been arranged. Seven groups had been trained to pass the top managers' national examination.

In 1990, the Institute planned to build up to over 1,000 students, plus those on short-term courses, with a faculty of over 400 full-time teachers. More attention will be paid to diploma and professional education. The foundation courses will be in the former, but more emphasis will be given to the latter. Adult, older students with work experience will be especially catered for, using continuing education methods.

Shanghai

The Shanghai Training Centre was set up in 1981, by the SEC and Shanghai Economic Commission. It acquired new buildings in 1985, with 20,000 square metres in all. A second phase, of 10,000 square metres, will complete the project. It had a total faculty of 95 teachers (full-time and part-time) by 1988. It comprised a library, teaching block, residential accommodation and a theatre. The Centre has organised ten sets of courses since 1981, with a total output of 2,400 students, excluding a foreign-aided programme from the West German government. The latter organised courses for separate groups on Enterprise Leadership, Marketing and Production Management. These first two normally lasted four and a half months and sometimes ran concurrently. The last ran for one and a half months. The programme attempted to apply West German management ideas to the specific problems of Chinese managers. After the course, the members were sent to enterprises in the Federal Republic.

Since 1986, four programmes were run and over 200 managers trained by the end of 1988. Each course had not more than 30 members, and not less than 20. The West Germans favourably evaluated this programme and continued its funding. Collaboration was originally planned to last from 1986 to 1990. Most of the money was spent on the foreign teaching staff costs, plus some equipment. There were altogether seven German professors and 20 Chinese teaching staff, seven interpreters and one Vice-Director on the Chinese side to run the programme. In addition to German, English and Japanese were taught.

Managers were also taught on an 'on-the-job' basis and 3,000 participants have been involved in this form of training to date. There were four courses for professionals in Enterprise Management, Finance, Planning and Statistics. Such courses were held outside the

Centre, usually 'in-house' in enterprises in the Shanghai area, using teachers from the Training Centre and associated staff.

There was also a Shanghai Enterprise Management Association, like the national CEMA also founded in 1979, with nearly 2,000 member enterprises. It organised services to firms, like providing information on training and other matters; it published useful materials on management topics, including a monthly magazine called *Shanghai Enterprise* (of which 50 issues have now been published); it also had set up a consulting company dealing with about 30 enterprise contracts per year. SEMA had 14 Research Institutes and 11 Research Groups under its auspices. It has organised 220 training courses to date.

The managers who came to the Centre had all passed a national examination for managers set up by the SEC, with between five to ten years' work experience. After four and a half months study, say on the West German course, they directly went back to their enterprises to apply what they had learnt, unless they went to visit enterprises abroad. Most students came from medium to large sized enterprises, with between 2,000 and 3,000 employees and a good proportion were trained engineers. The expenditure on the West German side was considerable and there has been considerable mutual learning in running this foreign-assisted activity.

Tianjin

The Economic Cadre Training Centre at Tianjin, a major port on the eastern side of China, started work in 1980 and ran both short- and long-term courses. The longest was ten months with 150 students; the shorter ones lasted for less than two months and had 350 participants. The Course Directors found it difficult and costly to recruit for short courses, so encouraged longer ones. The types of programmes they organised were responses to the 'market' since the economic reforms, such as those for senior joint-venture directors, hotel managers, publishing house editors, and so on.

A major influence on their training activities, and a special feature of the Tianjin Centre since 1983, was Japanese technical assistance. This provided teaching materials and books as well as training for faculty members. The emphasis was on Financial Control, Information Systems, Marketing, Production and Quality control. All the present Chinese teachers had been to Japan for a one-year course. The Japanese trained the Chinese teachers in the first two years of collaboration, who then compiled and translated the teaching materials from what they had learnt. All the teaching was done by the Chinese faculty, however, who numbered 25 in all; there were, in addition, part-time teachers.

The Tianjin Centre dealt with a student intake on a nationwide basis from 20 provinces and cities, and claimed to be more independent of the SEC than its Beijing counterpart. The Centre was, in addition, involved in in-house programmes and consulting, according to demand, in the following areas: Computers, Marketing, Production Control and Strategy. Consultancy and teaching were often combined. There was also an Alumni Association which is arranged and administered locally by the Centre. In addition, there was a Tianjin Enterprise Management Association, like CEMA.

The Tianjin Centre believed that its strengths lay in linking theory to practice, unlike the university level courses which they saw as too theoretical. They also felt that foreign experts did not always achieve the best results, because they did not know enough about Chinese conditions. The students all came from enterprises and had to have at least three years' experience, but did not need to know the Japanese language. Such managers were normally required to have a knowledge of technology, as well as management. The teachers were described as 'very flexible' and often had to prepare a short-course in four weeks, with the help of outside professors, who provided up to ten per cent of the curriculum. There was a serious shortage of management teachers, as some already had a 32-hour teaching load per week.

Wuhan

The Hubei Province Cadre Institute of Economic Management, with the Training Centre at its core, was located in Wuhan, a major industrial city in central China, and set up in 1983. It taught 1,100 students at a time by 1988. There were five departments and eight specialities, catering for cadres at all levels, although they had to have five years of practical experience and indeed there were many directors of enterprises on the many courses. Managers came from different backgrounds and industries. There were two main streams: first, a two-year college-level one, and secondly, short-term courses. The Institute had a total teaching faculty of 130, including seven professors, plus as many again involved in administration.

Each speciality taught had 24 to 29 courses over the two-year programme. Each term, the student had examinations in three courses and tests in four or five. For example, in Industrial Enterprise Management there were 24 compulsory courses and three optional ones, with around 1,600 hours of study over the two years. In the last six weeks, the students went out for empirical investigations in enterprises for over 200 hours.

Throughout the courses, there was an attention to basic knowledge and practicalities for the middle and higher level managers involved. In a typical week there would be 22 hours of classwork, held principally in the mornings. The teaching methods relied mostly on conventional lecturing inputs, as the faculty had to teach over a thousand students, but there were also seminar discussions and on-site work. Basic courses took up one-third of the faculty. The rest taught the other courses. All in all, there were nearly 70 courses taught. Several teachers were sent abroad for experience and many went on short-term teaching courses in the PRC. Several attended English-language courses to prepare for study abroad. The Institute tried to encourage the training of faculty members in countries such as Canada, France, Japan, West Germany and the USA.

On the short-term courses, the trainees were factory directors and senior officials from regional and prefectural level economic commissions of 26 provinces. The former studied for four and a half months and the latter for seven weeks. After this, a certificate from the SEC was awarded. The goal of the course was to enable the managers and officials to orient themselves *vis-à-vis* the latest economic reforms. The classroom input amounted to one-fifth of the course and the rest was for private study. The participants also analysed case studies and 'special topic' sessions.. They combined what they learnt from their reading, experience and the cases to write a short thesis. The cases were based on Chinese examples, with some reference to foreign ones where appropriate.

Given the previous experience of those on the courses, there were a variety of examinations. Some had an 'open book' exam, others exercises and some 'special topic' research projects. Students had to mix theory and practice in order to develop problem-solving skills.

DISCUSSION

The 'traditional' Chinese management model may be said to have fused over the years with the newer, 'political' models introduced after 1949 (Laaksonen, 1988, pp. 94ff.). Even the Soviet 'one-man management' model adopted soon after fitted the hierarchical predisposition of the system. In some ways, it has reappeared with post-1978 reforms. Seniority was also still built into Chinese management and administration according to recent analyses. Kinship relations have figured strongly in recruitment to factory jobs (Davis, 1988, pp. 223–42). Connections (or *guanxi*) have continued to lubricate the formal bureaucratic system and provided for informal lines of communication, allegedly verging on corruption in many instances (see *Le Monde*, 5 August 1988).

Up to 1949, China was very lightly industrialised. There were some 'modern' industries, concentrated in the large coastal cities trading with the outside world, such as Shanghai and Guangzhou (Canton). Only a very small percentage of production was derived from industrialised production, however, with small-scale enterprises dominant (Riskin, 1987, pp. 16 ff.). 'Modernisation' of the economy, it may be argued, only 'took off' during the 1950s and early 1960s (1987, pp. 16 ff.).

In reality, there were never clear 'ideal types', but emphases which were blurred at the edges. Traditional values were discernible throughout, for example. Leadership styles waxed and waned. Bureaucratic authority surfaced in various forms over time, particularly when the Soviet influence was strong in the 1950s. The basic criterion we must use is the institutionalisation and subsequent legitimacy of the characteristic form of authority. In contemporary Chinese industry, management has had to justify itself by overcoming the qualificational hurdles, in order to legitimise its aspired-to competence and expertise, as it imagined was the case in Western-style economies. Yet at the same time we must take note of theories like the one put forward by Boisot (1987) that China is not quite in the above position and is ready for more 'bureaucracy', albeit of the 'rational-legal' variety rather than the 'ideological'. In trying to make sense of China's administrative development, he used a four-box schema (see Figure 4.2). Boisot stated his conclusions as follows:

> In sum, if China's development strategy in the 1950's could be described as a move from quadrant 1 to quadrant 2, its strategy in the 1960's – if strategy it can be called – aimed at a shift from quadrant 1 to quadrant 4. Today's leadership is promoting a cautious move towards quadrant 3, the market quadrant. Clearly, however, this is very far from constituting a wholesale commitment

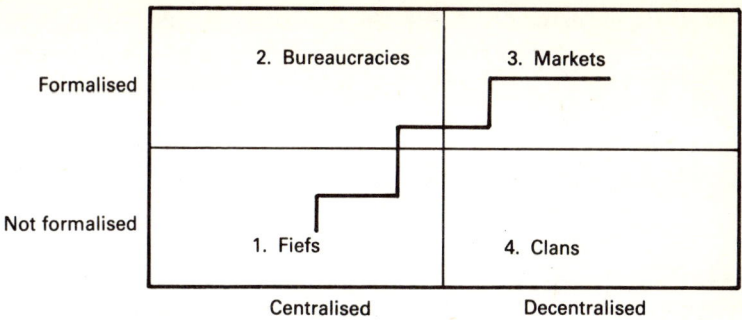

Figure 4.2   China's current modernisation strategy.
Source: Boisot (1987), p. 232.

to quadrant 3, which would indeed amount to a move towards capitalism. Pragmatism rather than ideology is in the driving seat, so that one may be witnessing a diversification of transactional strategies and a more dispersed configuration in the culture space.

(Boisot, 1987, pp. 232–3)

Indeed, we may argue that the cultural attraction of quadrant 1 has remained a strong one in China – the last forty or so years notwithstanding. The moves of the leadership to introduce an impartial legal system – with greater formalisation – and at the same time to increase the autonomy of industrial firms – with greater decentralisation – was designed to encourage 'market socialism'.

Whilst the 'managerialism' which embodied Weberian modern bureaucratic tendencies may now perhaps be encouraged, it should be remembered that almost everything in contemporary Chinese society has been seen as 'political', and that the term 'pragmatic' has a different meaning from its Western usage. Nonetheless, whether or not 'economics is now in command' the term must be interpreted in relative terms (Schram, 1988, pp. 177–97). Expressions like 'managerial revolution', as used in our own societal context, may be misleading if applied to 'one-party' states and economies which were 'market-oriented' only in constrained or limited respects. It has also probably been very hard for individuals brought up and socialised in a 'Communist' society all their lives to internalise foreign, Western management models and their appropriate managerial values.

Again, there may be *cultural* problems, based on China's age-old legacy. Laaksonen points out:

The main historical roots of contemporary management originate
from the hierarchical family (household) system, where the father,
the man, was the head. Because of the fights between the numerous early kingdoms, a strong central government was needed. Both
these systems – hierarchical family and centralised government –
were greatly strengthened by Confucius' thoughts.

(1988, pp. 332–3)

From these roots, the main aspects of contemporary Chinese
management have been set out, such as a hierarchical one-man
management system, masculine domination, respect for age, rigid
bureaucracy, special interpersonal relations systems, and importance of
'saving face', according to the above interpretation. Such a view must be
treated with a certain caution, however. Even if what was dubbed
'scientific management' was legitimised, it was hard to expect more than
a carefully measured response from those who knew how often the
political line has changed in the past years. The separation of the
managerial and the political as initially proclaimed by China's leaders
during the economic reforms period may, however, have been more
apparent then real in many cases, and therefore we must wait to see
hard evidence of fundamental changes in the way decision-making
has taken place (see Walder, 1986; 1989). It is perhaps a little too
soon for a full ex-post assessment.

As can be seen from the variety of courses offered, there has been
no clear strategy as to the respective roles the senior executive
training institutions should play. They have mostly concentrated on
training for practising managers, whereas the management schools in
universities have mostly focused on pre-entry training. There are,
however, considerable variations between the senior training centres
in programmes, size of student body, and faculty, and so on. Some
had considerable foreign assistance, while others have had much less.
The problem has partly arisen because so many schools have
been set up in so short a period of time, which was less than a decade
(Warner, 1986a, pp. 326–42). Moreover, internal and external
models of training were unschematically mixed up in the various
institutions examined. It was hard to disentangle the respective
influences of each regarding specific courses.

As the Chinese faculty members in the Training Centres responded
to open-ended questions when interviewed, it was rare for there to be
any extended statements on the philosophy of training, or indeed any
ideological points, other than endorsement of the economic reforms

and a naive belief in modernisation *per se*. 'Scientific management' was virtually regarded as a panacea (see Chapter 3). There was some ambiguity, however, regarding the transfer of Western techniques and a preference for practices 'with Chinese characteristics'. Sometimes, the Training Centre involved had a brochure in English, and in one instance there was even a briefing sheet which set out the objectives of the institution and described its organisational structure. There was usually only a limited account of comment on teaching techniques. More often than not, there was a great deal of explanation about courses, numbers of participants and teachers, curricula and so on (interviews in 1987 and 1988).

As to the rationale of management training, there was a geographical spread of coverage by the Centres, and often a local orientation, or a response to a specific industrial need or functional group of managers. After concentrating on basic studies related to the economic reforms (1979–82), the Centres then focused on general management for top enterprise directors (1982–86), and have now turned to professional training for staff specialists (1987 onwards). Which way will they go after this task is achieved? What will be their next main task?

CONCLUDING REMARKS

Management education in China thus faced a dilemma and many institutes sought a new role. Before, most managers were not trained and therefore needed preparation for the national examinations and diplomas (Lee, 1988). Later, there were many young graduates with BA qualifications in management studies who did not need to take the national exam. They might then be appointed by the appropriate local government, party and cadre bureaux, normally in consultation with the top managers of the larger enterprises to which they are going; smaller firms might take in less of these recruits and still need help in developing local talent. The Training Centres therefore had to concentrate more on professional training, whether for short or long courses. Many science and technology graduates did not have management training and therefore had to be developed either internally, or externally at university or institute, on, say, a three-month course.

The national examination system for top factory directors had completed most of its work by 1986. New exams for specialist levels were now *de rigueur*. We must remain sceptical about their impact on economic performance. The old national exam, as noted earlier, was not too difficult to pass (with most getting through) and some believed that it may have been a waste of time and money, although in its defence it may be said to have professionalised and legitimised management qualifications. Management training centres then had to worry about their future in that having trained most of the top managers available, they had increasingly to deal with lower level personnel. Managers were usually very busy and often felt that they could learn the elements of management at home from correspondence/distance learning schemes anyway. There was general agreement that China had to improve the standard of its training methods as well as the assessment of such courses, whatever the level of managers to be developed.

Finally, the strategic development of China's management training had to become more clearly promoted and put on a ten to twenty year time-scale (see Chen, 1988; Vermeer, 1988). To date, it had been focused on too short-term a perspective. If Chinese management training was to develop, it had to have a stronger strategic and organisational coherence, with better indigenous models, and a clearer division of labour between the centres involved.

5 China's University-Level Management Schools

INTRODUCTION

With the declaration of martial law in May 1989, the future of modernisation in China entered a phase of great uncertainty. Since the post-1979 economic reforms were introduced, management education had seemed to be expanding. Pre-entry management programmes, both undergraduate and postgraduate, as well as professional training, had been promoted. This chapter will concentrate on developments at university level, in Beijing, Shanghai and Tianjin (see map, Figure 4.1) over the decade 1979–88, and specifically focus on these schools as opposed to the broad range of cadre training institutions, all conforming to the SEDC degree regulations (see Appendix 2).

As we have seen earlier, the Chinese economic system overall had been critically hampered by a shortage of skilled personnel, partly due to the Cultural Revolution in the mid-1960s and early 1970s, when most formal education was greatly disrupted. The worst shortfall remained one of trained staff capable of managing modern enterprises and sophisticated technology, particularly in the context of an overstretched and overheated economy (see Tidrick and Chen, 1987). As part of the 'Four Modernisations' policy, foreign experts were brought in to hasten technology transfer and to train Chinese personnel in enterprises, as well as students. Considerable numbers (over 40,000 at government expense) were sent abroad to study between 1978 and 1987 (Gittings, 1989, p. 248). Most went to the USA, Western Europe and Japan. China claimed it has continued this policy, the events of 4 June 1989 notwithstanding (see *Beijing Review*, 18–24 June 1990 and *Times Higher Education Supplement*, 8 March 1991), but with of course greater 'selectivity'.

There has been a considerable expansion of higher education since 1949, but not enough to keep pace with economic requirements. The total number of institutions concerned has grown from 200 in the 1950s to over 1,000 in the 1980s. Student enrolment exceeded two million (see Table 3.1) with under 120,000 graduate students and a very small minority of doctoral candidates; it will remain stable until 1995.

Official statistics put the number of university-level graduates in China at over four million up to 1983, but as many of these qualified in the turbulent years of political upheaval with shortened and diluted courses, this may have been an overestimate (Orleans, 1987). Approximately three-quarters of the present graduate total have graduated since the end of the 1970s. China may in fact be seen as a Third World country in terms of the *percentage* of graduates in the population.

If Western countries have had skill shortages in the new technology area, the problem was compounded in China. There had been a virtual absence of applications engineers in the manufacturing sector, for example. The total lack of in-house engineering skills had been partly mitigated by the use of outside consultants; this development was in its embryonic stages (Khanna, 1986). Part-time university and institute assistance only marginally helped resolve the problem as this did not provide enough experts. Not only were science and technology graduates needed, but also trained technicians and skilled workers. Vocational education thus became a priority area as well, especially *vis-à-vis* high technology applications (Warner, 1989).

In addition, management training at many different levels became essential to help the more effective use of resources. Specialists were therefore relatively scarce, as were those trained to manage them. Indeed, the production of managers, as well as scientists and technologists, had been a priority for some time. Education was also encouraged to have greater 'relevance', and it was decreed that all graduates must have at least one year of work experience as part of their educational programme. Restructuring of state firms and government bureaux had, at the same time, attempted to cut down overmanning, but also revealed shortages of key personnel. Major problems arose in the output of graduates in foreign languages, especially English, as well as accounting and computing. This insufficiency represented a major concern for those estimating future needs of management. There were, however, over 300 higher education bodies offering management courses in China (see Table 5.1), under the regulations of the State Education Commission as set out in Appendix 2, presumably under broad headings.

Overall, the total number of students in 1988 in the wide variety of management-related programmes (see Table 5.2) not including correspondence and evening courses, exceeded 100,000. This number amounted to around five and a half per cent of the total number in higher education at the time. Of these, over 4,000 were postgraduates, 43,000 undergraduates and nearly 60,000 were vocational candi-

Table 5.1 Distribution and direction of universities or colleges with management-related specialties

University categories	Responsible authorities			Total
	State Education Commission	Other Ministries	Local government	
Comprehensive universities	12	1	22	35
Institutes of finance and economics	—	18	19	37
Engineering universities	13	65	17	95
Agricultural institutes	—	10	32	42
Medical colleges	—	1	1	2
Short-term institutes	—	—	82	82
Others	3	8	8	19
Total	28	103	181	312

Source: State Education Commission (1987).

dates. In 1986, the total output of such graduates was 16,000 (or just over four per cent of all higher education graduates) but this satisfied only 15–20 per cent of the demand of potential employers according to official estimates (see State Education Commission, 1987).

Let us now turn to a number of selected university management schools (in which we conducted research interviews in early 1988) in order to see how these were contributing to the needs of the Chinese economy and the manpower requirements called for by the enterprise reforms. In doing so, we may possibly conjecture as follows that:

(a) The rate of expansion of management training may have been a function of the pace of economic reform; innovations occurred from 1979 onwards because of the shortage of managerial personnel of adequate sophistication.
(b) The diversification of management training tended to follow Western models, such as the need for MBA courses, as these were associated with the achievement of an appropriately prepared industrial 'critical mass' to help implement 'technology transfer'.
(c) The development of management studies courses had expanded both undergraduate and postgraduate numbers as a form of 'import substitution', as it was cheaper than sending students overseas.
(d) The emphasis of management training was probably a function

Table 5.2　Summary of the 25 management-related programmes taught in Chinese universities

1.　National Economy Management
2.　Management Science
3.　Economic Information Management
4.　Industrial Enterprise Management
5.　Materials Management
6.　Materials Supply Management
7.　Machinery and Electric Products Management
8.　Customs Management
9.　Tourism Management
10.　International Economy Management
11.　Administration of Industry and Commerce Management
12.　Commercial Enterprise Management
13.　Industrial Economics
14.　Industrial Management Engineering
15.　Architectural Management Engineering
16.　Communication and Transportation Management Engineering
17.　Post and Telecomunication Management Engineering
18.　Economic Management of Water Conservancy
19.　Agricultural Economy Management
20.　Economic Management of Forestry
21.　Economic Management
22.　Materials Management Engineering
23.　Management Information Systems
24.　Management of Health Services
25.　Management of Medical and Pharmaceutical Enterprises

Source: State Education Commission (1987).

both of existing strengths in the universities concerned, as well as earlier experience in the subjects involved.

(e)　The balance of management studies intake as between full-time, and other kinds of students, such as those on short courses and on distance-learning type programmes, tended to depend on the need to widen the diffusion of managerial knowledge and expand the network of those drawn into its higher level study.

(f)　The potential applicability of managerial knowledge diffused probably depended on the recruitment of students with work experience, especially in management, as well as combining theory with enterprise-based practice during the courses.

It will, we hope, become clearer as we deal with the institutions at hand, how directly these factors related to the logic of developments in management educational policy since 1979. We shall look at them school by school, department by department, and see whether or not there has been a coherent outcome in terms of both strategy and/or structure (interviews in spring 1988).

UNIVERSITY MANAGEMENT SCHOOLS

Beijing

Beijing University

Beijing University had long been one of China's most distinguished academic institutions and was popularly known as 'Beida'. Founded in 1912 in its present form, it had over 12,000 students in 1988. It has had an Economics Department since its early days, and taught some Accounting, Finance and Banking subjects in its curriculum. It contained a College of Economics with three departments within it, namely Economic Management, Economic Theory and International Economics. As it was an 'elite' university, the students had to obtain very high marks in the national examination to enter; some also had prior work experience. The Department of Economic Management was previously a specialism, but became a distinct programme. However, there was a common core of courses for the three departments. Western Economics was taught parallel to lectures in Chinese Political Economy.

Many younger faculty members had been specially trained for the Economic Management Department and were particularly well-versed in the theoretical side of the subjects taught; some of them were completing their PhDs, albeit on a part-time basis. Graduate and doctoral students have also grown in number recently, as has the teaching staff. There were over a dozen professors out of the College faculty of over 100, of whom about one-third taught management. There were over 200 undergraduate students and 30 postgraduate ones, including a minority of PhDs.

The first two years of study were common for all undergraduates, with electives in the third and fourth years. The International Economics teaching greatly benefited from the contribution of Professor Hong Junyan (an expert on the US economy and China's first Fulbright Scholar). There was also a well-established American Studies Centre.

The department ran a number of short-term courses for managers during the summer vacation, with around 200 persons at a time. Another course trained government officials. Usually, they advertised in the newspapers in order to attract participants. Before coming, the latter had to pass a formal examination. Normally, the courses lasted one month and teachers were often sent out to the provinces to run them. Where they were held on campus, they were non-residential, with students principally recruited from the Beijing area. Often, those who sponsored the students institutionally were former graduates of the same establishment. The University also had its own Adult Education Bureau on campus and did not need to use the state equivalent. The above Bureau had over 7,000 distance-learning students registered for its courses.

Finally, Beida had strengthened its management-teaching related activities and had plans to set up a fully fledged Training Centre for ten-month programmes, as well as shorter courses for Directors and Deputy Directors of Enterprises. Research in management topics was also given greater prominence, with many projects sponsored by government organisations, especially where they related to applications of the economic reforms.

The People's University

The People's University was established in 1950, with Soviet assistance, and was principally designed to cover the social sciences and policy studies. By 1988, it had enrolled over 20,000 students. In the 1950s, a masters degree in Enterprise Management was introduced and taught by visiting Soviet faculty members. In 1959, lectures in industrial management were given at both undergraduate and postgraduate levels, but were discontinued during the Cultural Revolution. It had five management specialities and considerable experience in distance-learning. Its five departments in the area covered Agricultural, Commercial, Industrial, Information, and Investment Economics variations out of 25 departments in total in the University.

Due to expansion, there was restricted physical space at the University for the over 7,700 undergraduate (and over 1,300 postgraduate) student body. There were also over 10,000 distance-learning or evening students. In 1988, 250 undergraduates and 130 graduate students were enrolled in the Industrial Economics Department, which was the closest to the management teaching area. Additionally, there were seven professors and 32 other faculty members (with

120 altogether if Investment Economics is added). The University's plan was to create a fully recognised management school, with Canadian assistance, as in the other cases noted in this chapter (see Table 5.4 later).

There were also the beginnings of short-course activity and programmes have already been run for some of the biggest enterprises in China, such as Automobile Factory, No. 2 and Anshan Iron and Steel. These lasted four and a half months and to date have been sponsored by the State Economic Commission (SEC) which in spring 1988 handed over responsibility for management training to the State Commission for the Re-structuring of the Economy (SCRE). Enterprises were willing to continue such courses and pay for them themselves, but there were problems of good accommodation on campus. A Senior Executive Course, for example, had 50 members in addition to the other professional training courses. A distance-learning MBA for middle managers was launched with 20 students. Some experienced managers also took part in a full-time Masters course in Management, about 20 participants in all. Further, the University provided learning materials and classes for many of the 46,000 managers or more who took the SEC national management examination. There was also a separate Distance-Learning Department, with both undergraduate and professional courses, involving over 2,000 students.

Library facilities were substantial with considerable numbers of Western management and social science books and journals out of over 1,800 foreign language periodical titles in all. Computing facilities were also well-established. There were two main areas of research, namely Enterprise Management and Industrial Economics. In the latter, projects dealt with contracting systems, quality control and responsibility systems. The University published two journals of relevance to management, *Economic Theory and Economic Management (Jingji Lilun yu Jingji Guanli)*, and *Foreign Economy Management (Waiguo Jingji Guanli)*, both in Chinese.

Qinghua University

Qinghua University was one of two strong candidates to be named the 'Massachusetts Institute of Technology' of China (along with Jiaotong University, Shanghai) and unquestionably a centre of excellence for science and engineering. Founded in 1911, it had over 12,500 students at the time of investigation and was one of the seven named 'key' universities of the Seventh Five-Year Plan (1986–90). It consisted of 26 departments and four schools, as well as 27 research institutes.

The School of Economic Management was founded in 1984, previously having been the Department of Management Engineering as of 1978. It had taught Accounting in its Economics curriculum in the early 1920s. There was a Department of Economics, one of Management Engineering, one of Management Information Systems (MIS) and another of International Trade. Associated with these were two research groups and two doctoral programmes, in Engineering Economics and in Systems Engineering. There were over 250 undergraduates and over 200 postgraduate students in all, with around 20 doctoral candidates at the time of investigation. There were close on fifty faculty members (17 professors and assistant professors and 31 others).

Executive training programmes, such as one in International Trade (run with the World Bank), and short-term course activities completed its portfolio of activities. In the previous eight years, over 2,000 managers had been trained on them. There were also links with overseas institutions, such as the Canadian International Development Agency (CIDA) sponsored arrangement with MacMaster, Waterloo and Western Ontario Universities, with a budget of one and a half million Canadian dollars. Five students had been sent to Canada each year. A Joint Masters Degree with Waterloo and Western Ontario was planned.

Research activities in management were prominent, with around 40 projects each year, some government supported, some funded by foundations such as the Chinese National Science Foundation. Topics included Macroeconomic Modelling, Marketing Policy Analysis, and so on. Consulting was launched and the University had started to build a 'science park' to boost its revenues via industrial contracts in an open industrial zone with preferential status.

Executive programmes for managers from factories were run twice a year, with 40 people on each, until recently to SEC and local government sponsorship. There were also 'workshops' of a shorter duration dealing with specific topics, such as International Trade, Technology Transfer and topics related to current economic policies.

Qinghua's Management Engineering courses involved project-work and practice periods in enterprises during the summer vacation. There were *three* phases:

- *recruitment of enterprises*: for students' work experience;
- *consulting*: where the students carried out their projects;
- *thesis*: combining the theory with practice.

There were several kinds of examination for postgraduate entry. One group came from the five-year undergraduate programme. There were often selected from fourth-year students who still had to finish their fifth year of study, amounting to about 25 students. A second group came from enterprises and other universities. These had to have two years' work-experience at least and pass the national examinations in Maths, English, and so on, running to another 25 students. Third, there was a 'special entry' programme, like the MBA, requiring at least five years' work or managerial experience, with examinations by the School only, with slightly lower standards permitted, resulting in another 15 students.

Qinghua had extensively built up language-training facilities, not only for English but also French and German. Language laboratory facilities were on campus. There was a three-month preparatory programme for the 'special entry' group for English and Maths, which coped with 45 students at a time, including the normal intake of management studies candidates from the departments.

All the managers on courses were expected to return to their original enterprises, which paid 3,000 yuan a year (or about £450 sterling when investigated) for each student sent. There was not much experience of students changing jobs between enterprises and advanced recruitment is difficult. About 90 university institutions had Management Engineering courses, so resources were fully stretched. Qinghua faculty believed their school benefited by mixing students from different backgrounds, such as those from enterprises, government bureaux and university faculties.

Importantly, many Qinghua management courses stressed a technical orientation and work-based practice as part of their activities. There was also an interest in distance-learning via the short-term Vocational University Economic Management Academy, which was student-paid and non-resident, and used correspondence and other materials, similar to the Economic Management Periodical University nationally.

It is worth noting that to enter Qinghua a student had to have *the highest marks average attainable* in their chosen subject in the national examinations. Qinghua's strengths, however, were in the higher degree fields, with overall the largest number of doctoral students in China. As the University President, Professor Gao Jingde noted, the University 'hoped to become one of the key bases in China for both the training of high-level specialised personnel and the development of science technology and culture' (see *Qinghua University Catalogue*, 1986–1987, p. 3).

Shanghai

Fudan University

Fudan University was founded in 1905 and had over 10,000 students by 1988. The University had introduced management studies in 1917, had taught the subject within its Economic Department and had inaugurated a business school in 1929, although this was in abeyance form 1952 onwards together with most other academic management training institutions after the education reforms of that year. In 1977, however, a Department of Management Science was set up, which became a School in 1985. It consisted of three departments, namely Economic Management, Management Science, Operations Research and Statistics. There was also a Training Division and two Institutes of Economic Management and Operations Research, as well as one for Quantitative Economics. It had enrolled over 800 undergraduates and over 200 postgraduate students in management. It also ran a two-year programme for an undergraduate lower-level diploma, but the students could complete their thesis after they left. Degrees conferred over the previous six years covered six fields: Econometrics, Enterprise Management, Industrial Economics, Management Science, Operations Research and Statistics.

The School had around 150 faculty members, including 30 full professors and associate professors. It also conferred doctoral degrees. It was one of five national universities allowed to confer the MBA degree, and claimed to be the only 'comprehensive' university to do so. Since 1977, nearly 900 students graduated at either undergraduate or postgraduate levels, and about 1,300 executives have taken the training programme.

In 1987, the school inaugurated its MBA programmes, one for enterprise executives and the other for R&D. The candidates involved were specialists who had to have several years' managerial experience. There was also a Senior Public Administrators' Course. There were also international links through exchange arrangements to train faculty members abroad, largely in the USA and Japan. A Faculty Development Programme in Management Information Systems was sponsored by the World Bank. There were in addition, short-term training programmes of one to three months with trainees from local enterprises and the Shanghai Economic Commission, which had been given seven times now. A similar set of courses had been run for the State Science and Technology Commission. Both these programmes led to the training of over 60 per cent of the total number of managers trained. In 1980, the School started training teachers of management centres and around 200 personnel have qualified.

Short-term programmes of two and a half months were thought to be too long, as with the economic reforms, enterprise directors were given more responsibility and therefore could not be away from their posts for too many weeks. The School had strong links with enterprises and the managers on the courses came from 28 provinces and cities. Regulations for university degrees were decided at a high level, but as far as short-term courses were concerned, the university could decide how much to charge. Some executive courses were full-time, some part-time. The latter lasted for four semesters, some days per week, plus one semester on campus full-time. There was also Master's level training for the position of 'General Economist' – first instituted in 1985. Fudan was selected as the first faculty to run such a programme on a pilot basis for the SEC. The School had a library of over 20,000 management volumes and received over 300 periodicals, many from overseas, including the *Harvard Business Review*, *Omega: The International Journal of Management Science*, and so on.

Jiaotong University

Jiaotong University (or JTU as it is called for short) was founded in 1896 and is one of the oldest polytechnic universities in China with over 12,000 students in all. The name literally means 'Transportation University' (appearing in 1921), but is now interpreted very widely to cover science and technology. The Management School, which was preceded by its Division of Commercial Affairs as well as the Economics Department, dates from 1927, but its activities were in abeyance after 1952 and it was only set up again in 1979 as a department. A full School of Management was later established, in June 1984.

There were four departments in the School in 1988, namely Decision Science, Hotel Management, Industrial Management Engineering and lastly Foreign Trade. There were also four research institutes: Economic Management, Systems Engineering, Human Resources and Transportation. In addition, there was an Adult Training Division. The School awards BA, MA and PhD degrees with provision for post-doctoral study. Teaching staff included over 160 faculty, of whom 33 were professors and associate professors. The number of undergraduates was over 500, with 180 Masters candidates, 12 PhD students and one post-doctoral fellow at the time the study was conducted.

Several joint programmes have been inaugurated. First, from 1981–83 there was a dual Masters degree in Computer Science and Management Decision Science with the Wharton Business School, University of Pennsylvania, with half the courses given by US professors. Lasting three years, it trained 28 graduate students who mostly went abroad in the United States and West Germany for doctoral study. Second, there was an MBA in International Business and Trade sponsored by Canada (via CIDA) involving the University of British Columbia, and lasting three years. In 1988, there were 16 graduate students on the programme receiving extensive English training, with a dissertation in that language.

There also were two externally aided short-term courses at JTU in the management field. The first was the joint management course with the University of Constanz, West Germany. It had preparatory courses before enrolment; the senior course had German inputs on five courses (Accounting, Business Decision, Finance, International Marketing, Organisation and Planning). It took around 20 participants in all and lasted six months. It has been 'tried and tested' and has run three times up to 1988. The participants then went abroad for six weeks to Baden-Würtemberg to have experience of German advanced technology enterprises. Their average age was in the late thirties and they were recruited in Shanghai Municipal Bureau enterprises. After the visit to Germany, the faculty ran a seminar and the participants each gave a paper in English.

The second programme was the Shanghai Management Development Programme, with ten courses taught by Chinese University of Hong Kong professors as well as JTU faculty (some other academics were also asked by the former group to join in). It was taught in both Chinese and English and lasted six months. After the classroom-work, the participants went to Hong Kong for six weeks. All the course members came from the Shanghai Economic Zone.

In JTU courses, the student took core courses in his or her major field, like Micro- and Macroeconomics, Operations Research, Organisational Behaviour and Production Control, for example. There were also electives at advanced levels, mostly for doctoral students. There was a great emphasis on *quantitative* work. In Business Administration, which was usually under the heading of Management Engineering, some of the courses were common (Production Control etc.) but others were electives. There was generally a large input of Accounting, Finance and Statistics.

The *practical* side of the management degree was very much in evidence. Access to industrial and commercial enterprises was assured, as over 300 top managers in Shanghai were JTU graduates. Students got to know how to manage enterprises and obtained 'hands-on' experience with Production Planning and so on. They were asked to define problems existing in the enterprise, make diagnoses for the firm and then suggest solutions. The 'practice' period lasted for one semester, that is, over four months. The short winter vacation was used by first-year graduate students for this purpose. There was then oral feedback by the manager to the School.

While Fudan University was seen as more *theoretical* in this field, JTU saw itself as rather more *practical*. It had received many research contracts from the SEC and large industrial companies, including joint-ventures. Another interesting area of activity was the study of such enterprises in collaboration with the Technical University, West Berlin, on how much ventures could be made more successful. The project was underwritten by funds from the Volkswagen Foundation.

The view was held at JTU that their graduates in management had more of the qualities needed by the economic reforms *vis-à-vis* other management schools. For example, over 50 graduates in foreign trade were forthcoming in 1987, but over 200 enterprises sought to recruit them. There were special relations with enterprises because of the scientific and technological strengths of the university. JTU was chosen as an 'experimental university' for the new system of job allocation introduced in 1988, which tried to introduce greater flexibility in the choice of enterprises for new graduates, especially in the case of joint-ventures.

As for the future strength of its faculty, the School kept some of its brightest graduates and these were then often sent abroad for PhD study. The whole university retained around 100 each year, with six for the Management School. The 'special enrolment' route was encouraged in order to attract more students with work and managerial experience. They held onto their posts in their enterprises and received a salary while studying. The enterprise paid all their fees and other costs, but if they wanted to change their jobs, they then forfeited this support. One possibility was for the new unit employing them to pay for their education. For graduate school, the state regulations to date required 4,300 yuan per annum (over £650 sterling at the time of writing), apart from the salary and social security costs. For short courses, there was a 1,500 yuan fee (then, over £200 sterling) for tuition. The Constanz Joint Course had a 2,900 yuan tuition fee (then over £400 sterling).

Finally, a special feature of JTU was its Alumni Association which covered the whole university. There were over 1,000 members in the USA, but forty per cent of the total were in the PRC. Several government ministers and governors of provinces belonged to it. The founder of the well-known computer firm, the Wang Corporation in the USA, was an ex-graduate of the University, too. The headquarters of the Alumni body was in North America, but there was also a branch in Hong Kong as well as in the PRC. The Chinese mainland Alumni section was run from the JTU President's office and was unquestionably a very strong source of support for the University in general and the Management School in particular.

Shanghai University of Finance and Economics

SUFE was first established after the end of World War One as the National Shanghai Institute of Commerce, but only became a university institution in 1985. It had over 6,000 students in total, with over 200 professors out of about 700 faculty members in all, by the late 1980s. There were also 300 postgraduate and 10 doctoral students in all subjects. It was funded by the Ministry of Finance and the Shanghai Municipality.

There were nine departments, each related to five specific degrees: Banking, Finance, Management Information Systems, Trade Economics and World Economics. It had two main campuses, one (the old one) for postgraduates and a new one for undergraduates. It also had a Training Centre and the Shanghai Institute of International Economic Management which ran programmes with the support of the World Bank. The training courses included General Planning, Project Management, Urban Planning, and so on. These were run in collaboration with Australia and Japan. There was also cooperative work with Canada, the Netherlands and the USA.

There were, as elsewhere, four-year undergraduate programmes in Management, with around ten per cent of the student body, and three-year programmes for Masters students, covering over 600 undergraduates and about 50 postgraduates in this field. Fifteen specialties and three options for undergraduates were offered. In the Department of Industrial Economics, which in effect was one of Enterprise Management, the required Masters courses were, for example: Economic Management of the Soviet Union and East European Countries, Industrial Economics, Management of Industrial Enterprises, Industrial Management in Western Economies, Planned Administration of National Economy in the Soviet Union and East European Countries, and Planned Administration and Economic Forecasting of the National Economy, as well as Standardisation Management. The Department of International Economics provided courses in Foreign Trade and International Finance, and the Department of Trade Economics offered many topical electives of interest to management students. Accounting courses were also available.

Since 1949, SUFE has trained over 16,000 managers, many of whom play important roles in industry and government. The library had over 600,000 books, of which about 50,000 were in foreign languages. The number of specialised foreign language journals was considerable and probably greater than elsewhere in China, with a high proportion in English, French, German, Japanese and Russian. A substantial level of support for such purchases and subscriptions was provided by the World Bank. Two monthly journals were published, namely *Foreign Economics and Management* (*Waiguo Jingji Yu Guanli*) and *The Study of Finance* (*Caijing Yanjiu*), both in Chinese.

Altogether there were four Doctoral programmes and ten Masters courses; training at SUFE was also claimed to be more *practical* than at many university management schools. Part-time study was also given some emphasis. Most students already had a job in a bank or factory. The Evening-School Centre was located separately in central Shanghai, like the 'branch schools' in Beijing, for such 'walking students', as the Chinese call them. Seventy per cent of the students were chosen by Ministry of Finance dependent units, and thirty per cent from the Shanghai Municipality enterprises.

With close connections to the Financial sector, SUFE received extra support via the practical periods the students obtained in their enterprises. There were also close relations with the Ministry of Finance and the Shanghai Financial Bureau. Students spent such in-service periods in working on the job, but also wrote their theses there. Teams of ten students went to enterprises, with a tutor accompanying them, to carry out their management-related projects. They then presented their results in seminars to their professors.

There were extensive faculty links with overseas, to exchange faculty members and students. The University sent young teachers for management and related qualifications abroad. Candidates went to Canada, West Germany and the USA to obtain MBA and PhD degrees. Senior faculty members often went to give lectures in Hong Kong, Japan or North America, for example. Western professors were also invited to teach 'special topics'. The relations with the World Bank were close and their experts often came to lecture at SUFE. At graduate level, it was claimed that most students could closely follow lectures in English by such visitors, although this would not be true for undergraduates. All the theses at the Masters level in the World Economics department were also written in English.

Tianjin

Nankai University

Nankai University was founded in 1919 and nearly seventy years later had enrolled over 10,000 students. In its early days, it had a College of Economics, with Departments of Accounting, Banking, Commerce and Statistics, and it had inaugurated a management course in its Economics curriculum. In 1933, it ran an MBA course, claimed to be the first one in China. Its modern Management Department, as such, was set up again in 1979, as Commerce and Management teaching were in abeyance from 1952. Nankai's Economics Department had long enjoyed a high reputation nationally, with several research institutes, such as Accounting, Finance and International Economics (see Chan and Guan, 1986).

The Management Department had eight professors and associate professors, with over 50 faculty members in total. It offered a three-year postgraduate Management Enterprise Programme and four-year undergraduate programmes in the areas of Auditing, Economic Management and Management Information Systems respectively. There were over 200 undergraduates and over 65 postgraduates in management plus two PhD students. The main courses offered include: Accounting, Economics, Economic Management, Law, Management Psychology, National Economic Management and Technological Economics.

The Department had set up a collaborative programme with Canada for its three-year Masters degree. Canadian professors came to teach and 12 courses have been run to date by them, the others being run by the Chinese faculty. There were 35 students on the MBA programme. The Masters degree was awarded by Nankai, but the Canadians helped to select the students. When top students went to Canada, the Chinese authorities paid the travel costs to Laval, MacMaster and York Universities. The Canadian International Development Agency (CIDA) contributed the air fares and salary of the visiting Canadian faculty. Nankai paid for their accommodation and meals in China; the teaching materials and computers were contributed by CIDA.

Nankai had signed an agreement with the French government to run a programme for managers with work experience. This arrangement would involve the study of the French language for two years, followed by a professional study period of a further two years and a further six months in France. The five top students would be selected for subsequent PhD study. Initially, 15 candidates would be selected from enterprises, with all fees paid by the French side. Nankai University also trained personnel for enterprises and received payment for this service, covering all costs. All were trained on campus, not in-house, but had practice periods in their enterprises while studying. Short-term programmes of one year or six months were run by the Adult Education Department.

DISCUSSION

What then can we conclude from this account of a decade of Chinese university management education in China's three largest cities as presented above? Management training appeared to be *de rigueur* for most major universities. It had taken root in what too many outsiders looking at China, say, ten years or so ago might have thought infertile ground. Maoism and managerialism had then seemed to be a truly incompatible mixture. During the period of Deng's pragmatic policies, however, advanced management training had become relatively well-established, at least compared with earlier years, and probably reasonably accepted (see conjecture (a) on p. 61).

Yet there may have been an underestimation of the long-term implications of the new policy. Many officials thought that foreign experts could be brought in, pass on their knowledge and then hand

Table 5.3   Overview of university management schools under review

University	Founding date[1]	Total no. of students	No. of f/t mgt u/grads	No. of f/t mgt p/grads	No. of f/t mgt faculty members[2]	Main o/seas assistance and collab.
Beijing University	1912	>12,000	>200	30	33	USA and others
People's University	1950	>20,000	>250	130	120	Canada
Qinghua University	1911	>12,500	>250	>200	48	Canada, World Bank
Fudan University	1905	>10,000	>800	>200	149	World Bank, USA, Japan
Jiaotong University	1896	>12,000	>500	180	161	W. Germany, USA, Canada
Shanghai University of Finance & Economics (univ. status 1985)	(1919)	>6,000	>600	50	108	World Bank, Canada
Nankai University	1919	>10,000	>200	67	53	Canada, France

1. Founding date was of main university, not the earliest component college.
2. The official norm laid down by the SEDC was 1:6.6 for the teacher/student ratio.

Sources: Interviews, March–April 1988, and miscellaneous university handbooks/ catalogues.

over to their Chinese counterparts to teach indigenous students. This interpretation would, however, imply an overoptimistic view of the 'technology transfer' process or 'import substitution' (see conjectures (b) and (c)). Further, many courses were too descriptive of Western management practice, rather than linked to relevant Chinese experience, although the China–EC collaborative MBA programme, based at the Beijing Economic Management Cadres Training Centre, may have been an exception here.

Looking at the selected management training institutions which have been presented (see Table 5.3 for an overview), we can see they varied in student numbers and size of faculty. Variance in the teacher/student ratio may have been due to the presence of part-time and distance students. We also see how they built on their existing strengths and past experiences (conjecture (d)) that there were differences between the university management schools (UMS) and other economic management cadre training centres in China (described in the previous chapter). Most of the latter dealt with post-experience training, often of a short-course variety, although several

UMS had such activities and were increasingly developing them (see conjectures (e) and (f)). As in other countries, the UMS promoted both teaching and research, although it is hard to evaluate the second of these. The non-university training centres hardly engaged in research activities very directly. Computer and library facilities were disproportionately well endowed in the UMS, as might be expected, *vis-à-vis* cadre economic training centres for example, given that the former had access to university-wide resources (interviews in spring 1988).

As management studies was a relatively new subject in China in the 1980s, it was perhaps unrealistic to expect that the UMS have developed a distinctive approach, as say one might expect from a Harvard or a London Business School. Nonetheless, Chinese institutions clearly had enjoyed a strong reputation for excellence, such as Economics Analysis at Beijing University. Others had developed a quantitative approach and built on their reputation in Operations Research, such as Jiaotong and Qinghua Universities, respectively. The range of courses and electives was relatively wider in the UMS, compared with other training bodies, as were the opportunities for specialised advanced work, say at Masters level.

There was greater North American involvement in UMS programmes generally than from any other source, although greater Western European participation in academic links in the management studies area was envisaged by all the universities visited. The aid programme with the widest net was the Canadian one which had contributed to Masters and PhD level work at, for example, Jiaotong, Nankai and Qinghua Universities and described in detail earlier in this chapter, as well as at five others as can be seen in Table 5.4 (see Chan and Guan, 1986).

The 'flag-ship' American MBA programme in China was taught at Dalian. The initial announcement of the course was made in 1984 when Ronald Reagan, then President, visited the PRC. A five-year protocol was signed by the two countries committed to management education and funding was jointly provided by the US Department of Commerce and the PRC State Economic Commission. A budget of $2.1m was called for over the period.

The teaching was to take place at the National Centre for Industrial and Science Technology Management at Dalian, in north-east China. The US government had already sponsored executive management training on a higher education campus at the Dalian Institute of Technology, the name of the broader site, since 1980. Most of

Table 5.4   CIDA-funded universities in China for management education and their Canadian counterparts (up to 1985)

Chinese universities (location and special fields of concentration)	Canadian universities
Shanghai Jiaotong University (Shanghai: Management Engineering, Systems Management)	University of British Columbia
Xian Jiaotong University (Xian: Management Engineering, Machine Manufacturing Management)	University of Alberta University of Calgary University of Regina University of Saskatchewan University of Manitoba
Huzhong University of Technology (Wuhan: Management Engineering, Material Management)	University of Toronto University of Windsor Wilfrid Laurier University
Nankai University (Tianjin: Economic Management, Economics)	York University McMaster University Université de Laval
Qinghua University (Beijing: Management Engineering, Computerised Management)	Queen's University University of Ottawa
Chinese People's University (Beijing: Economic Management, Information Systems)	McGill University Hautes Études Commerciales Université du Quebec à Montreal Concordia University
Tianjin University (Tianjin: Management Engineering, Mechanical Engineering, Capital Construction Management)	McGill University Hautes Études Commerciales Université du Quebec à Montreal Concordia University
Xiamen University (Xiamen: Economic Management, Applied Economics)	Dalhousie University St Mary's University Technical University of Nova Scotia Université de Moncton Memorial University

Source: Chan and Guan (1986), p. 187.

these have had 180 registered participants for the six-month programme.

The goals of the course were to enhance management skills of
enterprise managers, to enable them to better cooperate with US and
Western joint-ventures and multinationals, and to train educators
and officials in this field. The broad mission was to introduce Western
management concepts and practices into the Chinese environment.

In the Chinese government's organisational structure, the State
Economic Commission supervised over 450,000 Chinese enterprises
up to 1988 and coordinated national economic planning among the
various ministries, with the State Science and Technology Commission in charge of most scientific and technical research institutions, and the Ministry of Education responsible for all the education
activities in the country. American activities in the programme were
administered by the US Department of Commerce, with the assistance of a contract organisation, the Asia Foundation in 1981 and
1982, Forecasting International Inc. in 1983 and 1984, and Chi
Associates Inc. in 1985.

Within the Department of Commerce, the programme was managed by Richard W. H. Lee, Director of Science and Technology
Programs, East Asia and the Pacific. All major academic issues such
as curriculum design and recruitment of US faculty were decided with
the assistance of a US Academic Advisory Committee. On the
Chinese side, Wang Hao of the Bureau of Economic Cadre Education in the State Economic Commission was the responsible official
in charge.

To support the Centre the Chinese organised a consortium of nine
institutions of higher learning in China. They included the Dalian
Institute of Technology, the People's University (Beijing), the University of International Business and Economics (Beijing), the Harbin Institute of Finance and Economics, the Hubei Institute of
Finance and Economics, and the Shanghai Institute of Science and
Technology.

The admissions net was to be cast nationally and enterprises had to
identify managers who would benefit from the course. A later selection was made after one year's study as to who was finally to be
admitted to the MBA 'core' activities. The programme was to extend
over three years, and to be taught in English. Each participant had to
write a project thesis, spend fourteen weeks on the US campus, and
up to four weeks as an 'intern' in a local firm there.

The structure of the course followed the fundamentals of a typical

North American MBA programme. The School of Management of the State University of New York at Buffalo was founded in 1927, by the mid-1980s had graduated 14,000 students in the field, and had a good reputation for both undergraduate and postgraduate studies. It provided the academic inputs for the programme. In the first year, both US and Chinese faculty members dealt with basic subjects, the latter teaching quantitative subjects, computing and social science. In the second year, American faculty members covered three modules of more advanced work. In the last module, part of the teaching took place on the Buffalo site.

The Dalian programme represented an experiment in direct North American educational intervention in management education and training for Chinese managers. Ongoing management problems were converging, as its mission statements emphasised:

> Although the American and Chinese economic systems are completely different in the role played by central planning, there is a great deal of similarity between the problems faced by managers day-by-day in the two systems. In China of course the means of production are publicly owned, in contrast with the US system based on private ownership. But the manager of the Chinese enterprise faces many of the same types of decisions as his American counterpart; the latter reports to shareholders through his board of directors, while the former reports to a government bureau. Both managers face certain rules and regulations laid down by the authorities in the government. Problems in cost accounting, production management, inventory control, personnel management, financial control and marketing, for example, all are remarkably similar in the two systems.
>
> (Dalian Programme Catalogue, 1985, p. 3)

An alternative model of intervention was provided by the joint China–EC Management Programme. It was taught at the National Management Centre in Beijing which was the home of the Training Centre for Economic Cadres (see Chapter 4). The first programme became operational in September 1984. The European contribution to the activity was managed by the European Foundation for Management Development on behalf of the EC. Although not on a university campus, the programme was at postgraduate level.

The programme was set up to address two concerns: first, to develop an interactive programme relevant to China's modernisation needs; second, to develop Chinese faculty members in management to be capable of adapting to a curriculum related to the first concern, and further adapt it to changing economic circumstances.

There were two main activities, namely the MBA and faculty development programmes. The central philosophy was to be as follows: 'Only by directly interacting with the real problems that Chinese industrial enterprises confront today . . . students (and teachers) will get a sense of which management methods will be of use and to what extent' (Programme, 1988, p. 2). The concept of 'hands-on experience' anchored the application of Western management notions to Chinese industrial enterprise practice.

The course had a conventional MBA format with a six-month English language input and eight teaching modules of eight weeks as illustrated in Appendix 3. These were each taught by European faculty members in English, and there was a period of placement in European enterprises for many successful students (see Figure 5.1). The programme took on a project-based approach with the students in 'consultancy groups' of five or six to 'advise' a Chinese industrial enterprise throughout the course. (Interviews, Spring 1988)

There were MBA intakes in 1985 (36 students), 1986 (66 students), 1988 (36 students) and 1989 (36 students). Almost all of these candidates graduated. A profile of one course's students is set out in Appendix 4. The MBA degree was awarded by an Academic Council composed of leading professors from European business schools. There had to date been two European Deans successively running the Programme, but it was envisaged that a Chinese Dean would eventually take over.

After the MBA course had been completed, a group of students were placed in European enterprises to enable them to see how Western firms work and to apply their management concepts. Each student was asked to work up a case study based on this experience, to be later used as teaching material in China. The project was jointly supervised by the China-EC Management Institute (CEMI) and a senior member of the firm in question. The cooperative arrangements for the placement were carried out by the Euro-China Association for Management Development (ECAM), as well as general activities involving China–EC collaboration.

In the summer of 1990, CEMI introduced a three-week executive training course for 60 managers, and in 1991 three such programmes a year would be run.

Taking into account the conjectures set out earlier in the chapter,

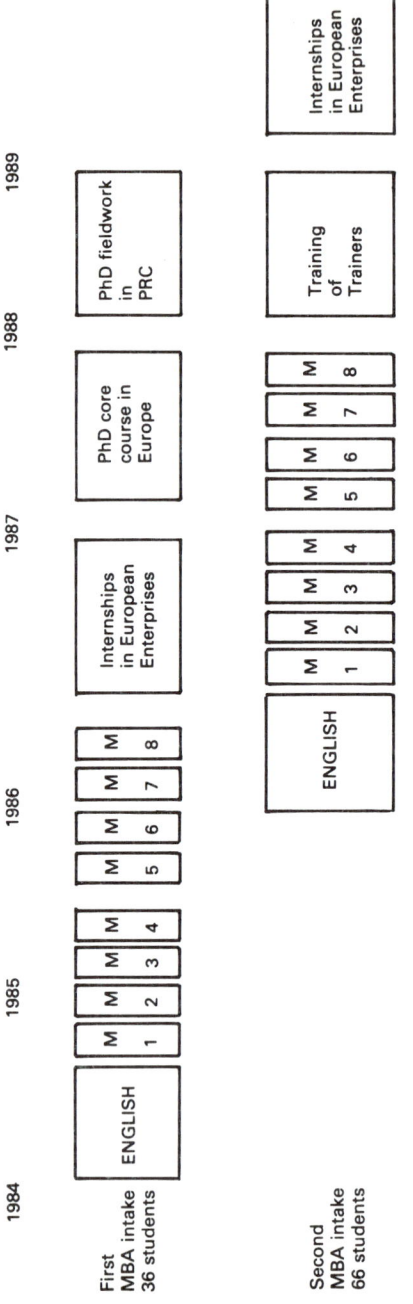

Figure 5.1   China-European Community Joint MBA Programme structure.
Source: based on Joint MBA Programme Prospectus (1986).

Chinese management education appeared to have had a less than fully coherent strategy, to the outside observer at least. It veered towards a set of reactive responses to, on the one hand, the perceived needs of the 'Four Modernisations' and 'Open Door' policies, and to, on the other hand, offers of quasi-technical aid from various Western countries and Japan. It nonetheless represented a fascinating variety of institutional responses to what appeared to be a critical shortage of trained managers and management teachers.

Taking the management teachers available (considerations of quality apart), there appeared to be a skewed age distribution. Since none were trained during the Cultural Revolution, they were either very old or very young, with few between 35 and 45 years old. Nearly half were young and relatively inexperienced. The teacher–student ratio in this field was higher than in other subjects on average. The solution was both to train more new instructors on Chinese campuses (and offer refresher courses to teachers in associated subjects), as well as to send only high-flyers abroad for advanced study.

The State Education Commission had hoped to pursue the following goals:

(1) To establish a development plan for management related courses and disciplines in accordance with the national economic and social development.
(2) To draw up a scheme for the training of teachers under the development plan.
(3) To seek additional sources of funds to improve the present conditions as much as possible.
(4) To accelerate reform and improve quality in education and teaching process.
(5) To widen the scope of international exchange activities.
(6) To strengthen research work in management related courses and disciplines.

(State Education Commission, 1987, p. 18)

However, only time will tell if the economic reforms will survive and whether management education will continue as mutually envisaged.

CONCLUDING REMARKS

To sum up, the management education programmes in China (in the UMS described above) represented some very useful organisational experiments, but were still some distance from a 'stable state' model. Since the earliest date of their initiation or re-establishment was no further away than a decade ago, it would, on the other hand, be unfair to expect them to have as yet resolved their strategic and/or structural problems. It was therefore premature to extrapolate the experiences of the decade, given the political uncertainty subsequent to the events of June 1989. The direction of management studies in Chinese universities remained an open question.

6 Industrial Training in Selected Chinese Enterprises

INTRODUCTION

This chapter will attempt to look at management and industrial training *vis-à-vis* new technology in Chinese enterprises and the degree to which there has been 'convergence' with comparable manufacturing organisations in Western advanced economies. It will focus on the interplay between microelectronics and manpower, as they influence variables affecting production in manufacturing. The role of 'culture' on this interplay will in turn be considered (see Sorge and Warner, 1986). In addition, it will try to give the reader a more informed understanding of how China is modernising its industries and what this means for both technical and management skills, particularly in the technically more advanced sector.

The development of a Chinese computer industry was an integral part of the 'Four Modernisations' policy, which sought, as we have already seen, to improve Agriculture, Industry, Science and Technology, and Defence (see Chapter 1). In terms of its external rivals the industry's history was short, but nonetheless it had established itself in a surprisingly short time. One of the reasons for its progress had been the drive for self-sufficiency, partly for strategic reasons and partly for economic ones. The nationalistic motive had also been a factor in the situation. Clearly, to develop a core of skills and expertise had been another important element. The electronics sector, as a recent World Bank Report notes, held a strategic position in economies like China's (see Khanna, 1986). It grew rapidly, and its progress was virtually synonymous with modernisation in the industry.

The 1950s saw the first phase basically consisting of straight copying; after this followed a period of emulating and adapting hardware. However, the early Chinese computers were made in uneconomic small batches, and were not very reliable. The late 1970s then saw a clear policy of encouraging science and technology and computers became a priority area (Simon, 1987). Looking eastwards to Japan, and even further eastwards to California's Silicon Valley, the Chinese realised that their economic takeoff would not be possible without developing both hardware and software in order to enter the so-called 'information society'.

By 1985, there were over a quarter of a million computers in the PRC, compared with five million microcomputers alone in the USA (Simon, 1987, p. 199). But China was moving quickly, albeit from a small statistical base, with very rapid rates of growth per annum. In one computer factory investigated by the present writer, for example, production of PCs was set to double in a year, by 1988. This was very fast growth by any standards. Many computers were and some still are more or less adaptations of foreign models, especially IBMs, and many parts were imported, as was for example testing equipment (interviews in selected computer factories, summer 1987). Nonetheless, specific advances in both hardware and software were aspired to. Adapting the models to Chinese usage and specific applications was given priority, as was developing Chinese Character Disk Operating Systems; CC/DOS, as it was called for short, was now very common.

Imports of computers, in mostly knockdown form, were an initial feature of the early stage, partly because of import duties and partly due to Western restrictive controls on exports to Communist countries. But dependence on foreign sources had led the Chinese to emphasise R&D in the electronics industry, particularly where there are military applications. It was clear that developments in aerospace had for example called for sophisticated technology in the electronics area, and missile and rocket advances have required indigenous skills in both the scientific and technological areas. In addition, a recent emphasis of government policy had been to increase the collaboration between industry and education, by direct sponsoring of students by firms, and contract research arrangements, and this has particularly been true of high technology enterprises.

China had now, according to World Bank estimates, about 3,000 firms involved in electronics manufacture, providing jobs for around one and a half million workers, and producing just under two and a half per cent of total industrial output (Khanna, 1986, p. 29). The more technologically advanced firms numbered about 600, employing over 50,000 workers. Such firms were, of course, only a *fraction* of the 450,000 enterprises overseen by the State Economic Commission. Given the low cost of labour, some believed China should continue with older technologies, as they were more labour-intensive. On the other hand, newer technologies offered notable economic benefits, as mentioned earlier.

Could China move into large-scale production of micro-electronics? The answer was probably positive, if a long enough time-horizon was allowed. As the four 'little dragon' economies of South-East Asia (namely, Hong Kong, Singapore, South Korea and Taiwan) moved upmarket, China may have been able to find a niche, given its labour cost advantages. Again, with its scientific and technological ingenuity, it may have found short-cuts in production methods, but any immediate leap was improbable. It is difficult to predict the future industrial policy of an emerging economy, and questions of whether or not there will be a flourishing home-base for production of microelectronics have concerned decision-makers in many Western countries, not only those on the road to development. In any event, the decision seems to have been made to take the high technology route, as part of the 'Four Modernisations' policy. It is clear that education and training would play an important role in such a move, and Chinese policy-makers have seen that higher education and research were vital components of this commitment.

Part and parcel of this development was the production of science and technology graduates, teaching undergraduate and Masters students at home, and sending advanced postgraduates abroad. However, now there was a shift in emphasis to increase the number of arts and social science graduates, as many kinds of students are needed to become tomorrow's managers. Next, sciences and technology had to become more closely linked with industry, and vice versa; enterprises too had to help to fund universities upon which they were dependent for trained manpower, and research via contracts.

Many Chinese high technology firms had links with specific universities and research institutes upon which they drew for new graduate intake and continuing education for existing graduate technical staff. Lecturers from such higher education bodies had to 'moonlight', to supplement their meagre salaries, by giving training courses in enterprises. It was a practice which was very commonly found in the high technology firms to be described below. Quite often the training bureau of the enterprise would employ a full-time core staff, and then bring in external instructors as needed (interviews, summer 1987).

MANPOWER

In order to build its own microelectronics sector, China had to have a 'critical mass' of both hardware and software specialists. This was no easy task given the general lack of skilled personnel in the context of the country's backwardness. The Cultural Revolution in the middle 1960s and early 1970s too had left its mark, with much havoc caused to the educational and training systems. As part of the 'Four Modernisations' policy, it was necessary to bring in foreign experts, a long-standing tradition in China, to hasten technology transfer and to train Chinese computer and information scientists (Spence, 1980). Technicians and students were also sent abroad to become familiar with Western knowledge and techniques. Most of these went to the USA, Western Europe and Japan, as noted previously.

As we have seen in Chapters 3 and 5, the number of university-level graduates in China was estimated at six million, but as many of these qualified in the turbulent years of political upheaval with shortened and diluted courses, this may not have been a very helpful yardstick. In short, China had a shortage of highly educated personnel, specifically in the areas related to science and technology, as well as general shortfalls at many other levels. There had, however, been a considerable expansion of higher education since 1949. The total number of institutions in this category had grown from 200 in the 1950s to over 1,000 currently. Student enrolment exceeded two million (see Table 3.1), but with under 120,000 graduate students and a very small minority of doctoral candidates.

If Western countries had skill shortages in the new technology area, the problem was compounded in China. As noted earlier, there was a virtual absence of applications engineers in the manufacturing sector. The lack of in-house engineering skills was partly mitigated by outside consultants, but this was a development in its embryonic stages. Part-time university and institute assistance could only marginally help resolve the problem.

Not only were science and technology graduates needed, but also trained technicians and skilled workers. Vocational education continued to be a priority area (Times Higher Education Supplement, 8 March 1991). In addition, management training for many different groups was essential to help the more effective use of resources.

China had not only a Higher Educational Commission (HEC) both at national and provincial levels, but also a Vocational Education Commission (VEC) which paralleled its work. Work at the provincial level was very important as the areas and populations covered are often as large as many Western European countries. The Guangdong HEC was resposible for a provincial population of around 60 million people; the Fujian VEC dealt with over 30 million. At city level, the local economic commission had its own education bureau, such as at Xiamen, responsible for a population of over one million.

At each of these levels, there was a growing emphasis on techno-logical expertise. At first, the SEC prepared a plan of overall man-power needs for the Seventh Five-Year Plan which was then broken down into specifics. Education was linked with the economy via the qualitative as well as the quantitative aspects of the plan. The provincial HEC then was responsible for implementing it, say, for Guangdong province, and local government has local control as it paid for most of the sub-degree and undergraduate students, who there numbered 84,000 in all. Enterprises made known their needs at local level, indeed over ten per cent of students were funded by enterprise (interviews, Guangdong Higher Education Commission, summer 1987).

Vocational education first started early this century, but after the 'Liberation' in 1949, progress was more rapid. During the Cultural Revolution, however, it came to a standstill (CEDEFOP, 1987, p. 38). Its promotion became part of the Sixth Five-Year Plan, and the government encouraged the building of technical schools and teach-ing teams. At provincial level, the foundations were laid. In Fujian, for example, the VEC made a plan for the province, coordinated the different departments and gives direction. Every bureau had an education office at all levels of local government and this was repli-cated in the enterprises. Around half a million students who lost out on their education and training during the Cultural Revolution needed courses and examining, and over two million were dealt with in workers' education classes, among other vocational education activities. About five per cent of the working population in the province had qualifications ranging upwards from a workers' edu-cation college diploma; technical school graduates constituted nearly nine per cent; middle school over 35 per cent; and high school over 22 per cent (interviews, Fujian VEC, summer 1987).

Advanced technical workers made up about two and a half per cent, with a technical qualification in eight parts. There were over 85,000 workers out of a total population of thirty million who had qualifications above technician level. Professional training was part of the most recent policy changes, with 84 experimental sites, in order to link more closely with the needs of enterprises. At factory level, the director had to make a plan for the four-year period of office, and spend one and a half per cent of the total wage bill on training, with an emphasis on technical and vocational education. How this worked out at enterprise level, particularly in the case of high technology firms, will be illustrated in the case studies which follow.

SELECTED CASE STUDIES

The research upon which this study is based was carried out in several Chinese high technology sector enterprises in the summer of 1987. It covered six sites engaged in the production of computers, advancing their research and development, and turning out consumer electronic goods and electrical equipment.

In each case, we look at the nature of the firm, production methods, management organisation, skills, training, and rewards structure.

The enterprises varied in size from 240 to 3,000 workers, and were located in the North (in Beijing) and in the South-East of China, (in Fuzhou and Xiamen.) The ownership varied from wholly Chinese to joint-venture and exclusive Hong Kong control. The skill level was, on average, high, with a range from skilled to very skilled. Wages were mostly higher than normally found in Chinese firms. Training was, on the whole, well above average. The percentage of graduates and technicians employed was also noteworthy. About half the firms had conventional three-year apprenticeships; the others were more flexible. Nearly all had trade unions in the workplace (see Warner, 1987c), but not all had Workers' Congresses (see Table 6.1).

An important example was the Beijing Computer Factory No. 3, making the 'Great Wall' PC. The factory dated from the mid-1960s, but had only started PC production in 1985. Originally, it had built a minicomputer, the DJS 130, but not any more. From 1982, it began PC production, with its main product the IBM PC/XT/AT 16-bit microcomputer with a 68000 Motorola chip. The export price of the machine was about US $3,000, against a domestic price of 32,000 yuan. As it used the Chinese character system, CC/DOS, the price was higher than other PC/ATs. The domestic price was relatively high because of the high import-content of parts and equipment. The basic model on sale has been the 'Great Wall' 0520, but a new model five times as fast was available called the 286 (see *China Daily*, 9 August 1987).

The factory had expanded as a result of government support for a 'Chinese' model and had around 800 employees on the payroll, making 10,000 machines a year. Nationally, the state-owned computer company to which the plant belongs made 25,000 per annum altogether.

The organisation structure of the enterprise consisted of four departments:

Table 6.1   Characteristics of the enterprises studied

Organisational characteristics	Case number					
	1 *Beijing Computer*	*2* *Beijing R&D*	*3* *Fuzhou Computer*	*4* *Fuzhou TV*	*5* *Xiamen Elect.*	*6* *Xiamen Tel.*
Size (employed)	800	600	984	900	3,000	240
Ownership	Nat.	Nat.	Nat.	Nat.	Joint	O/seas
Skill level	H	H	H	M	M	M
Training	H	H	H	M	M	M
Apprentices/yrs	3	3	2	—	2	—
Wages/av. month/Y (RMB)	> 66	>120	> 80	>80	>150	>200
Trade Union	+	+	+	+	+	–
Workers' Congress	+	+	+	+	–	–

Key: H = high; M = medium; + = present; – = absent.

Source: Interviews, summer 1987.

- Production
- Design
- Sales
- Service

plus ancillary departments of:

- Finance and accounting
- External economic relations
- Business management.

The labour force configuration was broken down in rough figures into over 200 employees as technicians, 100 in research and development, 130 in administration, over 100 in sales, 700 production workers, and 130 in the new products department. There were in addition over 100 management cadres.

The training function was given considerable emphasis. Thirty people had been sent overseas to the USA and Japan. Training for the others and customers took place in the factory. There were altogether five full-time personnel organising training, who mostly selected the tutors to be brought in from outside. Younger workers were trained on the job, by technicians and engineers. There were apprentices but no special 'masters' as found normally in Chinese industry. The technicians received continuous education from the prestigious Qinghua University, Beijing Industrial University, and foreign experts. Wages were standard as in the rest of the economy, with eight grades. The range was 36 to 110 yuan per month, but after finishing the first year of apprenticeship 40 yuan. Technicians got somewhat more, with 56 yuan, rising after one year to 66. Managerial rewards went up to 120 yuan basic. Bonuses were added at all levels. At the time the research was done, there were nearly 6 units of currency, the yuan, to the pound sterling at the official rate of exchange, in the form of Foreign Exchange Certificates, or FEC, which tourists and foreign visitors have to use, and about 50 per cent more unofficially. At the time of writing, the yuan has been further devalued.

The Director was appointed (for four years) and not elected; the Under-Director and Secretary could be elected, however, and the Workers' Congress would be involved in such elections. It would 'just discuss' several other matters such as the strategic plan made by the Director, wages, housing, etc., and met once a year or *ad hoc*. The trade union dealt with such things as workers' education, birth control propaganda and so on. Its main task was to carry out the policies agreed by the Workers' Congress. The Chairman of the union was considered to be at the same level as the Under-Director of the factory.

The Party Committee of the factory still played an important role, with one in four of the employees belonging to the Party. At the time, they were discussing a recent government document on 'How To Put The Party In Order'.

The future plans for the enterprise were most ambitious. Another site was being built for the Seventh Five-Year Plan, with a capacity of 50,000 units per annum. However, the workforce would not be enlarged, except by the recruitment of 20 college graduates a year.

The next case investigated was the Research and Development Institute for Computer Technology, in Beijing. It had been built in 1979 for the development of computers, but now its general direction was in the area specifically of micros and their applications. In 1980, it had been building 8-bit machines, and had then moved onto 16-bit IBM PC/XT compatible applications. In 1987, a new kind of model was launched (namely the BCM 0530, CPU 80286, which was IBM PC/AT compatible). The Institute carried out design and development as well as working on single-board computers. It was offering the BCM TT on the market, a special product used in video transmission for editing Chinese characters on the TV screen and used by national and local broadcasting stations.

Applications were mostly used in hotels, banks, manufacturing and so on. Enterprise uses included financial, office and planning functions. Recently, the Institute collaborated with the agricultural bureau for cataloguing ancient trees. It also developed a system for the exchange of housing. Chinese character processing was now being built into the hardware, to come up on the screen. Special applications for process control were also launched.

The Institute developed software for PC DOS and specific uses (the examples for business usage included BCM PC, BCM 3, and BCM 0530). The situation differed from Western countries *vis-à-vis* copying software, without copyright being applicable. Enterprises copied easily and cheaply and for their own use. Some customers gave specifications and the Institute produced machines and software at the same time. The clients often passed on the software to other firms.

The cost of a machine naturally depended on the model and enterprise concerned. One example involved collaboration lasting for one year with a large factory making electronic components which brought in fees of 20,000 yuan. A BCM PC model, for instance, cost 20,000 yuan, like the IBM XT, including a hard disk and two floppy disks, with the printer extra as it came from Hong Kong. This model was the cheapest in the range; the 'Great Wall' was about 20 per cent more expensive. The BCM 0530 was the only type still actually in production, with 500 units being made this year. The Institute basically concentrated on research and development, and did not manufacture in any volume. It was an autonomous profit-centre, with funding obtained from the banks and with no public subsidy.

The staff of the Institute was around 100 cadres, 100 technicians and over 200 workers. There were five research departments, and two workshops added more operatives to make a total complement of 600. New technicians were regularly recruited from universities and technical institutes, and about 40 each year joined the Institute in this way. Staff were also sent abroad to Japan, Canada and elsewhere for further training, some even paying for themselves. Several workers were enrolled in the TV University. Wages averaged 85 yuan per month basic; this was not very high due to the high number of very young workers in the unit, given its recent origins. Apprentices earned about 50 yuan over three years of training. Total individual average income per month with bonuses and benefits came to about 120 yuan.

Another interesting case was that of the Fujian Electronics and Computer Company in Fuzhou, founded in 1981. The computer division was part of a complex of four factories, making in addition TV sets, transistor parts and auto equipment. In addition, there were two research institutes, three technical service companies, two joint-ventures and a technical training school. The range of products in the electronics and computer side covered calculators, cassette re-corders, PCs and industrial applications. The computers ranged from a super microcomputer, to IBM PC/XT and AT models, and a cheap educational model. They also produced Winchester-drives. The total production consisted of 200 of the top-range models per year, selling at 150,000 to 200,000 yuan; 1,500 of the middle of the range PCs at 800 to 60,000 yuan; and the low-price educational models at 500–600 yuan.

The factory could keep its profits after tax to reinvest and distri-bute as welfare benefits. Its gross revenue in 1986 was 40 million yuan. The total number in employment at the four sites came to 3,400, and the computer site specifically had a workforce of almost 1,000. This was broken down into 360 cadres and technicians with 2-, 3- and 4- year graduate qualifications, together with 624 administra-tive and production staff. The percentage of highly skilled staff was very noteworthy. The training programme was very systematic and geared to the different occupational levels of cadres, technicians, skilled workers and operatives.

The managerial staff attended training schools for management cadres and had to take the national examinations. At department director level, they took either the TV University courses or went to the provincial-level management training school for four months, with one month for lower-level administrators. Many of the tech-nicians were trained in-house, and already had graduate diplomas. Some were trained by outside experts who came in to give lectures; others were sent to universities for further study. The skilled workers had to follow TV courses and in-house skills training classes. As for the operatives, they were usually from technical schools, and came in as apprentices after two years there. They came to the factory to train on the computer assembly line and after qualifying were able to work in other factories in the corporation. The apprenticeship period was one year here, with 40 yuan per month wages. The rewards structure for the workforce was as follows: 80 yuan basic per month for qualified workers, 110 for technicians, and 130 for those above these levels.

A case where the skill level was somewhat less high was the Fujian TV factory, which had been set up in 1958 in Fuzhou. It made TV sets and computer monitors, producing altogether 160,000 sets per year and around 1,000 monitors. The Factory Director here was a woman, originally trained as an electrical engineer. Black and white TV sets in China sold at about 400 yuan, which was three to four months' salary for industrial workers (about £65 sterling at the time of writing).

Its organisation structure consisted of 18 departments and four workshops, with the main Directors in charge of the main office, finance, production, and so on. The number of people working in the factory was over 900, broken down into 600 permanent workers, 200 contract and 100 temporary (the latter somewhat unusual, with part-time being even rarer). The Workers' Congress supervised the Factory Director in principle. It concerned itself with the strategic plans, wages and salary levels and overall product quality. The trade union carried out the day-to-day task of representation of workers' concerns, allocation of housing, recreation, educational activities, etc. Workers paid, as elsewhere, 0.5 per cent of their wages to the union, with three-quarters of the total amount collected passed onto the provincial office of the national trade union federation (ACFTU). All cadres had to take the management examination. If they had passed three courses they could work in the offices. No cadres, however, went on outside courses.

All cadres and workers were encouraged to take spare-time classes and many attended vocational schools in Fuzhou for these purposes. The skilled workers mostly went to night-schools, but the technicians went to technical school for two years on a spare-time basis, with a 50 yuan bonus per annum for this course, 100 for a three-year diploma course, and 150 for a university diploma.

The educational level was that of high school on average; if below this, workers had to take classes to reach the appropriate level. There were no apprenticeships, and employees signed labour contracts when starting with the enterprise. Wage levels were in the region of 80 to 90 yuan per month, including bonuses, for workers at grade 3 and 4, the average qualified level. The top cadres were paid 170–180 yuan per month including bonuses.

The next site to be considered is the Xiamen Overseas Chinese Electronic Company, one of the most successful joint-ventures in China since the new policy was launched in 1978. This firm was one of 128 such cases in the Xiamen Special Economic Zone in Fujian province, which now extended over the whole city, out of 700 enterprises in total. It mainly produced electronic consumer goods and component parts, with its capital equipment imported directly from Japan for the most part. About 10 per cent of production went for export, but the target was 70 per cent. The enterprise was relatively advanced technologically and had a great deal of computer-controlled equipment with integrated production systems. It had eight production lines in each of thirteen factory units. It was a large site with over 3,000 employees, a high proportion of whom were skilled.

The products ranged from TV sets, cassettes, radios, PCBs and so on. The Director of the enterprise was responsible for the seven departments, comprising production, marketing, accounts, etc., with five main directors and seven departmental managers. In addition, there were thirteen factory managers. These cadres were recruited from all over China.

Training was now being improved and several assistant engineers were being sent abroad to the USA and Hong Kong. Because the factory was still expanding, it was recruiting labour. It had enough specialists in most areas but there was a shortage of people with a knowledge of foreign trade, English and computers, especially to operate the IBM and Wang PCs in the administrative offices.

The salary structure for managers provided for over 170 yuan per month basic, but in excess of 200 yuan for technicians with university qualifications. Skilled workers with technical qualifications received over 150 yuan monthly plus bonuses. Labour contracts were for three years initially, and then for ten if permanently hired (see White, 1987). New workers came from technical schools and after two years' training were taken on (see CEDEFOP, 1987).

Engineering and technology specialists were hired from universities, the enterprise having special connections with institutions like Xiamen Science Institute. The personnel department did the hiring, as well as using the Xiamen SEZ Labour Service Company, especially for skilled workers and lesser grades. The Service attracted recruits via newspaper advertisements, but the company itself did the testing. There was a trade union in the enterprise, but no Workers' Congress.

The last case to be considered was a company making consumer electronics, Supertronics, in Xiamen. This plant was a subsidiary of a Hong Kong enterprise, and was established in 1984. It made telephones and speaker-phones, producing 600,000 units per year, all exported to the USA.

It was not a joint venture, as all its funds came from Hong Kong, and had a similar method of management to its parent firm. The latter set the production plan and sold the final products. The managing director controlled six departmental heads concerned with production, quality assurance, testing, etc. Next, came the workshop and group leaders in each of the four workshops. Some parts were produced outside by about 100 employees. There were altogether 240 workers in the plant itself, of whom 13 were cadres, seven were technicians and eight advanced workers.

Young workers received 140 yuan basic during a three-month training period, and henceforth the full wage per month of 200. Skilled people earned an average of 300 yuan, and technicians between 250 and 350 yuan monthly. Managers could earn up to 500 yuan per month. Most of the labour force were skilled, three-quarters being women who joined the firm after middle-school. They learnt on the job, and there were no apprenticeships. The remainder of the workforce were technical school products, plus graduate technicians and cadres. More attention was paid to the personality and work habits of the recruits than formal qualifications. At the end of the year (when the plant was less busy) management cadres, including workgroup leaders, were sent to Hong Kong for training.

There was no trade union and no Workers' Congress. Some foreign-owned firms in the SEZ had unions; others did not. There were labour contracts, but these were for no fixed period and there were no part-time workers. Ten per cent of the workforce were temporary labour, released when demand slackened. Recruiting was via newspaper advertisements or personal introductions. About 60 people applied for a couple of jobs last time they were advertised.

DISCUSSION

Whilst the range of products varied between the cases considered, there were many common features. None of the factories was highly automated; all relied on considerable labour-intensive manufacturing processes. None of the firms was self-contained in that they had integrated production systems, with one exception; all relied on high proportions of imported components. Nearly all the capital equipment used came from abroad.

Nonetheless, there was an attempt in several firms to produce 'new Technology with Chinese characteristics', the 'Great Wall' PC being a case in point. Merely copying foreign products was not considered enough, although many products were IBMs by any other name. Some TV production was for the home market, but others were marketed explicitly with foreign brand-names, as were many other consumer electronic products.

As for organisational characteristics, the firms conformed closer to indigenous forms than Western ones. Wages were often much higher than would be the norm in Chinese industry, given the higher levels of skills involved and the greater preponderance of technicians and technologists. This latter feature reflected the relative complexity of the technology and the occupational structure of the enterprise was closer to that of a Western firm in the high technology sector than might have been imagined initially (see Warner, 1986d).

This latter factor was mitigated, however, by the cultural constraints on the enterprise, both because and in spite of the norms of the 'Four Modernisations' policy. The economic reforms would 'pull' the enterprise towards relative convergence, but other values in the system would 'push' towards relative divergence with comparable firms in the West. With the former, technological and economic necessity would shape organisational behaviour towards great differentiation *vis-à-vis* other firms in the economy, but the latter would prevent the actors stepping beyond the boundaries laid down by the system. Thus, Chinese high technology firms still looked more like their non-advanced counterparts than the nature of the technology and products would lead us to expect, and dissimilar from Western firms in many significant respects. However, this observation may have rested on the alleged technological and managerial backwardness of Chinese enterprises generally, even high technology ones.

Walking round Chinese high technology plants, one could not have failed to be struck by a specific *couleur locale*. The very first day of the very first visit, there was no electricity all day as there had been a power cut in that part of the capital. It was therefore not possible to see any of the machines or products working. The factories ranged in appearance from fairly modern to positively old-fashioned and drab. The layout too was, with some exceptions, very conventional. Working conditions were reasonable, and given the extremely high temperature when the factory visits took place – it was often over 35 degrees Centigrade – the workplaces and offices were quite well ventilated. Nonetheless, workers on the line and in the offices had fallen asleep and were given a gentle prod by the supervisors as we passed by.

Convergence was clearly a myth in such circumstances. The reality was that comparisons of organisations and their socio-technical systems have shown up subtle and less subtle cultural dimensions in the workplace (Maurice, Sorge and Warner, 1980). Whilst there may be many archaic factories in China, and whilst the ones using newer technologies, or even advanced ones, to make microelectronic, electronic and electrical products may be very much less backward, it is hard to see where convergence had taken place. In one important study using a methodology which had been extensively used in firms in twelve Western European countries, Chinese enterprises were found to have experienced a shift away from ideological norms towards economic ones (see Laaksonen, 1988). In this sense, they were less like socialist-type organisations, but how far their managers can be compared to Western ones has yet to be seen, and is at least debatable.

In terms of human resource management, greater professionalisation and training were now visible in Chinese enterprises, as I have argued elsewhere (Warner, 1986). In this sense, there had been a move away from the Maoist norms which of course made the Chinese workplace very distinctive indeed.

CONCLUDING REMARKS

The case for convergence has, in the investigation described above at least, not been upheld. True, there were resemblances between Chinese high technology firms and their Western counterparts, but the intervening variable of national culture, indeed of social system, modified the relationship between technology and organisation, as well as between itself and the manpower configuration of skills and training. There was, as in other studies, no clear one-to-one relationships. The 'societal effect' was noticeable in that 'Chinese characteristics' were very much present in all the sites visited. Technology transfer was in any case only partial. Hardware may have travelled better than software, and if management training is included in the latter, or in what one may call 'peopleware', only limited transplantation may have taken place, whether intended or otherwise.

Part Three
Comparisons and Conclusions

7 Comparisons with Other Countries

INTRODUCTION

In this chapter the emergence of different models of management education and training will be discussed *vis-à-vis* that of the Chinese. We shall describe and analyse their respective characteristics in their industrial and cultural contexts, and ask what lessons might be derived from their development.

In contrasting Chinese with the European, American and Japanese and other approaches to management training, we must note that there was no identifiable optimal training 'model' as such: there were a variety of approaches, *each* related to a *national* context. Thus we can, at best, speak of a British or a French or a German model in this specific field, which in turn related to the general education and training institutions to be found in those respective countries. Consequently, the countries will be considered *separately*. Trying to conflate the wide spread of management education models into meaningful subsets was problematic. Critics have noted that the members of any subset have idiosyncratic characteristics. The reader is thus reminded to bear in mind *national* differences throughout.

Specific variables which might have permitted comparisons (and which will be discussed in turn) include lateness of industrialisation, the nature and pace of industrialisation, the social and cultural norms which preceded the industrialisation process and their associated patterns of elite formation, the nature of the socio-political system, the social class system and the rate of social and geographical mobility, amongst others (see Figure 7.1).

The approach which follows is mostly exploratory, but hopes to suggest a pattern of development of management education models, nonetheless. Aware of the difficulties of developing a methodology robust enough to deal with the variance described, we have therefore limited ourselves to some cautious comparisons. It is probably not feasible in this context to go beyond an institutional analysis when one is dealing with such macro-phenomena, and indeed it may not be appropriate or desirable, given the nature of the data available. The

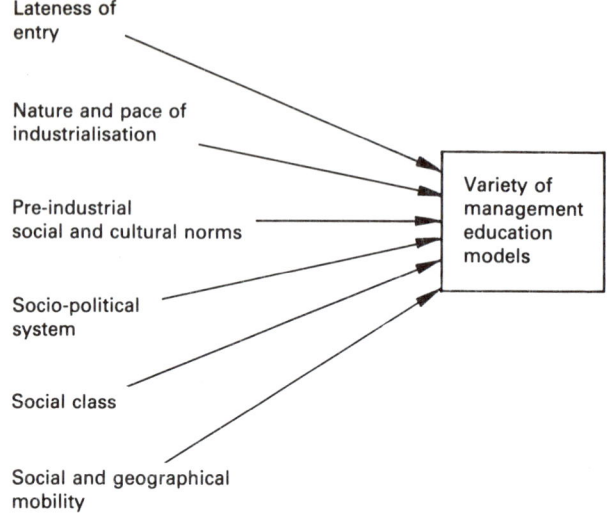

Figure 7.1 Possible explanatory factors relating to the variety of management education models.

reliance on mostly secondary data for many of the countries in the comparison could be defended on grounds of limited research resources. However, most of the data on Japan and Yugoslavia was collected at first-hand, as was that on China.

This chapter will concentrate on the comparative and analytical aspects of management education across a number of country contexts. It has relied heavily on a limited number of settings, namely the earlier developers such as the British, French, German and American, as well as the later Japanese, Yugoslav, Soviet and finally Chinese 'models' (to which we will give greater attention and detail for the purpose of comparison). This emphasis did admittedly not do sufficient justice to a number of geographical areas like South America, Africa, the Asian subcontinent or Australasia for example, but it was felt that it was better to consider only the countries of which the author had either recent first-hand acquaintance professionally or for which more accessible secondary data was forthcoming. A noteworthy attempt to deal with some of these areas (Cornwall-Jones, 1985), however, described cases where the Henley (at that time, the Administrative Staff College) model had been diffused, in India, Pakistan, Bangladesh, Australia and New Zealand, Ghana, the Philippines and so on, in the period 1948–84.

Finally, we hope to say something about the contemporary problems of educational 'technology transfer' in so far as the 'software' of management training was involved. If there is the possibility of transfer from other countries, how would this be feasible and what would be the attendant problems?

SELECTED NATIONAL MANAGEMENT EDUCATION SYSTEMS

The British case

In the early stages of capitalist development, for example in the experience of Britain during the Industrial Revolution in the eighteenth century, economic growth was not accompanied by very formal management education and training; British managers, like British gentlemen, were born rather than made (Whitley, Thomas and Marceau, 1981, p. 31). Britain had started earlier and had become the 'first industrial nation' by 1750. Its growth may be said to have been based on raw empiricism: problems were 'met and solved *ad hoc*' (Pollard, 1956, p. 189) with innovations developing slowly, often over several decades, 'with no sets of principles to guide the innovators' (Warner, 1984, p. 34).

If we examine the link between the Industrial Revolution and management education, we see that there was the development of a parallel stream to the secondary and higher education system, namely the evolution of new training institutions. The Nonconformist Academy was prominent, being 'vocational in objective' (Pollard, 1965, p. 141); later, new universities emphasised the 'new' subjects and opened their doors to social and religious groups excluded from the traditional universities of Oxford and Cambridge. But the educational monopoly of the latter delayed the onset of the newer higher educational institutions except in Scotland. There was a second stream of activity directed towards the skilled artisan, namely the Mechanics' Institutes, but these 'quickly became swamped by the demands of white collar workers and lost the support of the artisans' (Pollard, 1965, p. 145). But formal management education 'was so rare as to be negligible' (1965, p. 147) – managers were trained by 'practical work in the firm'. The larger and more progressive firms carried out more than a negligible amount of in-house training: in the commercial sphere, the East India Company had its own Staff College.

During the nineteenth century, and for part of the twentieth, British enterprises dominated world markets without evolving a national management education system (perhaps one might argue they did not need to) and this state of affairs persisted until the Second World War. Before 1939, it is true there was a limited output of graduates in commerce from universities such as Birmingham and Edinburgh. The post-war years, however, saw business courses developing at the undergraduate level. Yet it was not until the 1960s that the need for state-supported postgraduate management education was realised (with the setting up of the London and Manchester Business Schools), although recently called into question with a demand for 'privatisation' (Griffiths and Murray, 1985). The universities were producing about 1,000 MBAs a year by the 1970s, a mere drop in the ocean *vis-à-vis* the one and a half million managers in Britain, or 6 per cent of the total workforce (Rose, 1970, p. 14), and this had probably not increased beyond 1,250 MBAs by the mid-1980s. By this time, there was a call for an annual output of 10,000 MBAs (*Financial Times*, 15 July 1985, p. 14) by the late 1990s. However, there was a good chance this number might be achieved. There were at the time of writing 2,500 full-time MBA places (as well as 2,700 part-time ones, with 2,800 distance-learning Masters candidates).

To expand the quantity and quality of British management education will not be a straightforward task. As the Principal of the London Business School lately pointed out:

> To achieve balanced excellence is never easy. It is particularly difficult in Britain at the moment. Employer-led developments, such as the Management Charter Initiative, are calling for greater 'practicality' and 'relevance' and for greater emphasis on 'training' and 'development' and less on 'education'. At the same time, business schools are increasingly becoming privatized organisations that are expected not only to earn their keep but also to contribute to general university funds by engaging in a wide variety of income-generating activities.

Difficult or not, however, balanced excellence is the goal that British business schools need to strive for. It would strengthen their position both inside and outside universities. It would also help them to provide managers with what they really need: a broadly-based foundation for life-long learning in careers that, given the increasingly dynamic and global nature of modern business, are likely to be pursued in more than one organization, in more than one industry, and in more than one country.

(Bain, 1990, p. 13)

If we look at post-experience courses established (particularly from the late 1940s onwards) the numbers were greater, but the courses were of limited duration. By the early 1980s, such courses were becoming shorter and numbers on each fewer. Over 40,000 were attending these programmes at that time, with up to 60,000 on internal training courses, respectively just over 2.5 per cent and 4 per cent of all managers.

Western Europe: the French and German cases

We have already seen that Britain clearly industrialised first in the eighteenth century, ahead of France, with Germany (and the USA) well behind until the 1840s in their share of world industrial output (see Hobsbawm, 1969, p. 342). The USA was, in turn, to shoot ahead of Britain in the 1860s (1969, p. 342). But it was not until 1870 that Germany began to grow level with Britain in steel production (but not yet in pig-iron production) with the USA a poor third. By this date, Britain was still well ahead of the USA in cotton goods production, with Germany well behind (1969, p. 347). It was not until the 1890s that the Americans clearly led the British in coal, pig-iron, steel and cotton output (1969, p. 343).

Comparing Britain with France and Germany, the roots of the latters' systems appear to be: (a) medieval craft apprenticeships, (b) state engineering schools, for which France was the pioneer during the late eighteenth century, and (c) the classical universities. The contrast with the USA is apparent. These institutions could be seen as centres of gravity, each exerting a pull which has been *different* in each of the three nations (see Maurice, Sorge and Warner, 1980; Sorge and Warner, 1986; Lane, 1989). Apprenticeships were most strongly developed in Germany, where they eventually formed the core of professional training in handicrafts, industry and commerce (Porter, 1990, p. 369). Furthermore, Germany absorbed a modified system of public higher technical education from France, separate from the classical universities, but which was more decentralized (see Locke, 1989). French education and training was based on the prestigious higher schools of engineering which formed part of the *grandes écoles*, with a leaning towards higher level training. Intermediate schools for technicians and master craftsmen often developed into such *grandes écoles*. The apprenticeship system weakened in France and the training now occurs via full-time state education in *lycées techniques* and *collèges d'enseignement technique*. But this forms only a small portion of training which is mostly done in a less coordinated way by enterprises, by successive learning on the job and promotion from one job to another, and by shorter enterprise-specific courses (*formation-maison*).

In Britain, there was much less formalisation and certification of training than in Germany and France (and the US). The apprenticeship system was kept, but not developed and expanded as in Germany. It was linked with the training of engineers and led to the establishment of professions as qualifying associations; but this reflects the traditional gaps in British technical education, which arrived later than in the other countries and which was often taken by a 'pull of gravity' from classical universities and academic education. In the area between worker and higher training, Ordinary and Higher National courses and exams played a major part; these were run by local technical colleges and polytechnics (Maurice *et al.*, 1980, p. 74).

Until recently, as we mention later, the French did not develop business schools on American lines, although the *École des Hautes Études Commerciales* (HEC) was founded as early as 1881. The main training for many managers was through the mainly engineering-oriented institutions (see Boltanski, 1987; Crawford, 1989) outside but parallel to the university system such as the *École Polytechnique* (established earlier in 1794) and similar bodies. The total in these *grandes écoles* was about 5 per cent of all those in higher education.

These graduates were a very distinct elite and were very conscious of the fact, self-confident and intellectual in outlook. What was unusual about the French elite emerging from the top *grandes écoles* was that they were very mobile between government and business spheres, unlike the British educational high-fliers who tended to be trained in the classics, and once selected for top Civil Service posts, in the past rarely moved into industry (see Whitley *et al.*, 1981). However, inter-firm mobility may have been low in the past for managers and engineers (Crawford, 1989, p. 145).

Within France, but apart from the French system, the European Institute of Management (INSEAD) at Fontainebleau which began in 1958 (Whitley *et al.* 1981, p. 72) aspired to be the Harvard Business

School model on this side of the Atlantic with 450 students (see Table 7.1). It drew on a Europe-wide clientele of management students and offered teaching in English, French and German, with a heavy reliance on a North American style MBA Programme approach: 'The course as developed at INSEAD follows a delicate path between the development of the "man" and the development of the "managerial" man' (Whitley *et al.* 1981, p. 78), to lead to an emerging European corporate elite (Marceau, 1989).

The Euro-manager of tomorrow must be multilingual:

Although English predominates as the language of instruction, students are expected to speak other European languages. At the Institut Européen d'Administration des Affaires (INSEAD), where 80 per cent of tuition is given in English and 20 per cent in French, students who are not bilingual are required to do a month's crash course before starting the MBA programme. Such schools are proud of their multi-cultural mix, which they believe affords students maximum exposure to differing approaches to business.

(Thomas, 1990, p. 21)

Germany did not (and still does not for the most part) spawn North American style business schools offering MBAs (Sorge, 1978; Randlesome, 1988). Their commercial schools originated in the late nineteenth century; the first *Handelshochschule* opened in Leipzig in 1898. They operated mainly at the undergraduate level, but such courses have existed longer than those in Britain. Business economics (on its own or as part of engineering training) coloured the development of the best German managers, and until the 1970s was dominated by accounting subjects (Locke, 1984). These days, the 'business economics curricula are not dissimilar from MBA curricula' according to one opinion (Randlesome, 1988, p. 138).

In management, the German qualifications were mostly those from the middle and upper brackets of engineering and chemistry training, as noted above. Usually, technical and management qualifications were related; an engineer was seen as a likely manager, and a manager had to be competent in the firm's technical affairs. This link was most evident in Germany, while the engineering generalism found in France was based on 'encyclopaedic' as opposed to 'specialised' training (see Locke, 1984, p. 42), with more emphasis on abstract mathematics rather than practical laboratory work. By contrast, British management and technical qualifications were more

Table 7.1 Selected European business schools

	France (INSEAD)	Spain (ESADE)	Italy (BOCCONI)	Switz. (IMD)	Switz. (IMI)	UK (LBS)
No. students	450	655	130	65	38	240
Teaching language	Engl./ French	Spanish	Italian	English	English	English
Percent. women	15	60	20	15	9	20
Average age	28	26	28	30	30	27
Length of course (months)	10	24	16	12	24	24
Cost ($)US	20,000	15,534	16,247	17,000	17,000	7,515–10,985

Source: Adapted from The European, 8–10 June 1990, p. 21.

dissociated, especially in mass production. Fewer engineering qualifications were found in management (see Locke, 1989). Instead, one
found more natural science degrees or management diplomas (see
Maurice *et al.*, 1980; Lane, 1989).

The American case

The American system was the main one to concentrate on *general*
management education among the countries coming after Britain but
not as late as Japan. On the other hand, European countries such as
Germany developed managers more within a context of *vocational*
training, where education was rooted in engineering, applied science
and quantitative subjects (Lane, 1989).

The Americans were the first to set up business schools and
professionalise management. As Chandler (1977, pp. 46–7) points
out:

> Central to the professionalisation of management in the new
> multiunit business enterprises were modern business schools. Their
> appearance marked an educational development that was at that
> time unique to the United States. In the late nineteenth century,
> business education did not go much beyond the teaching of book-
> keeping and secretarial skills in small private commercial schools
> and, to an increasing extent, in public high schools. The University of
> Pennsylvania's undergraduate Wharton School, founded in 1881, was
> the only one offering courses in business, which mostly covered
> commercial accounting and law. But after 1899, business subjects
> entered the curriculum of the nation's top colleges and universities.
> The University of Chicago and the University of California then
> established undergraduate schools of commerce in that year. In
> 1900, New York University and Dartmouth (along with the Amos
> Tuck School of Administration and Finance) joined the others.
> Then Harvard opened its Graduate School of Business Adminis-
> tration in 1908, and professional postgraduate business education
> was already off to a good start.

By the 1920s, the model had been extensively diffused – and a system
of professional management (societies, business schools, journals
and consultants) was well-established, as diversification and division-
alisation in large corporations continued.

The aspiring manager in the American system typically aimed for the MBA. One estimate suggested a figure of 65,000 such graduates in the early 1960s, which rose to over 70,000 fully accredited MBAs per year by the late 1980s (more if part-time courses are added in). This number may be set against the even greater number of undergraduate business majors graduating annually, perhaps nearly a quarter of a million in all (Harris, 1984).

Whether the American business school model was appropriate in terms of sustaining economic growth even for its own society was problematic. Harris (1984, p. 122) has suggested that the decline in American industry's performance may be correlated with the period of ascendancy of professional schools of management and their (in his view) misguided emphasis on economic rationality as defined by economists, especially as in the 'neoclassical ideology' (1984, p. 124).

In the North American context, it should, however, be noted that postgraduate business schools constituted only a percentage of management and industrial vocational training. There was a great deal of vocational training with the numbers involved probably exceeding that of their entire university student population. In the United States, government has played a role in vocational training since the Smith-Hughes Act of 1917 (Doeringer, 1981, p. 2). Federal budgets, including military vocational training, exceeded $17 billion. Workplace training expenditure in the private sector went beyond a total of $30–40 billion a year by the 1980s (Doeringer, 1981, p. 3).

Eight million adults were enrolled in corporate training programmes, carried out in 400 campuses or more. Remedial courses were deemed necessary because of low school standards. Courses were also offered up to Masters degree level (to compensate for perceived deficiencies in the college system), such as the one in computer software taught by Wang Laboratories in Massachusetts (*Times Higher Education Supplement*, 8 February 1985, p. 9).

Not all North American management scholars have had a rosy view of undergraduate business or MBA courses. Mintzberg (1989), for example, observed:

> I have long had concerns about undergraduate education in management and have not done it for many years (although I do believe in accounting training at that level, since accounting really is a profession). More recently I developed similar concerns about the conventional MBA. Increasingly I have come to believe that it is wrong – socially as well as economically – to train relatively inexperienced people in management. A few years of prior experi-

ence does help, but that does not resolve the fundamental problem. We cannot afford to have a society of elitist managers, preselected at a young age on the basis of academic criteria and then promoted on a 'fast track' outside of the difficult work of making products and serving customers. Thus, I have come to believe that management training should be directed at people who have substantial organizational experience coupled with proven leadership ability as well as the requisite intelligence.

(Mintzberg, 1989, p. 80)

Most MBA courses, according to this view, were over-analytical and abstract. The use of 'judgement' and 'intuition' based on experience might have been more appropriate. Young managers (and anyone working) ought to have developed a clearer idea of how organisations *really* work, as opposed how they *should* work.

The Japanese case

The end of an inward-looking Japan in the early 1870s led to eventual Japanese industrialisation, with the State playing an important role in promoting the growth of basic manufacturing industries. By 1900, Japan was an emerging industrial power; by 1920, it had arrived. After 1931, an increasingly militaristic regime mobilised the economic structure for armament production and war. Later, the Japanese 'takeoff' after the Second World War was, amongst other things, to see new methods of management brought in during the period of Allied Occupation. But in the 1950s and 1960s, there was an increasingly widely held view that American methods did not suffice and that Japan must continue to develop its own model with a premium on technical competence.

An authoritative study of Japanese industrial training summed up as follows:

Historically, large modern industries in Japan have relied upon within-enterprise training programs, rather than outside schooling to generate high and middle level skills. These programs emerged largely through the initiatives of management, except for the highest administrative and technical personnel, who received their education in elitist universities, through overseas study, and at specialised professional academies. Although the programs varied considerably in scope and coverage from industry to industry, they demonstrated the success for the individual firm of training its own core groups of skilled manual employees who began their work careers usually with no more than elementary schooling. One wonders whether this enterprise-based training system might have had more extensive application beyond the modern firms themselves had the government pursued an active manpower policy throughout the economy.

(Levine and Kawada, 1980, p. 186)

The main strengths of the Japanese model were held to be: first, a high standard of general education with a strong emphasis on mathematics (up to forty per cent of school leavers go to university or college) for entry to employment, followed by very rigorous selection by and competition for recruitment to the big firms that dominated the Japanese economy, with over half the companies providing in-house continuing education for their employees; and second, a concentration on in-company training both for technicians and engineers as well as managers (see Karsh, 1984; Dore, 1988; Dore and Sako, 1989).

The training programmes in Japanese firms depended on such variables as organisational structure, nature of the industry, resources available to training and the firms' tradition (Tesar and Suzuki, 1984, p. 23). The programmes fell into *four* categories:

- programmed training
- cafeteria-type training
- combination of above
- cafeteria-type training with supervisor's advice.

Promotion, in most cases, was based on seniority in the lifelong employment firm, but some firms expected the passing of specified courses before advancement could be approved.

A major institution providing such certification was the Japanese Management Association (JMA), the oldest management education body in Japan. It was set up in its present form during the Second World War, when the Nippon Industrial Management Association and the Nippon Scientific Management Association merged in 1942. Unlike the British Institute of Management, it had relatively few individual members, although it had over 2,000 corporate participants, as well as about 500 individuals and 300 associates. Both big and small firms were represented in its membership, as well as government agencies and academic institutions. It ran over 1,400 courses for 60,000 'students' a year in all, employing 1,600 employees, of which 800 were involved in educational work (interviews, summer 1989).

Taylorism came to Japan just before the First World War. By 1912, Kanebo was training its textile factory managers in the rudiments of scientific management. In 1915, the School of Technology at Port Arthur (now Dalian) in Manchuria started to teach similar courses when it was occupied by the Japanese. On the mainland, Otaru College of Commerce in Hokkaido copied this in 1917. In the 1920s and 1930s, companies like those in the Mitsubishi Group started in-company training along these lines. The Navy and National Railways also began industrial engineering training. In 1937, the Nippon Industrial Management Association offered the first production management course. After 1945, with the Allied Occupation, numerous American courses were on hand, and eventually indigenous ones began to predominate, such as Total Quality Management.

In addition to the JMA, many other bodies offered public management training programmes; perhaps a couple of hundred organisations were in the business of putting on courses. Those available to the public ran to 5,000 each year, with a similar number on hand from large manufacturing companies to their subcontractors and distributors (interviews, summer 1989).

The JMA's activities were broken down into:

- open programmes
- in-house training
- distance-learning
- publications.

Let us now closely examine each of these in turn, as Japan is China's biggest neighbour in East Asia.

Open programmes

Foremost was the two-week Executive Development Course, which was established in 1959. It has attracted over 1,000 managers since that date. The JMA also offered specialised computer-integrated manufacturing (CIM) and related programmes, as well as broader based Industrial Engineering Methods Courses. An Annual Marketing Conference activity was also offered each January, attracting 600 executives.

In-house training

Each year, as well as external programmes, over 2,500 training courses were offered to companies in-house by JMA's own teaching staff. These covered management development, motivation, etc.

Distance-learning

A further activity consisted of distance and correspondence courses, with 120 individual types of programmes available, including 20 in the English language. These covered leadership skills, use of computers and other study topics.

Publications

Japanese managers probably have been keener on self-study than their Western counterparts – with 3,500 publishers all told in the country as a whole. Since Frederick W. Taylor's classic *Scientific Management* was first translated into Japanese in 1913, a vast stream of business books has come onto the market. Since 1958, there has been a boom in business publications, with 50 to 80 new titles a year, offered by the JMA. After 1982, a *JMA Journal* monthly with a circulation of 50,000 copies superseded *Management* started in 1952, although its roots go back to *Efficiency* launched in 1942 when the JMA paper was founded.

The JMA Management School has been the 'umbrella' organisation which offers its main public programmes. Under its auspices, managers may find the activities of the following bodies:

- The Japan Institute of Plant Maintenance (JIPM)
- The Japan Physical Distribution Management Association (JPDMA)
- The Japan Society for Technical Communication (JSTC)
- The Japan Society of Office Automation (JIOA).

Another important training institution has been the Japan Productivity Centre (JPC) which dates from the 1950s and set up in its present form in June 1954 as part of the Productivity Movement, with US technical aid assistance. It directly received its budget from government funds. Unlike the pre-war rationalisation movement, it promoted worker participation, although the Japanese labour unions were suspicious of any activity supported by the US government. Since its inception, it has sent 26,000 participants on study-tours to the USA, whereas only 700 Americans have been to Japan. Participants have included executives, union leaders academics and others.

The International Labour Organisation (ILO) resolved at Philadelphia in 1944 that it should aim at the 'programs to achieve labour–management collaboration in continuous improvement of productivity as well as labour–management cooperation in preparation and application of social and economic measures'. The ILO further resolved in 1952 to give 'advice for conference and cooperation of labour and employers in enterprises'. It stressed that (a) conference and cooperation of labour and employers are indispensable for increase of productivity of enterprises; and advised that (b) contribution to social and economic welfare of labour should be recognised, and (c) labour–management conference in enterprises should be recognised as a national benefit and recommended by governments.

The JPC emphasised these aims, hence: 'Concrete measures for the increase of productivity must be studied and discussed in individual enterprises in view of actual conditions through Labour–Management joint consultation systems.' On this basis, the JPC promoted the modernisation of labour–management relations. It consequently organised a Labour–Management Joint Consultation System Committee, consisting of representatives of labour, management and people of experience or academic standing. The committee engaged in the popularisation of reformed labour–management relations. In 1964, the Committee proposed a 'Standard for the Realisation of Labour–Management Joint Consultation System in Enterprises'. Today, most large Japanese companies encourage joint labour–management committees.

By 1969, the JPC had proposed the establishment of an industrial labour–management conference for persons in charge of labour–management relations across the country. The Committee suggested that both labour and management should be aware of their respective social responsibilities and should communicate with each other in order to cope with changes in economic structure and the trend towards internationalisation. Since that time, a large number of joint labour–management consultation systems have been set up in most industrial sectors, such as automobile construction, textiles, and about nine out of ten large companies have them.

The JPC has regional centres as well as its Tokyo headquarters, and runs seminars, courses and so on to build up a network to diffuse the productivity 'message'. As part and parcel of its activities, the JPC has run a wide range of post–experience management training programmes. Amongst these are senior executive courses which ran for three or four days, often at a suburban hotel. These covered economic, social and political topics relevant to its activities. Seminars geared to management functions have also been held, running from one to ten days. These have covered personnel, marketing, finance, corporate planning and other activities in the company and how these related to enhanced productivity.

An Academy of Management Development was also set up in April 1965 to mark the tenth anniversary of the JPC. Its goal was to 'meet the need for a more formal approach towards intensified education as achieved by the Harvard Business School'. The Academy's market was middle managers and specialists at various levels. It specifically emphasised:

- understanding the latest theories;
- developing advanced levels of expertise;
- intellectual creativity and practical adaptability;
- leadership and corporate responsibility.

Altogether, there have been ten one-year courses, organised in four programmes. Some were held in the evening, and others by day. The courses have been taught by academics, other specialists and researchers. In addition, the JPC carried out in-company training, like the JMA. It dealt with practising managers in affiliated companies, new entrants to management, and follow-up courses.

The JPC also ran the Management Consultant Leaders Training Course, which trained over sixty would-be consultants every year. The clients ranged from industrial firms to banks and government bodies. The course covered all the general management topics found on similar Western courses, but involved two months in-plant training. A three-month 'Basic' course has been an alternative to the one-year programme, which was a condensed version of the wider course. A distance-learning one-year version was also available, with reading assignments, a two-week residential module and a three-week in-plant training assignment.

It is widely believed that Japan has not had business schools, although one exception has been frequently noted. The educational system did, however, make provision for both postgraduate and undergraduate management education, as we shall shortly see. The one business school proper which is cited, that of Keio University, has rarely been discussed in any detail.

The Graduate School of Business Administration was established at Keio University in April 1978, with an MBA Programme which lasted for two semesters over a two-year period. The campus, with 20,000 students in all subjects, was built in the late nineteenth century. The Business School was the first full-scale, professional management school of its kind in Japan when it was set up in 1962. Keio University had entered into a collaborative arrangement with the Harvard Business School to do this. Their Japanese counterpart used the case method, with industrial study, group discussion and class discussion. There were five courses in all for practising managers:

- Management Development Seminar (3 months);
- Advanced Management Seminar (10 days);
- Middle Management Seminar (2 weeks);
- Junior Management Seminar (2 weeks);
- The Distribution Seminar (6 days).

McMillan (1984, p. 132), for example, claimed that:

> The absence of the US-style MBA professional management school in Japan's universities – Keio University perhaps comes closest to a US model – has meant the Japanese companies prefer to 'make' management education through company training programmes rather than 'buy' through university education.

In his view, this choice of model was not accidental, but stemmed from Japan's educational traditions and underlying cultural values. Japanese firms, he asserted, have stressed direct recruitment of school-leavers and have trained them themselves; the same policy as used with graduates, unlike recent Chinese experience.

Japanese managers and professors typically made a major distinction between education and professional training. Another author noted that:

> The purpose of a university is to develop a rounded personality while providing the student with a general academic background. They believe that it is not their responsibility but rather that of the employer to offer graduates specialised professional training . . .
> (Cited in McMillan 1984, p. 132)

While training courses within firms have been specialised, higher education has been generalist. Many top managers started out at centres of excellence like Tokyo University, which became the 'Imperial' university in 1886, and often took liberal arts courses. Tertiary education in Japan was used as a filter rather than a training-ground (see Dore and Sako, 1989, pp. 13–32). The Japanese system graded human potential through merit-based higher education, so that the 'best' people went to the 'best' firms. The companies believed that the ability of these graduates to learn and what they can be trained for internally was good for the corporation.

However, several authors (such as Gow, 1988, p. 42) have underestimated the scope of Japanese undergraduate and postgraduate business training, in my view. They claimed that there was a virtual absence of such departments in at least national and prefectural universities. Several universities, however, taught this subject at undergraduate level at both state and private institutions. Altogether Japan turned out about 70,000 economics and business studies graduates a year (Dore and Sako, 1989, p. 48). Kobe University, for example, had a large number at the lower level, and was proposing to start an MBA course, as opposed to the academic Master's level qualifications to date available there (interviews, summer 1989).

Often universities have recruited many hundreds of Business Administration and Commerce students at the undergraduate level, but only a few dozen at the Master's or PhD levels. The latter were probably going into academic teaching or research rather than employment with the large corporations. This pattern had clearly been the case at the private Chuo University near Tokyo. It was also typical of the public Kobe University, where there were 1,553 candidates at the undergraduate level in 1990 (1345 males/208 females) out of 11,414 first-degree students in total. There were 93 graduate students in Business Administration altogether (of which most were attempting a PhD) out of a total of 710 in all subjects in the University in 1990.

At Chuo University (which had a total recruitment of over 30,000) there were large numbers of undergraduates in Commerce in 1990. Daytime students totalled 4,650 (ten per cent female). Evening attendance came to 1,562. In other departments, there were nearly 1,500 students specialising in Industrial Economics and over 700 in Industrial Management. In the graduate school, there were smaller numbers, 29 in total in Commerce at master's level and 18 at doctoral level. At Kobe, the Business Administration faculty totalled 49 in all (of which 17 were professors) over the same period. At Chuo, there were 256 such faculty members (of whom 80 were professors).

It was nonetheless the case that merely looking for American-style 'business schools' as an indication of activity in management education was unsatisfactory. Business Administration, Commerce, Industrial Management and Industrial Economics were widely taught at university level. Even so:

> Japan's spectacular wave of overseas investments has encouraged a growing number of the country's most promising business men to learn foreign management and marketing methods at Western business schools. Attending overseas MBA courses provides company employees with a better knowledge of Western business strategies and sales techniques. But the overall number of students with MBA qualifications, thought to be around 2,700, remains low by international standards.
> (*Times Higher Educational Supplement*, 27 April 1990, p. 13)

The Soviet case

The Soviet Union, however, pursued yet another approach, related to the economic planning model which emerged in the late 1920s, establishing a pattern which has more or less persisted. Soviet training academies for managers emerged as industrialisation got underway (Warner, 1984, pp. 108 ff.) and specialised professional managerial skills were needed. Many of those who had run enterprises before the Bolsheviks seized power had of course gone into exile or had been removed from their posts. In the heat of revolutionary enthusiasm, workers initially occupied factories in 1917, but eventually State bodies took over the operation of enterprises. Pressure from below towards workers' self-management was discouraged, and such experiments were not seen as compatible with democratic centralism.

Lenin had at first bowed to 'workers' control' but deplored syndicalism, and believed that the existing capitalist enterprise management could be run by workers. But as the revolution ran on, he became convinced that a management hierarchy was needed. Lenin believed that Taylorism combined with Socialism would lead to Communism. By the 1930s, differentials had been brought back by Stalin. There was a shortage of trained managers and foreign technical workers poured in. In the absence of other training bodies, trade union colleges were used as schools of management. Incentive schemes, and 'Stakhanovite' methods – called by some Taylorism in Russian guise – were encouraged.

In the post Second World War period, as Granick (1961, p. 5) has noted, students of Soviet business administration schools with work experience progressed faster than those straight out of school; however, the children of white-collar parents were more likely to become managers. Soviet managers were trained in technical institutes, narrowly geared to a single industry (1961, p. 5) in the initial stages of their industrial careers. Probably nine out of ten Soviet managers today are graduate engineers, with a substantial minority gaining an added administrative qualification.

The Soviet management schools in the mid-1980s consisted of State Economic Institutes, Finance and Marketing Institutes, and Engineering Economic Institutes. As Constable pointed out:

> Management education is carried out within the Soviet Union through four main channels. At the top of the pyramid, there are prestigious national institutions, which train managers drawn from all sectors of the economy. Secondly, there are national institutions under the aegis of individual ministries, which train the managers from a particular industry. Next, there are regionally-based institutions within the individual Republics which train managers from all industries within the region. Finally, management training takes place at the enterprise level. In Western terminology, this would be 'in-house training'. It probably represents the greatest single volume of activity and deals with the lowest levels of management.
>
> (1984, p. 81)

Many new institutions have been created in recent years, and the Soviet Union has signalled that it intends to expand and improve its management education. By 1989, as many as 100 new business schools had sprung up (see *Financial Times*, Special Supplement, 12 March 1990), most of untested quality.

Faced with the problems of their economy, the Soviet planning apparatus has tried to decentralise decision-making. They have needed more and better managers to cope with the problems of low labour productivity, and other workplace problems. They have thus tried to improve their top management:

> At the elite level, a good example is the Academy of the National Economy, which was founded in 1978 in Moscow. Its two objectives are to upgrade existing top managers (500 a year on three month courses) and to train future ones, with greater emphasis

through its major programme being given to the second objective. This major programme involves an intake of 100 people a year on a two-year, four-term postgraduate course. Candidates are typically about 40 years old and will already be senior managers or engineers, heads of departments from national ministries or deputy ministers from Republic ministries.

(Warner, 1984: 81)

By 1989, however the Academy was training 1,200 bureaucrat/ managers a year. (*International Herald Tribune*, 18 May 1989, p. 14) It has also set up an overseas MBA course for Soviet managers at Duke University's Business School in South Carolina.

Another development has been the 'Leningrad International Management Institute' (LIMI) which is a joint-venture between Bocconi University of Milan and Leningrad State University. Its target was the creation of a Graduate School of Business Administration in Leningrad. It was important in view of the opening up of the Soviet economy to international markets. LIMI was managed, on the Italian side, by the Bocconi University Business School and supported by top-ranking European and Soviet institutes such as ENI, Conf-cooperative, Zhylsotsbank (the second Soviet bank), the Institute of World Economy for the Socialist Systems, and the Institute of International Economy of Academy of Sciences. It aimed to carry out extensive training and updating for Soviet and Western managers in economics and international management. The teaching and research programmes were to be carried out not only by Soviet and Italian experts but also by well-known Western scholars in international business, financial and academic world. The main objectives of LIMI's activities have been to create a complete programme of *management training* through courses, seminars and the foundation of an MBA in Leningrad, to promote knowledge through *research*, and to deepen *information and expertise* about the Soviet economy.

A further Italian management educational joint-venture with Italy has involved 'Mirbis', the embryonic Moscow International Business School and the Bologna-based 'Nomisma Institute'. It hoped to run three types of courses:

The 'Master' course of 45 weeks for younger managers draws from the bureaucracy and industry those who are at an early stage of their careers. The first stage will admit 60 people who will be reduced to 40 after intensive training in English and information technology. These will then go on to learn about organisation of labour, regional development theory, industrial economics and production theories as well as international finance, marketing and management controls. The 10-week 'Top Manager' course is tailored for company managers and senior bureaucrats who cannot be spared for longer periods. This will include two weeks experience abroad and two weeks on a practical exercise in the workplace.

Short courses of four or five weeks are designed to satisfy the specific requests of companies and state organisations providing the students. The aim will be to teach the latest institutional and economic developments in the Soviet market and also foreign markets.

(*Financial Times*, 4 April 1989)

The Swiss-based Institute of Management Development has also set up IMD-Kiev with the Ukranian Academy of Sciences. In addition, a small group of Soviet managers have been enrolled at the Harvard Business School on the MBA Programme. There has also been similar collaboration with executive courses at the London Business School.

In any event, data has not been available on Soviet training in the same detail as for most other countries. Even so, their commitment to management training has been considerable with a past emphasis on quantitative approaches, such as operations research, cybernetics, and so on, although since the 1960s an interest in applied social science and job design has been observed, if only in a minor key; since the mid-1980s, an emphasis on decentralised decision-making and managerial incentives has been highlighted. It would be hard to argue that the American model has until recently had any noticeable impact on the USSR's method of management training, however, other than the indirect influence of Taylorism noted earlier.

The Yugoslav case

The development of management education in Yugoslavia, in order to achieve improved managerial performance, has been long overdue. Even though the country was one of the earliest examples of 'market socialism' by any account (see Warner, 1984) it was slow to set up management schools, either at university or post-experience levels. Still, it is better late than never, and they opened one in 1986 before the other Eastern Europeans (see Table 7.2). This observa-

Table 7.2 Opening dates of Eastern European business schools

Ljubljana	Brdo Management School	October 1986
Budapest	Hungarian Management Institute	November 1988
Budapest	International Management Centre	March 1989
Kiev	IMD-Kiev	August 1989
Moscow	Mirbis	September 1989
Warsaw	International Business School	October 1989

Source: Adapted from *The European*, 8–10 June 1990, p. 21.

tion does not mean that executives received no training, either within large enterprises, for example, or, in a small number of cases, by being sent abroad to the USA or Western Europe. Even so, the extent of management training was limited compared with both the Soviet Union and more recently China (interviews, autumn 1989).

The mainstream preparation of Yugoslav managers has previously been through, first, their university education, often as engineers, which parallels the German model, and second, through learning on the job. Management was not seen as a profession in Yugoslavia but it was believed by some that a manager needed management knowledge and skills (especially related to the specific enterprise involved). Often leading cadres have had a horizontal career-track anyway and moved from running enterprises to government organisations, the Party and its satellite bodies, even trade unions. The faculties did not keep close track of their alumni so career data was sparse. Most went to 'branches' of the economy. Engineers, or equally economists (as well as lawyers), eventually became general managers.

There were altogether 24 schools of economics in Yugoslavia in the late 1980s, a good number of whose graduates became managers. Before the Second World War, there was only those in Belgrade and Zagreb, following in the Germanic/Hungarian tradition of the economic and commercial Hochschule. After the War, the Soviet influence was widespread and the enthusiasm was for central planning, leading to an emphasis on macroeconomics. In 1950, two schools were added in Sarajevo and Skopje. There were at that time few foreign, even Soviet professors teaching in the economics faculties.

Six schools had emerged by the late 1950s and a new wave in the 1960s completed the score or more now teaching. These were based on the Belgrade/Zagreb model and taught Macroeconomics and Political Economy. The initial development was the 'triangle' of Political Economy, History of Economic Thought and Economic

Policy. The second phase involved the teaching of 'branch' and Industrial Economics. Then, the theory of the firm was introduced, which was closest to the Managerial Economics approach. In the 1960s, with the interest in the socialist market economy, interest developed for other areas, such as Enterprise Economics.

In Zagreb, there had been an attempt to set up a management programme at undergraduate and postgraduate level at the university. Up to now, there was limited amount of teaching of business subjects in the Faculty of Economics, where among the sub-departments are those which offered third- and fourth-year special subjects, such as Managerial Economics, Microeconomics and Accounting. There were about forty faculty members involved, and three-quarters of third-year students (about 200 each year) took these specialities. The proposal for a business school in Zagreb appeared (as of the time of writing) to be still in the discussion stage. It was to be jointly financed by Slovenia and Croatia but the former wanted their own school. There had been offers of practical assistance from the University of Florida at Talahassee (as well as from Manchester). There were several problems other than the political ones; for example, there were question marks over whether there were enough local competent management studies teachers, and there were also language problems if foreign faculty members were to teach. There have been university financing difficulties, as well as a limited enthusiasm from many of the Zagreb University faculty.

An executive training centre has been set up in 'go-ahead' Slovenia, in Cranje to the north of Ljubljana, which has been operating for about five years now. The institution was set up by the Slovene Chamber of the Economy, under the direction of its founder, Dr Danica Purg. Since 1986, she has seen 4,000 or more managers pass through the doors of the Centre. The core staff has been mostly from Slovenia, with North American and Western European visiting faculty members helping. The Brdo Management School (see Table 7.2) as it was called, has run 30 to 40 specialised programmes a year and has been used by course members from other republics. In 1990, it launched an MBA programme.

In Belgrade there has been *no* business school as such. There have been special management seminars held recently, but these were only short post-experience courses. There had been a course in the 1970s in the Faculty of Organisational Sciences, but it had been abolished due to party anxieties about 'technocracy'. Like Zagreb, the Belgrade Faculty of Economics offered a selection of management courses for third- and fourth-year undergraduates, for example. There were altogether 130 full-time faculty members, 95 per cent of whom are graduates of the same Department. From the initial intake of 500 full-time students for undergraduate Economics, the 300 or so who stay in the running have taken the seven specialisms for the last two years of the four-year course (Accounting, Macroeconomics, Marketing, Microeconomics, and so on). There were also 250 post-graduates, mostly taking the three-year Masters course.

A limited proportion of management training has been done by the Yugoslav Chamber of Economy (rather like the CBI in Britain) which represents all the enterprises in the country. They had to affiliate *directly* by law, not federally, but there were Republic and local Chambers and the latter do sponsor management training es-pecially in Slovenia (also to a limited extent in Croatia and Serbia). The Chamber itself ran a few courses, such as a five-day programme for management trainers, with instructors from North America and West Germany. In 1989, it held a short course for top managers, with speakers of the calibre of Dr Wolfgang Poeck, president of the Dresdener Bank; Dr Edgar Cartwright who used to be president of Lockheed; Dr J. Fred Bucy, former head of Texas Instruments; and Dr William Agnew, who was until recently director of programmes and planning for General Motors. The Chamber had plans to build a permanent training centre outside Belgrade to run week-long specialised courses, but did not envisage setting up an MBA pro-gramme. Such a school would not be part of the University. In-house training has been carried out by large enterprises, such as GenEx-port, Iskra, Energovinvest and others. They had permanent training staff and also used experienced and retired managers. Training budgets were, however, hard to estimate.

The Chinese case

The People's Republic of China, as we have seen, industrialised much later than the USSR, although after 1949 the Soviet model initially influenced its development. One author has doubted where China had found 'a route to modernisation without bureaucratisa-tion, or that the Maoist ideal solves the problem of how to modernise without sacrificing revolutionary social goals' (Whyte, 1973, p. 163). There were, in his view, similarities between Maoist and Western organisational notions: Chinese organisations still had goals, special-ised roles, rewards and rules (1973, p. 163). Even so, Chinese management training is only now progressing beyond the dire state it fell into during the Cultural Revolution. In the past, most Chinese managers had virtually no professional qualifications beyond middle school (Warner, 1987a).

Comparing data for Soviet managers in the 1930s (Granick, 1964) with contemporary China, we can see that the educational level of the Chinese counterparts in the 1980s lags far behind. The influence of the Soviet model on Chinese management was clearly tempered by the negative experience of the 1950s. There was no desire whatsoever today to learn from Soviet example amongst Chinese management educators, even if they appeared to be willing to look at many other countries' experience, although a number of Chinese management educators and managers studied in the USSR at that time. Additionally, Soviet personnel were the main, possibly the only foreign advisors in the PRC until 1960. Nonetheless, apart from the vestiges of Soviet industrial-bureaucratic structure and practice still found in Chinese enterprises, management practice has now decidedly changed.

In 1981, a policy decision was made by the Chinese leadership that between then and 1985 all cadres should be trained on at least one 'course' (however short) in enterprise management, as part of the policy of the Four Modernisations (see Chapter 3). A major target group has been the nine million 'cadres', that is first-line supervisor and above, in manufacturing industry, transport and communications overseen by the State Economic Commission. After 1982, 36 university-level academic institutes were re-established and 59 departments in universities and similar bodies were set up. Several experiments in distance-learning were also launched, particularly the 'Economic Management Periodical (Joint) University' which has a formal enrollment of 30,000. By the mid-1980s, just over half of the nine million industrial cadres had been on at least one short training course in enterprise management. Examinations were also introduced for all cadres and a qualifications commission set up, as we have seen outlined in Chapter 4.

There was also a shortage of management teachers and a limited start has been made to train people for doctorates in management. In addition, an Association of Chinese Industrial Enterprise Management Education (mostly teachers and researchers) was set up. There was an enormous way to go as far as providing trainers was concerned to cope with the 450,000 or so enterprises in the state sector. With the post-1979 economic reforms, it was seen as essential that managers be trained to cope with decentralised decision-making (as has already started to be the case in Hungary).

All kinds of training, however, have been given greater priority in Chinese enterprises although the proportion of resources devoted to such specialised training varied from firm to firm, with usually about two per cent of the budget devoted to this activity. The decision as to *who* went on training courses was usually taken by the head-office of the corporation as far as heads of workshops and branch corporations were concerned. If the employee was at a lower level, the factory manager decided who went. The influence of the party bodies was now claimed to be minimal. There were several kinds of internal training courses. First, there was remedial general education for people who were disadvantaged by the turmoil of the Cultural Revolution period and this includes those who had lost years of university-level work. Second, there was general technical education to keep people up to date in the industry. Third, there was 'economic management' training, in Accounting, Personnel Planning, and so on. Such courses lasted from between six months to one year (some full-time, some part-time) with other advanced courses lasting longer.

In order to coordinate external management training activities at the national level, the Chinese Enterprise Management Association (CEMA) was established in March 1979. As we saw in Chapter 3, the Beijing Training Centre had been set up by the State Economic Commission and served most of the main cities and provinces. It claimed to be *the* training-centre for *top* managers and seeks to update their proficiency in the shortest time feasible. Also, parallel to the managerial system, scientists and technologists appeared to need distinctly specialised management training courses. It was said that there was a considerable demand for this kind of programme, since the economic reforms have required increased levels of technical innovation because so much of China's industrial capital is out of date. According to Professor Ma Hong (a Chinese economist who has been the *éminence grise* of the new reforms): 'The production technology in China's light industry generally belongs to the level of the 1940s and 1950s abroad, with some even dating back to the 1920s and 1930s' (Ma, 1983 p. 36). To help the modernisation process, the Institute of Industrial Economics in Beijing, for example, set up a Computer Applications Training Centre in late 1984 to teach students drawn from the enterprise level. Several Ministries were experimenting with different ways to train their managers. For example, Directors of Textile Bureaux in the provinces (equivalent of Corporations) were sent to the Institute; or the State Economic Commission arranged cadre-training courses for the above directors, which usually lasted two to three months.

A good example of how management training was utilised at the micro-level was at the prominent Machine-Tool Corporation. There were altogether 1,600 managers in the Corporation, about 16 per cent of the work-force, and about half of these had been on a course in the mid-1980s. The average length of course was 2 months if full-time, one year if half-time, with 'systems' training taking over three years, full-time, in a Worker's and Staff University. Thirty managers were enrolled in the Correspondence University. It should be noted, in passing, that even during the Cultural Revolution some in-house technical training continued, of which the main Shanghai Machine-Tool factory has been used as a national model for work-force technical training.

Most Chinese enterprises had, by the mid-decade, reintroduced extensive training programmes. White (1982, pp. 620 ff.) alleged that there had been 'an inherent tendency towards *hereditary* transmission of jobs within state-enterprises', which he thought had a bad effect on efficiency. Reform of the Labour Allocation system was designed to alleviate these shortcomings, and therefore the selection procedures of such enterprises was of particular importance. Apprenticeship training then became the norm, as China moved to a more vocationally orientated education and training system, starting at middle school level and continuing into the initial work period. Adult education, with an emphasis on self-study, had also been given considerable emphasis. Many managers who went on formal courses could supplement their knowledge with self-study, although the numbers relying exclusively on such after-work activity was clearly more numerous.

However, until recent times, it was common for even the most modern enterprises in China to use a closed shop approach to recruitment of new personnel. On retirement, often early by Western standards, parents would bequeath jobs to their offspring. All this took place in a context of considerable levels of youth unemployment, general underemployment, low labour efficiency, etc. Lately, there has been a zero intake of apprentices in many firms because of overstaffing.

Apprenticeships became increasingly geared to specialised training. Newcomers are trained for one task, but after several years they can learn other skills. The 'production' apprentices were not allowed at first to do repairs, but might do so when qualified. Although the Japanese multi-skill model was well regarded, Chinese training was limited to single skill/task training according to each workshop's requirements in production. If in 'repair' functions, however, they might have acquired multiple skills. Conditions of work for apprentices were the same as for operatives, with the same work hours and contracts of employment. New recruits were to be placed on contract rather than lifetime employment (see Chapter 6).

In most cases, a one-year period of apprenticeship ensued if he or she went to technical school; if not, two or three years was the norm. If a technician, promotion was based on examinations, not on years at work. The trainees usually made a 'master–apprentice contract' and at the end of the period involved there was an examination. If they passed, the masters and apprentices received a bonus; if the trainees failed, the period of contract was lengthened and the master penalised.

Criteria for promotion have therefore now changed in China. There was to be a greater emphasis on managerial and vocational professionalism (see Appendix 1). There was, nonetheless, a fair degree of variation between firms as to criteria such as age, ideology, knowledge, professional skill and educational qualifications. Laaksonen (1988) stressed the importance of personnel decisions in Chinese enterprises to control the use of exams (*pace* Confucian bureaucracy) to assess fitness for jobs and hence promotions.

Promotion criteria has become more generally related to organisational effectiveness. Young, 'go-ahead' managers were favoured; if you were over 45, you would not be promoted to be a factory or branch head. It became national policy not to promote to certain grades anyone above a certain age, presumably to counter the traditionalist variable (see Lockett, 1988, p. 486). Ideological factors were also important, in so far as you had to support the modernisation policy but did not have to be a party member. The requisite level of knowledge was crucial, which increasingly included a university degree and practical experience for key management posts. Last, a professional qualification was called for, usually of a specialised kind. For the top job of corporation director suggestions filtered up from the branch and plant levels to a standing appointment board at the headquarters level of the organisation. To be promoted to be the head of a national industrial corporation, you had to be under fifty by the late 1980s.

We can now derive some qualified conclusions from the Chinese data on management training presented above. Chinese industry has now evolved an industrial-bureaucratic structure, partly based on norms and practices in operation in the 1950s and mid-1960s, but which lapsed in the late 1960s due to Maoist attempts to weaken hierarchical relationships and which came back into operation in the late 1970s and early 1980s, as well as adding new responses to cope with the rapidly changing environment stimulated by the economic reform policies.

By the late 1980s, the Chinese were developing recognisably 'modern' responses to the problems of training human resources in enterprises. In doing so, Chinese managers pragmatically attempted to work out organisational solutions according to their perception of national requirements, which could be ideologically justified in the then current climate of thought, as far as human resources management was concerned. To sum up, *training* was given greater emphasis, *promotion* was increasingly based on ability, and flexible *grading* was extended. It may be expected that greater professionalism and specialisation, an increase in in-house training, as well as greater reliance on external skills training, will persist rather than diminish as long as China continues to pursue the 'Four Modernisations' policy.

TOWARDS A COMPARATIVE FRAMEWORK

We hope in this section to deal with a number of possible explanatory factors which would help devise a defensible framework which might cope with the sheer variety of management education and training systems described above, and help place the Chinese example in perspective.

Lateness of industrialisation

The early entry of Britain into the industrialisation process produced an 'entire world economy. . . . built on, or rather around Britain' (Hobsbawm, 1969, p. 14). The earlier the success, the greater the subsequent obsolescence of social and educational structures, with the accompanying need for the reform of training such as is involved in management education. The later the economic development, the newer the investment in physical and human capital and their reproduction processes. Newer economies will have newer 'interface structures' (Whitley *et al.*, 1981, p. 8) where the economic system meets the education system. In so far as we can divide the above systems into meaningful sub-sets, we might classify Britain as a case of *early* development and Japan as a *'late* developer', to use Dore's (1973) phrase, followed by the Soviet Union, Yugoslavia and then China as the latest emerging example.

We might conjecture that the later the system, the more it was *vocational* (as opposed to educational), and *specialist* (as opposed to generalist), as one possible approach. If we pursue this supposition, then the *later* the system, the more likely it was to be more broadly based in terms of the numbers of managers trained and the social groups from which they are drawn. The earlier set of countries, especially Britain and France, would have tended to an *elite* model of education generally. Germany cast a wider net for its managers and the USA did so even more. Japan, the Soviet Union and China may have developed possibly broader-based systems, if in different ways. Yugoslavia seems to have been an exception. We would generally characterise an *elite* model in management development as likely to be *generalist, educational* and *residential*; a broad-based model would by contrast tend to be *less generalist, vocational, non-residential*. In the former, the training centres would be *small-scale*, in the latter *large-scale* (see Table 7.3).

Such similarities within sub-sets may be, however, at best only superficial. The lateness of entry into the industrialisation process was clearly only one variable which might help to cope with all the variety. It is indeed possible that no comparative framework has been devised, yet on the other hand, we have made comparisons of the societal contexts in which business organisations have developed (see Maurice *et al.*, 1980) and then compared their differences, so why not their derivative management education systems?

Nature and pace of industrialisation

The nature and pace of industrialisation, however, also governed the need for trained business elites. The older type of industrialisation required a quite different generalist *vis-à-vis* the newer kind of specialist with an emphasis on professionalised, knowledge-based skills. Where fewer members of the administrative elite could run the hierarchies of the business world in the former, a wider managerial elite was called for in the case of the latter, often with technically based training in engineering. If growth was very rapid, bottlenecks could be overcome by 'mass production' of technical managers as in

Table 7.3   National management education models

Stages	Time	Country	Model
Early	18–20th century	Britain	Initially in-house, now university business schools
Intermediate	19–20th century	France Germany USA	*Grandes écoles* Technical universities and Institutes Business schools
Late	Early 20th century Mid 20th century Late 20th century Late 20th century	Japan USSR Yugoslavia China	University/in-house Economics/Engineering Institutes Economics/Engineering Institutes University/Management Institutes

the case of command economies, regardless of quality. Again, fast economic growth has come about without industrialisation or technological advance (Locke, 1984, pp. 12–13). Thus, rapid growth could have occurred without the business elite having, or having to have, an advanced technological education. With the second industrial revolution, however, the development of the chemical, electrical and mechanical engineering industries required the application of science to product development and innovation, fields in which Germany made great strides in the period up to 1914: 'The graduate engineer has the attributes that are indispensable for the factory man,' observed Locke (1984, p. 64).

Training systems evolved with this growing need to professionalise management on a large scale. The development of the Business School/MBA Programme model in the USA, for example, might be ascribed to the growing demand for general managers to run the newly emerging multinational corporations. Such firms had emerged in the USA because of the size and nature of the domestic market. Geographic size also was clearly an important variable in distinguishing the American model from, say, the French and the German, and even the British, if the Empire was excluded. As Chandler (1977, p. 498) pointed out:

In the second part of the nineteenth century the American domestic market was the largest and, what is more important, the fastest growing market in the world. In 1880, the nation's national income and its population were one and a half times those of Great Britain. By 1900, they were twice the size of Britain's and, by 1920, three times the size.

He went on to argue that the rate of growth of the national product and population had been consistently greater than that of other advanced nations – France and Germany as well as Britain – between 1860 and 1914.

If it is true that the North American business schools were a response to the rise of large, divisionalised firms in the fast growing domestic market, one explanation why Britain was less prone to train the new management professional was that there were fewer large firms there and that these were in low technology, such as the food, tobacco and consumer sectors. Large German firms were also less keen to develop the highly integrated, multidivisional structures, but did try to coordinate production, marketing, research and investment functions, and hence needed university-trained graduates (Locke, 1984, pp. 306–7).

Pre-industrialisation social and cultural norms

The social and cultural norms of the pre-industrialised order had a pronounced effect on the development of business education and training. Where traditionalism was strong, even though industrialisation proceeded apace, 'aristocratic' and hence anti-commercial values or imperial preoccupations dominated British and perhaps French thinking until quite late in the day. The debate on the topic is still open, but if the above was true, it may be held to be an explanation for why the appropriate business training response was grossly delayed. Japanese society may have been a special case in the development of its management education as it industrialised later than the others, and the delay was less obvious.

Nature of the socio-political system

The nature of the socio-political system may explain some of the difference between the European responses and that of the United

States. If Alexis de Tocqueville, writing in the early nineteenth century, was right in seeing American society as more open socially and politically, this might have been an important factor. The difference in socio-political systems was possibly reflected in the Soviet and Chinese developments, although the Japanese case cannot be easily fitted into this thesis except for stressing the role of the State in all three instances. The change in the socio-political arrangements may have led to new forms of management education as in the cases of Hungary and Poland.

The State was weak in the British case and government took very little interest in management education until the 1960s. The State was more influential in the French and German systems from the start, but less directly so in the United States. Looking at Japan, the USSR, Yugoslavia and China *vis-à-vis* those which evolved earlier, there seems to have been an even greater tendency to gear their management training to a *vocational* model, irrespective of the types of different socio-political system involved.

Social class system

Britain and France have often been held up as cases of societies where social class has been a crucial variable in explaining access to educational opportunities, and this has extended to management education. American society, on the other hand, was more homogeneous. Income distribution was less skewed there than in other nations, and markets were less divided by class lines than in Europe. Furthermore 'the newness of the American market – much of which had been unsettled wilderness a few decades earlier – also meant that business enterprises were new and business arrangements had not had time to become routinised and rigid' (Chandler, 1977, p. 498). There was also the wider access to American technical and higher education, compared with the situation in Britain and France. French higher education, especially via the *grandes écoles*, was very selective, partly because of the *concours* entry system. In Germany 'any student with an *Abitur*, and many without, could study in a technical institute' (Locke, 1984, p. 45). By 1910, France had 20,000 day students in the lower level commercial and technical schools, whilst Germany had close on 330,000 (1984, p. 153). The German system, if not as open as the American, had wider entry to managerial positions without the intermediary role of business schools (see Lane, 1989, pp. 62 ff.). The early Soviet, Yugoslav and Chinese ideological emphasis on egalitarian values in varying degrees was reflected in the different social origins of their trained managers compared with certain, but not all, Western countries. Japan, whilst a society where social hierarchy is central, educated a higher proportion of its school population for advanced study than any other country (Dore, 1988; Dore and Sako, 1989).

Rate of social and geographical mobility

Social and geographical mobility rates may have been important in shaping the management education system. Where rapid, this pro-duced a larger and more widespread elite group than where both kinds of mobility were more static. Some have argued that at the time of the Industrial Revolution, Britain was an energetic and mobile society, but these things are hard to measure; later in the American case, social mobility appears to have been greater, as indeed it was to be later in the Soviet, Yugoslav and Chinese cases. Germany and Japan did not exemplify this kind of explanation easily, but defeat in the Second World War may have disturbed their earlier pattern to produce significantly new elite entrants.

Relative mobility in the American case and the need for a univer-sally recognised MBA qualification may be more closely related to the rise of the business school model, although this may hint at a functionalist explanation. The absence of business schools on Ameri-can lines may have reflected conversely the low inter-firm mobility of Japanese firms with the lifelong employment patterns for senior male participants, although geographical mobility of managers within the divisions of the same enterprise may have been required. Again, younger workers and managers may have been more inclined to 'shop around' since the labour market had shifted in the 1960s and 1970s, but probably this was not yet a major factor (Levine and Kawada, 1980, p. 124).

By the early 1990s, Japanese top managers were still afraid of inter-firm mobility:

Japanese businesses continue to view managerial training as some-thing that should be done within the company rather than achieved externally. Companies are also afraid that employees sponsored for MBA programmes may be head-hunted for posts with rival companies. Other company heads have questioned the need to learn Western business strategies when Japanese ones have proved so effective.

(*Times Higher Educational Supplement*, 27 April 1990, p. 13)

Assessment of possible explanatory factors

It should be clear from the preceding discussion that any one system may not have easily compensated for early entry into the industrialis- ation process, the nature and pace of its industrialisation, or its pre-industrialisation social and cultural norms. It might have changed the nature of its socio-political system, reformed its social class system and improved its social and geographical mobility, but not very readily. On the other hand, early entry into the industrialisation process might have left room for subsequent expansion of pro- fessional management education, and having once gone through rapid industrialisation, a system might then have been able to de- velop training for a subsequent phase of development. Older social and cultural norms might have stood a better chance of being jolted into modernity, if the shock of being bypassed industrially in the new technologically based industries occurred – and they seemed to have been if we consider the response of European economies *vis-à-vis* Japan, with its possible implications for management and other forms of training.

A societal approach which had a fair degree of plausibility was that which emphasised 'traditions in higher education which are non- economic in origins that, when the conditions of entrepreneurship changed during the second industrial revolution, became educational forms of greater or lesser use to an economy' (Locke, 1984, p. 310). If the key variable was held to be the German university tradition with its emphasis on applied research, it may be noted that its influence was also noticeable in the North American and Japanese academic training. German educational philosophy methods of instruc- tion were stressed in Japanese universities after 1885 (see Levine and Kawada, 1980, p. 50). The vocational model spread from nineteenth- century Germany and had a wide diffusion elsewhere, yet others have argued that the economic success of Germany (and more recently of Japan) may have been due to factors outside the educational system (McCormick, 1985).

If the Japanese have used their universities as a filter, China may have been going down the same path as the latter rebuilds merit-based higher education. The other part of the difference between Japan, China and possibly the USSR on the one side, and other countries on the other, was the degree to which management education output was directed towards the enterprise. In the United States and the United Kingdom, for example, the MBA became a passport to higher economic status in the market. In Japan (and now in China) the individual often went from the enterprise to a management education institution and back to the enterprise for which he or she was working initially. Training for the market, on the other hand, was likely to be more generalist, by definition, and because less tailor-made conferred market status (communication from Professor Ronald Dore, 18 July 1985).

FEASIBILITY OF 'TECHNOLOGICAL TRANSFER'

Why did the American educational 'technological transfer' of management education take so long to diffuse in the first place? The American model was clearly known to those outside the United States for many years, but appears to have had little influence. Why was this the case?

It was not until well after the end of the Second World War that Western Europeans started to enroll in American business schools in any numbers, often to become teachers of management, as McMillan (1984) pointed out: 'The fear of *Le Défi Americain* in the late 1960s and the view that the productivity gap between Europe and the US was in fact a management gap, largely explained the growth of management schools both in Britain and on the Continent' (1984, p. 132). France, for example, sent a large group of university teachers and doctoral candidates to North American business schools, then reorganised a network of *Écoles Supérieures de Commerce* in major provincial cities. Unlike their American equivalents, the French business schools were only loosely linked to universities, if at all (see Whitley *et al*, 1981, p. 63). They were often connected to chambers of commerce, and were relatively elitist in student enrolment, with a strong emphasis on international business in their curriculum (which includes language training). In Germany, however, business education has not to date been restricted to an elitist group as we have already seen. One may only speculate whether, as more closely integrated European markets develop, there will be an ultimate convergence of systems.

A high proportion of the chief executives of top French business corporations have graduated from Harvard, and many others have attended other top North American business schools. These alumni have clearly created a favourable climate to the growth of French management education in new directions in the older *grandes écoles* like HEC, or newer ones like INSEAD and ESSEC (see Marceau, 1989). Amongst these management schools, HEC was rated first in its field by peer-group preferences, with ESSEC in second place and INSEAD in fifth (see *Le Monde de l'Education*, July–August 1985, p. 85). The return of British, Belgian, Dutch and Italian postgraduates with MBAs and PhDs from the other side of the Atlantic has similarly influenced the development of contemporary business education in those countries, with some business schools inside and others outside the university system. In 1990, there was a projected annual output of over 5,000 full-time MBA graduates in Western Europe, of which just over half were in British business schools.

There were clearly advantages for such aspirant managers:

> From the student's point of view, an MBA carries the promise of immediate rewards: like their American cousins, students can typically expect to double their salary on graduating, and rest assured that various job offers will come their way. An MBA also offers a unique opportunity to change jobs, most commonly from a technical to managerial function within the same company, but also across sectors.
>
> (Thomas, 1990, p. 21)

However, a given system would be wise to choose *selectively* in establishing its model of management training and to take from external models that which seems to fit best with its own *cultural norms* as China has been doing, although sometimes these may be a barrier to change. We must bear in mind that in most nations, an unlimited trust has developed in general and scientific education as the way to professionalisation. This was likely to create a well-educated generalist frustrated by his work task, which had to be specific since he was not equipped with the practical skills to perform varied work from the outset (see Maurice *et al.*, 1980, p. 83).

A new consensus seemed to be emerging amongst those interested in such matters that vocationally related education systems might perform better in the competition for world markets (see NEDO/

MSC, 1984; Handy *et al.*, 1988; Porter, 1990) based on examination of the American, German, British and Japanese training systems. As far as managers were concerned, their training could not be seen in isolation from that of the rest of the workforce. What distinguished training in, say, Germany or Japan was a common philosophy of work, and a stress on what we have called 'institutionalised competence'.

In advocating the above strategy *vis-à-vis* the Chinese case, we must be careful not to mistake the presence or absence of professional business schools as representing the whole picture of management education or training. Other training institutions may have acted as surrogates for their role. Furthermore, the rest of the training pyramid of which they formed the apex were just as relevant, and sometimes more important. For example, the Army Staff Colleges provided a model for management training and after the Second World War for post-experience courses for managers in Britain before the London and Manchester Business Schools were set up. Within the Western European context, lower-level and higher-level commercial schools taught sub-graduate level work which may have been as important as the higher-level courses for almost a century, especially in Germany and the German-speaking areas of Switzerland as well as Austria.

To translate this discussion to the sphere of business school level management education has not been easy. Given the dominance of American-inspired MBA training in many British and a limited number of European business schools, the question was not whether to transfer this educational technology as such. Indeed, there was one view which questioned whether it was really appropriate at all (Griffiths and Murray, 1985) and whether a more practical type of training should not be given at this level. The same dilemma has faced Chinese management educators.

To have taken the Japanese route would be to promote greater 'in-house' management training which was an ongoing trend in Britain and the USA, at least for post-experience training and indeed in the latter for some MBA courses. A German or Japanese approach would have probably bypassed the existing elite business school structures. Again, this was something for the Chinese to consider. Building a management element into existing undergraduate and postgraduate engineering courses might have been one option, as in the German model – thus taking the existing business schools into engineering faculties. Relevant specialist technical training for all

supervisory and managerial staff may have been increasingly necessary, but generalist training may have been needed as the manager
ascended the hierarchy.

CONCLUDING REMARKS

To sum up, any conclusions *vis-à-vis* the Chinese case to be drawn
from the preceding description and discussion will only be tentative.
Training systems which developed at given levels of social, economic
and technological change may not have always been able to adapt to
new circumstances rapidly enough. Assistance may have been sought
from an *external* training model, for example as the Chinese have
recently looked to the North American, European or Japanese
models. It was, however, unlikely that models could have been
transplanted *en bloc*, given that they developed in quite different
cultural contexts, although specific characteristics were adapted, as in
the Chinese example.

8 Summary and Conclusions

SUMMARY

In this final chapter, we first summarise the main contents of the respective parts of the book, covering both post-experience and university-level management education as well as relevant vocational training in the PRC over the last decade. After this, we then go on to present some general conclusions, and attempt to evaluate the training structures and practices which developed as a result of the economic reform policies.

In Chapter 1, the main problems facing the People's Republic of China were set out as it embarked on the 'Open Door' and 'Four Modernisations' policies in the late 1970s, *vis-à-vis* the need for more trained managers and other highly skilled personnel. There had been a shortfall in the numbers of students specialising in economics and management. The shortage of such managers was pinpointed together with the issue of whether to choose an external model of training or develop one with 'Chinese characteristics'. In seeking to understand how Chinese managers learn to manage, we asked if general or more specialised management skills were needed to deal with the challenges of the economic reforms. The chapter concluded with a series of searching questions which would guide the investigation regarding the why, how, when, and so on, of management training.

In Chapter 2, the economic parameters of the modernisation policies were outlined for the decade 1979–88, as they impinged on the training requirements of Chinese enterprises. Several phases of economic development were examined. A high rate of industrial growth had already ensued from 1953 to 1978 averaging over 11 per cent, rising somewhat after the latter date until recently at an average rate closer to 13 per cent, but slowing down with the recent 'stagflation'. Last, the reversion to tighter control from the central authorities in 1989–90 was noted. The rapid growth of the industrial sector required more and better trained managers, particularly in the one per cent of very large firms whose profits contributed to over 40 per cent of state revenues.

In Chapter 3, the emerging infrastructure of management education and training was described as a response to the fast economic growth rates described in the previous chapter, and its main features illustrated. The overall coordination of management training at national level, which was mostly in the hands of the State Economic Commission until 1988, was sketched out and the nationwide examination system, which it had instituted, described. The work of the Chinese Enterprise Management Association (CEMA) was then examined, starting from its inception in early 1979 and covering its work in diffusing management knowledge across the country. The Economic Management Periodical Joint University, an example of distance-learning, was then mentioned, and the role of other self-study and adult education programmes was discussed.

In Chapter 4, senior executive training programmes were examined, especially in six major centres of population, namely Beijing, Chengdu, Fuzhou, Shanghai, Tianjin and Wuhan, based on interviews carried out in these training centres in 1987 and 1988. These institutions mostly ran short courses and conducted very little research.

In Chapter 5, the principal university management schools were dealt with, focusing on six major campuses in the three biggest conurbations in China (namely Beijing, Shanghai and Tianjin), as well as comparing these with the externally aided training programmes, particularly highlighting the contribution of the Canadian International Development Agency (CIDA). Developments at Beijing, the People's and Qinghua Universities were described, as well as those at the Fudan, Jiaotong, SUFE and Nankai campuses. Undergraduate, postgraduate and post-experience courses in management were examined, based on interviews carried out in these key universities in 1988. Research activities were beginning to develop, with collaboration with Western experts prominent. Several programmes designed for practising managers were also being set up.

In Chapter 6, examples of industrial training were discussed in the technologically more advanced sector, namely selected firms visited in 1987 producing electrical and microelectronic products, particularly computers and related equipment. Management and technician training were found to be at higher levels than in most Chinese factories.

In Chapter 7, we looked at management and vocational training practices in other countries, namely (in order of treatment) Britain, France, West Germany and the USA, followed by Japan, the Soviet Union and Yugoslavia, *vis-à-vis* comparable developments in the

PRC. Both the advantages and drawbacks of late development were discussed. The need for broader-based recruitment and vocationally geared, and widely diffused courses in management was emphasised. The main conclusion was that models could not be transplanted *en bloc* from one country to another.

In the present chapter, we attempt to evaluate Chinese management training, and offer concluding observations in the subsequent section.

CONCLUSIONS

Evaluation criteria

The problem of evaluating the effectiveness of management education and training in general has generally been a difficult one. One authority in the field (Easterby-Smith, 1986) has noted that in recent years there has been 'a renewed interest in the "evaluation" of such activities, particularly when some see in it the possibility of demonstrating that the goods or services provided by these institutions are of genuine value to the organisation, or to the wider society' (1986, p. 3). A major difficulty here was the sheer heterogeneity of management and related courses available since 1979, and external contributions, that is from North American, European and Asian countries (such as Japan), and this factor alone suggests caution.

It must be noted that throughout we will be using the term management training in the broadest sense. As others have pointed out 'in practice the distinction between training, education and development is rather blurred' (Easterby-Smith, 1986, p. 10). One reason for this was that the Chinese have largely ignored separating out these functions (see Chapters 1 and 3) although there was a 'rough' division of labour between the executive training centres and university management schools, as we have seen exemplified in Chapters 4 and 5. The notion of management development has received much less attention.

Two dimensions of evaluation have been suggested (see Easterby-Smith, 1986, p. 25). The first is the scientific-naturalistic one, essentially contrasting the 'harder' and 'softer' criteria of investigation. The second is the research-pragmatic dimension highlighting the 'hard' and 'softer' methods of data collection. These are set out in Figure 8.1.

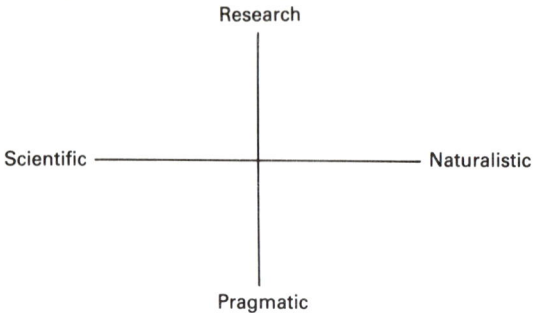

Figure 8.1   Dimensions of evaluation.
Source: Adapted from Easterby-Smith (1986), p. 25.

Evaluation on 'scientific' grounds using quantitative methods and operationalising variables was probably inappropriate to the heterogeneous nature of Chinese training developments. A 'naturalistic' approach emphasising significant focuses for investigation was likely to be most fruitful (1986, p. 23). We have avoided a 'research' approach emphasising survey methods, rather using a 'pragmatic' one which restricts data collection to the appropriate kind needed (1986, p. 24). The approach used has been less guided by theory than practical interests, and lasting generalisations have been subordinated to operational considerations (see Figure 8.2).

It is evident that a *qualitative* rather than a quantitative approach was the most sensible in the circumstances in which the present research was carried out. The evaluation has therefore been *judgemental* throughout. It would not have been feasible in any case to have undertaken a 'before and after' study for the whole system. It may have been possible for individual schools to have done this for groups of students, but as far as is known no attempt was made to

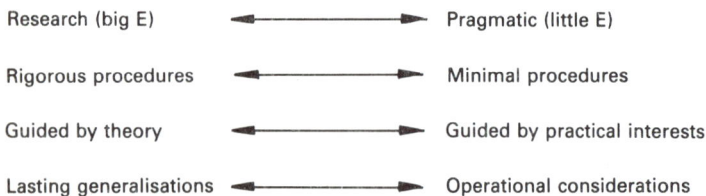

Figure 8.2   Contrasting styles of evaluation.
Source: Adapted from Easterby-Smith (1986), p. 24.

Table 8.1   Official governmental norms in higher education

Employee: student ratio	1 : 3.3
Teacher: student ratio	1 : 6.6
Floor-space per day student, inclusive of staff residential buildings	36 to 44 sq. metres
Average costs per student over four-year course	RMB 10,000 (yuan)
Salaries	40% of all university expenditure

Source: State Education Commission (1988).

achieve it. Given the relative laxity of the examination system and the desire to avoid the 'loss of face' in the specific culture, it was likely that it would have been avoided even if it had been available. The authorities therefore were reduced to citing the *rise in numbers* taught before and after key dates, and generally concentrate on the *output* side, playing down the inputs. Estimates of both inputs and outputs have been made elsewhere in an unpublished report to the European Commission compiled by a Dutch colleague and myself (parts of which are cited in Vermeer, 1988 and in Warner, 1990). Official Chinese governmental guidelines for expenditure per student, physical space per student, and staff–student ratios were available for higher education generally (see Table 8.1).

It is clear therefore that the difficulties must not be underestimated when trying to estimate the *costs* and *benefits* of such education and training in the PRC. Nonetheless, international funding agencies (like the World Bank, for example) have at least tried to set out criteria for effectiveness. To some degree, however, the Chinese authorities have very much taken the value of imported 'scientific management' at face-value, even as an act of faith. It was evident from the beginning of the Four Modernisations that obtaining 'foreign know-how' was an essential part of investing in Western technology.

Placing China now in the five-phase model of management education and training developed by Tanton and Easterby-Smith (1989), namely (1) starting up, (2) growing, (3) establishing, (4) consolidating and (5) integrating, we find it located between Phases 2 and 3, although nearer Phase 1 in terms of teaching methods (1989, p. 19). Almost all teaching was initially based on the lecture method, with little or no discussion or practical work. In Phase 2, foreign experts were brought in as we have seen. As China moved into Phase 3, teaching was increasingly based on case study methods and research was built up. There may also have been clashes in style and philosophy here between older and younger faculty members, especially where the latter have been trained overseas and bring in their externally inspired expertise. There was not therefore always a match of organisational expectations or cultural assumptions and this made assessing the impact of management training difficult. In the next section, we shall see how 'alien' training practices were sometimes perceived and how misunderstandings could arise.

Cultural factors

A major problem to be faced in evaluation was that training methods which have functioned effectively in one culture have not necessarily worked well in another. Foreign experts in China have not always recognised this possibility. The educational tradition in East Asia has been very often organised on Confucian lines, with great respect for those teaching and passive subordination from those taught. The acquired abilities of the taught have been loaded towards the 'spatial' rather than the 'verbal', probably due to the difficulties encountered in learning the written language (see Redding and Wong, 1986). The assumptions of Western educational theory have not always been valid.

Confirmation of the above proposition was contained in an American account of an early joint-venture in the field (Lindsay and Dempster, 1983). The study showed up the problems of assuming Chinese management students were just like North American ones. It was clear that a considerable degree of cross-cultural exposure and experience, as well as interpersonal sensitivity, was needed to teach in an 'alien' learning environment. The authors of this report described very vividly the 'painfully learned lessons' about working in the PRC (see Lindsay and Dempster, 1983). They had the advantage of being applied psychologists but nothing prepared them for what they were to encounter in China. The whole cultural, political and ideological climate led to 'conflict and isolation' (1983, p. 268). The trainers' perceptions did not fit the realities of the Chinese environment in the early 1980s and their expectations were essentially unrealisable.

An Institute for International Economic Management had been set up in Beijing in the early 1980s, under an agreement between the University of California (UCLA) and the Beijing Institute of Foreign

Trade. Its structure consisted of two sections, one to teach management and the other to develop English language skills. No one had told the prospective students in advance that they would be required to study in English. Nor did they know of the exclusive concentration on management topics over the ten-week period of the course.

The programme had adopted a rather *simplistic* approach, which betrayed the naivety of both parties to the original accord. The strategy was probably well-intentioned but the operationalisation appeared to be unsubtle:

> The agreement that launched the Institute stated one major objective: to facilitate and promote the exchange of students and research scholars for research, training and educational purposes. Before entering China, the members of the UCLA team refined this objective into a set of more manageable goals grouped into several phases of development. We worked only with the first phase of this development, which focused on preparing students to attend graduate schools of business in the US. For this reason, it was decided to conduct the training classes *exactly* [italics added] as if they were being presented in the US. UCLA intended to use American ideas, methods, materials, and trainers without making any adjustments for the Chinese setting because it felt that any accommodation to Chinese constraints would reduce the chances of the project's success.
>
> (Lindsay and Dempster, 1983, p. 267)

The result was that the Chinese students rebelled against the scheme, held meetings and denounced the management trainers. Due to the clash of social and organisational cultures, there had been a plethora of misunderstandings. The Chinese enterprise involved, alas, had sent the wrong kind of personnel on the course (for example, interpreters and engineers) and not senior managers. They had passed initial tests in the English language quite well, but lacked management experience and/or motivation to study management. The three ten-week study periods had therefore to be modified. Student participation in classroom work on case-studies and the like proved to be an unwise choice: they expected the teacher to know best. Respect for the teacher was a clearly defined Confucian cultural trait.

The authors, with hindsight, believed that Chinese culture was almost too hard to come to terms with:

Information becomes altered by incentive systems that support incomplete information, face-saving communications, and the practice of informing. Furthermore, central policies shift continuously in an attempt to maintain the balance between socialism and industrial expansion. Change is the most enduring aspect of the Chinese system. The American preoccupation with planning, organising, and controlling results in rigid allocation of resources and support. If the American organisation's plans, resource allocation and support systems cannot change in response to changes in China, the organisation will likely fail. More complete pregathering of information, more elaborate planning, or more tight control will not solve the problem.

American organisations need a flexible, unplanned, decentralised structure that can adapt easily to change.

(Lindsay and Dempster, 1983, p. 275)

An analysis of the problems suggested several lessons for future programmes. Simply inserting North American management educational 'software' and hoping the programme will work was not enough, they concluded. Organisational adaptiveness was required on the foreign experts' side:

To achieve this, the organisation entering China would have to do the following: 1) employ flexible nonspecialists with broad bases of experience and knowledge; 2) provide a link to alternate resources or provide resources that can serve multiple functions; 3) delegate to the employees substantial control over procedures, rules and processes; and 4) have a loosely defined hierarchy of authority capable of shifting in line with the changing intersection of resources, expertise, and need. This design would allow for maximum uncertainty and minimal resistance to change.

(Lindsay and Dempster, 1983, p. 275)

The experience of experts from the USA was sometimes successful, however, as the Dalian experiment clearly demonstrated. The Canadian business academics, on the other hand, fared much better. The experience of the Western European (and Japanese) foreign experts also seems to have been more positive, in many under- and postgraduate training as well as post-experience courses (see Chapters 4 and 5).

It is hardly surprising that the experiments in Western-style management training in the early 1980s should have experienced problems of the kind described above. Both sides had little idea of what to expect. It is rather odd, however, that most of the foreign programmes to be introduced were initially from North America, when there was a wide range of management training professionals, both academic and practitioner, from Hong Kong or Singapore, long familiar with Chinese cultural and organisational norms (see Redding and Wong, 1986).

It is important, however, to note that there was a Chinese-American business academic involved in the running of certain programmes such as the Dalian one, where the Dean at one point came from this ethnic community. In addition, several UMS and senior executive programmes have had major inputs from Hong Kong and other overseas Chinese professors, as can be seen in previous discussions (see Chapter 4 and 5). One managers' course in Chengdu (Sichuan province) took its students to Hong Kong. Several training activities have taken place in the Shenzen Special Economic Zone (see Henley and Nyaw, 1990), so that PRC students could see what was involved in working in this kind of environment (Chapter 4). Assistance from Japan also might have been closer to the psychological environment in which the training was to take place, and indeed substantial support was available from this source, particularly in Tianjin, for example (as is noted in Chapter 4).

To sum up, it was clear that Chinese management training had a lot of catching up to do. In the 1960s and 1970s, many educational courses in economics and related subjects were closed down. After 1980 most of these opened their doors again, firms were exhorted to boost their in-house training efforts and foreign experts were brought into Chinese training bodies to advise, teach and even set up special collaborative programmes (see Vermeer, 1988).

Economic effects

The main reason why Chinese management training expanded was that the nature of macroeconomic policy changed. In place of central direction of the economy, qualified as this had been *vis-à-vis*, say, the Soviet equivalent (see Chapter 2), there was a move to decentralise decision-making power to lower levels, in effect to municipal bureaux and those in charge of enterprises, amongst whom were top managers. Given the dead hand of years of state regulations, and the lack of market signals, Chinese managers were to say the least rather uncertain as to how to react to efforts to train them (see Chapter 3). Even with the new enterprise responsibility system, it is hard to say whether, in reality, top Chinese managers were yet fully accountable for profits and losses. The change of emphasis in macroeconomic policy after summer 1989 only undermined any relative autonomy which they might have achieved in the preceding couple of years. The State once again appeared ready to resume control of the levers of economic power as the 'storm signals' appeared, and to cover the losses of key enterprises.

We can assume here that a modicum of training may have a positive, if limited, degree of effectiveness. The authorities have clearly *legitimised* personal and vocational training, and together with education, its progress was set out in the Prime Minister's 'State of Nation' statement each year. Thus, improving management skills was an official goal, although it did not take precedence over macro-political and macroeconomic policy considerations. It was clear that training strategies followed the latter. Once a macro-policy was to be followed, there were infrastructural consequences for training (as Chapter 3 has clearly brought out): hence the new kind of management education required to deal with the shift from a centralised to a less centralised economy (see Chen, 1988). For the former you needed one kind of manager; for the other, you needed a different breed. The command economy needed economic cadres (*ganbu*); the socialist market economy called for enterprise managers, capable of reacting to 'market signals', even if these were relatively weak as yet.

A leading younger management educator in the PRC, Chen Derong (1988) has argued that 'the current reforms represent a modest shift from *bureaucratic coordination* to a system of *market coordination*' (1988, p. 38). The former had been a modified version of the Soviet model (Model One) and a more responsive decentralised one based on Maoist lines (Model Two) was put into place subsequently. Bureaucratic coordination with limited market forces involved a mixture of Models One and Two, but the second option was more radical. To shift from one kind of coordination (A) (whether the one model or the other) to a new kind (B), required economic reform. The management implications involved seeing actors in their economic role, changing the value system, emphasising management concepts and knowledge and developing management skills (1988, p. 44); it was these aims which shaped the training programmes described in Chapters 4 and 5, reflecting those in Chapter 7.

The analysis points out that: 'During the transition from one system to the other, it is very important for managers to understand the basic principles of the impersonal macro-control instruments . . . and to understand how different markets function' (Chen, 1988, p. 49). Different coordination systems call for different skills in managing. They may be summed up as follows:

- System A requires little need to formulate business strategy, whereas in System B it is central.
- Managers in System A carry out detailed plans externally provided; in System B they have to identify and solve problems.
- The structuring and use of information is very different in System A from that in System B where they have to generate information for their colleagues, customers and others.

From the above, it may be concluded that a *different* system of management training was called for. With the 'Open Door' policy, managers were needed for foreign trade activities and joint-venture enterprises. Managerial abilities had to be emphasised, as well as foreign language skills. The 'political' constraints on those running enterprises changed as the reforms extended their range, although they might regress if the reforms were to slow down. A new generation of enterprise directors was required with enhanced qualifications and more open attitudes than their predecessors. Certification of competence was now essential, at least on paper.

The result was the setting up of an infrastructure of management training (as described in Chapter 3). The creation of the Chinese Enterprise Management Association (CEMA) took place not long after the Dengist economic reforms got under way. Whilst CEMA was not an executive agency, it had acted both positively and prominently to promote management education and training. If one was critical at times about its effectiveness, it was true to say that its Western (or Japanese) counterparts did not carry out essentially different operations, and were also often taken to task by their detractors. The national examination system for managers followed. It probably had laudable goals and it covered a wide sample of senior middle managers, even if it had rather low and unexacting standards. The high pass rate would have been unacceptable in both Western and Japanese management circles. As for the 'Professional Title' examinations, there was little hard evidence to suggest they would have fared better, *vis-à-vis* the very rigorous comparable Japanese tests (see Dore and Sako, 1989). What was more important is that competence became the official formal bench-mark at least. Together with the promised ending of the 'iron rice bowl' policy, such a change held out hopes of macro- and microeconomic regeneration.

The notion of top managerial accountability in theory became policy after the mid-1980s, although there was only a low probability of its literal application due to the complex and shifting nature of decision-making in the Chinese enterprise. As Dwight Perkins (1988) pointed out:

> What is required is not movement all the way to an unfettered market system with or without private ownership of industry and commerce. Expansion of the role of the market is an essential part of the reform package, but large areas of bureaucratic control and direction will remain. Of equal or greater importance than expanding the scope of market forces are efforts to improve the functioning of the market forces that are allowed to operate. To achieve that goal enterprise managers need to gain more autonomy from China's economic bureaucrats and to pay attention to cutting enterprise costs, increasing sales, and raising product quality.
>
> (p. 342)

If there was any chance of this succeeding prior to June 1989, it has now more or less receded due to the reassertion of Party control in many enterprises (see Child and Xu, 1989; Walder, 1986, 1989). In this sense, there may have been a relative regression from competence and accountability criteria. Whilst the new formal goals of the system have not fundamentally changed, that is managers now have to be 'expert' rather than 'red', the 'Four Cardinal Principles' may carry at least as much weight as the 'Four Modernisations' (see Chapter 2). A period of greater political influence over management and economic austerity followed the summer of 1989, although as is typical of recent Chinese history, the ebbs and flows of policy led to a relaxation of the monetary policy if not political control a year later.

The implications for management training have not been too detrimental, but in any event it had to toe 'the Party line'. No major executive training programmes have been shut down, or university management schools downgraded. The joint Chinese-EC Management Institute in Beijing has survived the 'freeze' in diplomatic relations, and most of the other programmes cited in Chapters 4 and 5 continue, even if academic exchanges between Chinese and overseas universities have been greatly reduced for the moment. Managerial ambitions stayed strong: for example, CEMI's two-year MBA course had over 800 applicants for about 40 places in 1989. It was arguably the EC's biggest single investment in human resources development.

The main platform for the diffusion of management practice, namely the Chinese Enterprise Management Association, was also given considerable prominence when the Party General Secretary Jiang Zemin and Premier Li Peng attended a prize-giving ceremony for the ten best enterprises and the 20 most successful entrepreneurs nominated by CEMA in the Great Hall of the People on 7 April 1990 (see *CEMA Newsletter*, April 1990, p. 1).

In his address, General Secretary Jiang pointed out that:

> '[E]nterprise leaders should pay attention not only to production but also to political and ideological work. They must pay equal attention to both material civilisation and cultural civilisation.'
>
> (*CEMA Newsletter*, April 1990, p. 2)

Similarly, in his speech, Premier Li Peng added to the above with the observation that:

> The basic difference between socialist entrepreneurs and capitalist entrepreneurs lies in the fact that the interests of socialist entrepreneurs coincide with those of the broad masses of the workers and also with those of the country.   (Ibid.)

Their respective speeches no doubt tried hard to reconcile the economic necessities of modernising with the political and ideological slogans of the day. Nonetheless, it might be concluded that the top leaders' very presence underscored the importance of managerial achievement within the values of the system.

Summing up

A model to highlight the value of management training (Wallace, 1989, p. 171) was set out as follows:

$$\text{Value} = \frac{\text{Short-term effectiveness} + \text{Long-term effectiveness}}{\text{Cost}}$$

It mapped, albeit in a rudimentary way, the relationship between effectiveness and cost: the lower the cost, the greater the value. The short-term effectiveness was the impact on individual performance after the candidate had been on the course, whether as a student of management studies or practising manager. It was the 'quick return' to the specific enterprise and/or broader economy. Often this was based on a subjective estimate by the manager or sponsor in question. Long-term effectiveness depended on whether the capacity and performance of the organisation and/or economy was enhanced, however, and was harder to judge.

The value of specific managers to specific organisations was possibly easier to estimate in so far as a new way of working or a new product may have been profitably introduced (as was the case in the advanced sector firms described in Chapter 6). The effect on the broader economy was more difficult to estimate, although this problem was not uniquely Chinese (as the comparisons with other countries in Chapter 7 shows). The long-term effectiveness may have been more diffused as the work of individual managers was aggregated and may have been cumulative over time. The question of whether the course was internal or external was also important, as external ones often carried a public subsidy. Generally speaking, the benefit may have come either from a very high 'pay-back' (short or long-term) even though the cost was considerable, or possibly a modest degree of effectiveness *vis-à-vis* a relatively low cost: we remain sceptical.

It is fairly clear that the latter was probably the case in the Chinese circumstances, other than for those managers and/or students sent abroad for training. In all cases, the opportunity cost must be taken into account, although this was relatively less of a problem in a labour surplus economy. Nonetheless, the relative shortage of trained, effective managers raised the opportunity cost, especially for senior key personnel.

The monetary cost of courses, even of senior executive programmes, was rather low in RMB terms (see Chapter 3). The 'real' explicit cost was even lower given that the currency is probably overvalued at the official rate of exchange. If all expenses are to be taken into account we must include the course fee, plus accommodation and subsistence cost, plus the subsidy, plus the salary of the manager, transportation, and the opportunity cost. Compared with the equivalent paid for the training of Western managers, the Chinese costs were modest even if all the above was included. Similarly, the cost of training a management student at university was quite modest by comparison with many other countries. It was higher if they were sent abroad and there were added costs if they did not return.

The 'elite' MBA courses, such as those at Dalian or CEMI, were, however, relatively more expensive to run than other postgraduate programmes in China, given the superior facilities and overseas faculty (see Chapter 5). If the course members were destined for key positions in joint-ventures or Ministries, then their enhanced future effectiveness would compensate. The 'foreign' subsidy may have been essential (as was the 'domestic' one for such courses). For example, the total contribution of the Canadian aid programme for management studies was over $30 million, up to the late 1980s.

The bulk of training, by contrast, including that of managers, took place, as in most countries, 'on the job'. Such training costs were very difficult to estimate for the Chinese economy. In a 'labour surplus' situation, they would have tended to be rather low. Explicit overall training costs in the PRC at the enterprise level were often stated as around $1\frac{1}{2}$ per cent of the wage bill and in some cases higher, although this may have been due to the previously high percentage of apprentices employed (see Warner, 1986b). In any event, the costs of management training were more than balanced by the high rate of industrial growth over the early and mid-1980s, as can be seen in Chapter 2. There was a tricky 'chicken and egg' problem of causality involved. It could be just as easily argued that an upsurge in management training was a consequence rather than a cause of economic growth. It is likely that at least part of the increase in training expenditure was due to an *anticipation* of long-term effectiveness, as is the case with most investment decisions.

A show-case heavy industrial enterprise with 185,000 employees which has an impressive training base illustrated this point:

> To raise both the cultural and technical knowledge of the workers and staff, the Shoudu Iron and Steel Co. operates a full-time university and a vocational mine school. By 1988, it had developed 54 specialities in which 4,660 students had enrolled and 31 specialities in cultural education for 9,759 students. The company has trained 4,205 university graduates and the number of its computer personnel has grown from eight in 1982 to 3,100.
>
> (*Beijing Review*, 11–17 December, 1989, p. 22)

It claimed to be a model of enterprise contract system, with a 20 per cent annual increase in profits over the last decade, but in this context it was arguable that it could have afforded to train this percentage of personnel. Nonetheless, there was probably be a positive feedback into company performances, although possibly with a time-lag.

It can hardly be argued that education and training expenditure in the economy as a whole, low as it was *ex ante*, could have been a major explanation of post-1978 economic performance. This debate was not unique to the Chinese case, for the same point could have been made for British management training and its relation with the economy over the same period. As the economic reforms got under way, management training expenditure by the SEC was concentrated on the 8,000 or so largest state-run industrial enterprises, so it might be easier to narrow down the benefits as well as costs, but only if accurate, disaggregated accounts were available for each of these firms. Moreover, the lack of lateral managerial mobility ensured that the potential benefits were available only to those specific enterprises.

If the costs of post-experience and university-level courses were relatively low (see Chapters 4 and 5), the costs of distance-learning and adult education (via, for example, the Central TV University) were minimal. Even where these were specifically focused on management topics, as in the case of the Economic Management Periodical University (as described in Chapter 3), the numbers recruited were large and the fees very small. Management texts and magazines were also inexpensive, which made home-study or evening classes a very low-cost option. The widespread nature of this kind of diffusion represented a fairly high potential payback for limited inputs. Two per cent of workers' wages was deducted and turned over to the trade unions. One quarter of this was allocated to adult education by them. Some of this huge sum of money was spent on 'training for leadership in enterprises', with spill-overs into supervisory training in effect (see St John Hunter and McKee Keehn, 1985, p. 59). As we have already seen, there was probably a duplication or even triplication of facilities at local level between the different educational/training bureaux (firm, union or municipality), so there was most likely a degree of waste. Still, the coverage was vast, with over ten per cent of the workforce reported as involved in full-time refresher course or day-release study (1985, p. 132).

CONCLUDING REMARKS

Looking forward, it would be difficult to estimate the full impact of management training on the Chinese economy by the end of the 1990s. A great deal may depend on the continuation and duration of economic reform. Given that the present direction of strategy (namely, modernisation and external trade) broadly persists, we may expect the effect of consistently training managers over two decades to be cumulative. If, however, it was difficult to identify the measures that had the greatest productivity growth from the late 1970s onwards, as between the various classes of inputs (see Perkins, 1988, p. 631), it is even more problematic to weight residual factors such as improved management. It is nonetheless plausible to conclude that its contribution has been, on balance, relatively positive, if limited, in its effectiveness.

Appendix 1
Policy Document:
Training and Building Up a Mighty Contingent of Socialist Economic Management Cadres to Meet the Needs of the Socialist Modernisation Drive (October, 1987)

Source: Education Bureau, State Economic Commission (1987) (edited version).

A. THE DEVELOPMENT OF EDUCATION IN ECONOMIC MANAGEMENT SINCE THE FOUNDING OF NEW CHINA

Since the founding of New China, great progress and achievements have been made in the country's educational cause. The same is true with education in economic management, which forms a major component of the national education. In the course of more than thirty years, the country's education in economic management has roughly undergone the following three stages:

The first stage: From the 1950s to the middle of the 1960s, with the restoration of the national economy and the inauguration of the First Five-Year Plan, a large number of cadres were transferred from government departments at all levels and the army to the economic front. In view of the fact that most cadres at that time did not know how to run the cities and lacked an understanding of how the economy functioned, Comrade Mao Zedong called on the whole Party to do their utmost to learn production techniques and enterprise management. On the one hand, many cadres were sent to institutions of higher learning and middle-level technical schools to acquire an elementary education, learn technology or economics; on the other, more than thirty colleges and universities of finance and economics were set up one after another. Moreover, some polytechnic universities and colleges of engineering began to establish management departments, or to offer subjects of finance, economics and management. In the meantime, many industrial ministries of central government and local governments set up a number of cadres training schools. Also, some measure of progress was made in evening universities and correnspondence education. All this laid the foundation for the country's education in economic management. During this period, training of economic management cadres was given a high priority. A great number of economic management personnel were turned out, basically meeting the needs of the large-scale economic construction. Today, many leading cadres as well as key professional people in government economic departments at all levels and large enterprises were trained in this period.

The second stage: During the ten years of the 'cultural revolution' the entire educational cause suffered devastating damage, and more so with the training of economic management cadres. Among the colleges and schools of finance and economics that were newly-founded soon after New China was born, some were closed down, others simply eliminated. A great number of training schools for cadres were turned into 'May 7th Cadre Schools', i.e. they became places where the cadres performed manual labour. Three generations of people, the old, the middle-aged and the young, were gravely affected in their efforts to study and develop themselves. This led to the present situation in which the level of political theory and professional knowledge on the part of economic management cadres seriously falls short of job requirements. The proportion of financial and economic majors in the entire university student body fell from 11.5 per cent (equalling 22,000 students) in 1952 to 0.6 per cent (equalling 1,100 students) in the early 1960s.

The third stage: After the Third Plenary Session of the 11th Central Committee of the Communist Party of China, which was held in 1979, the country began to enter upon a new period of development, in which the focal point of the nation's work was shifted towards economic development, and the socialist modernisation drive started. A general policy marked by reform, opening to the outside world and enlivening the economy was put into operation. Under the new historical conditions, the Party Central Committee, in its 'Decision on the restructuring of the economic structure', pointed out that in order for the efforts at restructuring the economic structure and the development of the national economy to be successful, it is imperative to foster a large number of economic management cadres, enterprise executives in particular, who have the knowledge of modern economics and technology and are, at the same time, innovation-conscious, and capable of introducing and implementing new ideas. As a strategic task, the training of economic management cadres was, therefore, given primary importance. Thus, education in management began to embark on a period of fast recovery and major development.

B. THE FACTS AND DEVELOPMENTS OF ECONOMIC MANAGEMENT CADRES TRAINING IN CHINA

Let us now focus on the in-service training of management personnel in the sectors of industry, transport, trade, finance and related organisations in the last eight years.

Since the Third Plenary Session of the 11th Central Committee of the Party, the Party Central Committee has attached great importance to the training of cadres and has conducted a number of discussions about it. A resolution of the Third Plenary Session stated in explicit terms that the re-education of cadres constituted a strategic task which bears on the country's overall situation; that Party committees at all levels and leading organs on various fronts must take the training as a question of vital importance in the Four Modernisations drive, and must handle it with great seriousness. Furthermore, it made a series of instructions and rules, identified some guiding principles governing the cadres' training in the new period. Some of them were as follows: cadres' training must contribute to achieving the aim that cadres in general must be revolutionary, young, knowledgeable and professionally competent and must serve the socialist modernisation drive. Similarly, it made clear that the fundamental task of cadre training was to study Marxist theory, professional knowledge, the knowledge of science and technology, the leadership and managerial skill so that they might become qualified personnel of the Party and the state who would stick to the socialist road and acquire necessary professional knowledge.

The key to success in the socialist modernisation drive lies in the availability of talent. The modernisation drive not only requires a large number of professional technicians, but to a greater extent, tens of thousands of people who know well how to manage and have a proper understanding of economics. Years of practice have demonstrated that solely relying on regular universities and colleges for replenishment of the needed reserve is not enough. During the more than thirty years since the founding of the Republic, the total number of undergraduate students turned out by regular universities and colleges who have majored in finance, economics and management has come to only approximately 150,000. A well-run in-service training for cadres has proved to be a feasible and efficient way to bring about quick changes in the irrational structure of cadres on the economic front, achieve the aim that cadres as a whole must be revolutionary, young, knowledgeable and professionally competent and be able to meet the requirements of the national economic development in the shortest possible time.

In 1979, in order to give more effective leadership of cadre training, leading comrades of the State Council clearly demanded that the State Economic Commission should take charge of economic cadres training. As a result, appropriate administrative organs were set up. In 1983, the central government established a leading group for cadre training, whose responsibilities included: giving unified leadership and administration to cadre training; formulating guidelines, policies, regulations and making overall plans concerning cadre training; and coordinating the efforts by different departments to supervise cadre training of the whole country. Ministries and commissions under the State Council are required to share out the work according to the principle of 'having each leadership echelon and each channel of organisation share the responsibilities of administration'. As far as cadre training is concerned, the State Economic Commission, in its capacity as an economic coordinating organisation, is chiefly concerned with the following responsibilities:

(a) Drawing up overall training plans for economic cadres in the fields of industry, transport, commerce, finance and banking, examining the implementation of cadre training in the above fields and organising conferences on exchange of experiences of cadre training.
(b) Studying and making, in collaboration with departments concerned, specific guidelines and policies for training in an attempt to give more effective overall leadership.
(c) Conducting the training programmes for leading cadres of economic commissions at provincial and prefectural levels.
(d) Organising and guiding the development of training schools for economic cadres and developing a system of cadre training.
(e) Arranging for the teachers to engage in advanced studies and to compile teaching materials for economic cadres.
(f) Cooperating with foreign countries in training management personnel, systematically introducing foreign modern economic management science and experience.

Closely combined with and centring around the task of economic development and the needs of social development, cadre training, during the last eight years, gradually unfolded itself in a way that was marked by the approaches of 'spreading over the whole area from one point' and of 'from top to bottom'. Specific measures adopted include:

(1) Turning out a large number of cadres by making unified programmes while having each leadership echelon take up its own responsibilities

In view of the fact that China has a large number of economic cadres who are spread over a vast area, and to give more effective leadership to training, the State Economic Commission has worked out different training plans for each period in the light of the needs of the national economic development and the requirements for building up a force of cadres. In the plans, types of programmes laid on cover such matters as the training task, contents, and training objectives for cadres at different levels. In the meantime, in cooperation with the State Educational Commission and other ministries in charge of cadre training, the State Economic Commission has worked out related policies and taken some measures to ensure the smooth progress of cadre training. With unified plans and requirements, bearing in mind the differences in the actual conditions, the various regions and departments set out to organise training programmes of their own. It must be noted, however, that in the ten years of the 'cultural revolution', management in enterprises was thrown into utter disarray, rules and regulations were abandoned and no one dared mention management, with the result that a considerable number of people failed to learn management and their vocational knowledge became rusty. Considering this situation and in the light of the demands the state had placed on the task of restructuring, reforming, rectifying, and improving the national economy, the State Economic Commission in 1979 put forth the task of conducting a widespread rotation training for the majority of cadres in several hundred thousand enterprises and economic administrative departments at all levels, to be completed in three or four years' time. Under the unified plan, the various regions and departments, by bringing into full play the initiative of different quarters, surmounting difficulties by every means, and doing whatever they could, succeeded in getting a teaching force organised for the task of providing all kinds of rotation training courses and seminars. By stages and in groups, cadres were sent to attend off-the-job training courses, each course lasting for two to three months, where they would focus on a study of various strategies, principles and policies formulated at the Third Plenary Session of the 11th Central Committee of the Party, socialist economic theories and basic enterprise management. Generally speaking, [where the] needs of the particular [groups] in specific sectors were involved, training would be provided according to the professions of the trainees. In most cases, it was the responsibility of the various provinces and municipalities, ministries and commissions under the State council to provide training for enterprise executives and economic cadres, while training for middle-level cadres, enterprise managers and supervisors would fall on the authorities of prefectures and enterprises.

The practices had the advantage of aiding economic departments at all levels in their efforts to give more effective leadership to training. Similarly, it would facilitate the promotion of the training activities and make it easier to supervise and examine on the performances and results of training. By 1983, a total number of 4,900,000 cadres of all levels and types had been trained, accounting for more than 50 per cent of the entire body of the cadres in these fields. About 80 per cent of the leading cadres at all levels had received training. Never before, since the founding of New China, had any training been conducted on such a great scale, with so many participants who displayed such great zeal in their studies.

Through the training process, the trainees came to have a better understanding of the Party's principles and policies. The training also played a positive role in helping the trainees divest themselves of the influence of the 'Left' thoughts and draw the distinction between right and wrong. As a result of the training, the great majority of the trainees were able to catch up with new situations and came to understand the importance of scientific management. Many of them, based on the new realisation that while engaging in the modernisation drive, it would be impossible to organise properly large-scale social production without scientific management, applied what they had learned in the training course to practice, and achieved good results both in terms of the effectiveness of management and economic benefits.

(2) Instituting the system of the state unified examinations of factory directors and devoting great efforts to building up a reserve of young and middle-aged cadres

On the basis provided by the basic completion of the extensive training, with the unfolding of the economic reform and in order to achieve the aim that cadres in general must be revolutionary, young, knowledgeable and professionally competent, the focal point of economic cadre training was shifted to training factory directors, management personnel, and young and middle-aged cadres during the period from 1983 to 1985. In May of 1985, the central government declared that the system of state unified examinations was to be applied to the directors of state-owned factories of all types, and management personnel, and demanded that all current directors take the examinations. Besides, before taking examination, all candidates shall be by stages and in groups given a four-month training, during which time they shall devote themselves to a systematic study of the guidelines and policies concerning economic work promulgated since the Third Plenary Session of the 11th Central Committee of the Party as well as a study of enterprise production and operation management. By the first half of 1987, seven examinations had been successively conducted, with a total number of 16,000 examinees. These examinations served to arouse the zeal of the examinees in their studies, to make them to be [more] mature politically, [to] raise their organisational and leadership ability, and provide an impetus to the training of the rank and file in enterprises.

Leading cadres in enterprises at that time were fairly old and it was predicted that sixty to seventy per cent of them would have retired by the late 1980s. Moreover, in most enterprises, the leading cadres were experiencing a process in which the older were being replaced by the younger. In view of the above situation, while providing training to the current leading cadres, we must take as an urgent task training outstanding young and middle-aged persons. Meanwhile, the enterprises were urged to select and send, in a planned way, a number of young cadres to institutions of higher learning or middle level technical institutions to receive a systematic education in management. By the end of 1984, 13,000 persons had graduated from the various vocational colleges, while 24,000 had been granted middle-level specialised school diplomas. In addition to this, we had arranged for more than 36,000 persons to take courses offered by television universities and correspondence universities, without withdrawing them from work. All this helped to bring about great changes in the schooling structure of the management cadres, and to ease, to some extent, the shortage of management personnel in enterprises.

(3) Initiating post/job-oriented training to enhance the overall quality of the leadership of enterprises

The in-depth development of the socialist modernisation drive and the economic reform has placed even higher demands on the majority of the economic management cadres, enterprise executives in particular, and called for the kind of political and professional quality that will qualify these cadres for their jobs. Meanwhile, with the reshuffle in the leading teams in recent years, a large number of professional technicians have taken up leading posts. Familiar as they may be with production techniques, most of them have not received any systematic education in management and are relatively new to modern management and market economy. Furthermore, they lack the ability to synthesise, coordinate, command and make decisions. In the light of this situation, the State Economic Commission and the Central Organisational Ministry have decided to provide, in a planned way, post/job-oriented training for leading cadres in enterprises – an undertaking of vital importance in reforming the cadre educational system. This kind of training as envisaged will enable the trainees to broaden, deepen and improve their knowledge and enhance their abilities so that they may be better equipped with the requirements of their posts and jobs. At the same time, the practice will serve to link the cadre's training with his or her appraisal and appointment.

Recently, the State Council has endorsed the document 'Decision on the reform and development of adult education' promulgated by the State Educational Commission, in which the development of post/job-oriented training is seen as a major task of adult education. The post/job-oriented training falls under two categories: The first category refers to pre-post or pre-turnover training. The second is concerned with on-the-post training provided to persons, who, according to job requirements, need to be trained in a way that will orient them to the requirements of the posts they hold. The post/job-oriented training has just started in China. In order to gain greater economic and social benefits, at the initial stage, it will be conducted on a trial basis, confined to the leading cadres in large and medium-sized enterprises. It will be taken as a major concern in economic cadre training in the period of the Seventh Five-year Plan. In China, there are 8,258 large and medium-sized enterprises, which make up only one per cent of the sum of the enterprises of the country. However, these very enterprises form the main source of the country's financial revenue. In 1985, the profits and taxation they turned over to the state in money terms accounted for 42 per cent of the country's financial revenue. These enterprises are the main creators of social wealth as well as major producers of the daily necessities of the people and important items and commodities for the national economic development. They are the leading force in technical improvement and the backbone for developing new technology, new products, crafts and materials. They form a major base for introducing, digesting and assimilating advanced technology and popularising the results of scientific research. They are in a position to tap manpower resources and groom modern economic management personnel, and are a major source of talented people to be provided to Party and government departments. Therefore, more effectively managed large and medium-sized enterprises with added vitality would play an important role in achieving the objective put forth at the 12th Party's Congress of quadrupling the country's annual industrial and agricultural output before the end of the present century, establishing an economic system with Chinese characteristics. . . .

As the above situation shows, the leading cadres in large and medium sized enterprises are shouldering a historical task in the socialist modernisation drive and in the restructuring of the economic system. Consequently, efforts must be made to make their training more effective and help them really acquire the qualities that mark a socialist entrepreneur. Here lies our purpose in taking the post/job-oriented training of the leading cadres in large and medium-sized enterprises as the focal point of economic cadre education. At present, the leadership system in these enterprises takes the form of the factory director responsibility system. The leading team in an enterprise consists of the director, the Party secretary, the chief engineer, the chief economist and the chief accountant. To do a good job of their training, we start with investigations, making a detailed analysis of the existing status of the more than 11,000 enterprise leading cadres and their training needs. Then, basing our projections on the respective responsibilities and range of duties of these five different posts and the corresponding structure of knowledge and abilities required of these five different types of cadres, we have worked out five different teaching curricula. In order to make these curricula more scientific and standardised, we have set up a committee for the direction of the teaching and training of the leading cadres in large and medium-sized enterprises. The primary concern of this committee is to review and examine the feasibility of the course offerings, the syllabus, the allocation of academic hours, and the examination and checking methods respectively contained in the five different teaching plans. These teaching plans will be able to provide guidance which will ensure that all the colleges and universities that undertake training will place uniform demands on the post/job-oriented training so that training standards can be guaranteed. Meanwhile, by taking into account the varying features of the various professions, the differences that exist in various places and the actual conditions that differ from one leading cadre to another, the teaching plans also allow for some measure of flexibility. Only by so doing, can the post/job-oriented training strictly conform to the requirements of standardisation.

The training contents are summed up to include the following four aspects:

(a) *Training in the basic theory of Marxism and the lines, guiding principles and policies of the Party*, which form the theoretical basis for improving the political quality of the leading cadres of enterprises. As the leading cadres in large and medium-sized enterprises they must have a deep understanding of Marxism. Only thus can they correctly understand and implement the guiding principles and policies of the Party, maintain the socialist orientation of the enterprises and lead the enterprises along the right track.

(b) *Training in modern management science*, which forms a major part of leading cadres training. The development of the socialist modernisation drive and the deepening of the present economic reform will place increasingly high demands on the managing quality of the leading cadres of enterprises. Among all the existing leading cadres, only a few have received a systematic education in management. Without sufficient knowledge of management, it is impossible to effectively manage a socialist modern enterprise and properly organise large-scale social production. Therefore, we must promptly help these executives to fill in the gaps in their education.

(c) *Emphasising of managerial skill and enhancing their abilities through training.* Since the five types of trainees are top leaders of enterprises, basic management concepts, and skills alone are far from enough for them to run their businesses, so efforts must be made to develop their leadership ability and the ability of operation and decision-making.

(d) *Training in related knowledge.* As leaders of large and medium-sized enterprises, they are supposed to have a wide range of knowledge which will enable them to cope with the complexities of the external environment and raise their ability to meet a contingency. Consequently, special lectures are incorporated in the teaching plans. Starting from the latter half of 1985, there have been more than 90 schools, including some cadres management institutes with relatively high teaching levels, regular colleges and universities and some Party schools subordinate to the provinces, which have undertaken the training tasks. Nearly 5,000 enterprise leading cadres have been involved in the post/job-oriented training. Since all of them possess a schooling above university or college education, the post/job-oriented training they have undergone is virtually a kind of continuing education after college. Moreover, the training is an important way to groom higher-level management personnel. The training courses are so favourably received by the leading cadres that the opinion is shared by all that the training is suitably directed, the teaching contents have proved applicable, and that the whole process fully represents the principle of 'Giving instructions according to needs'. The four-and-a-half-month training resulted in the following advantages: (i) Every one of them systematically studied and grasped the basic theory of Marxism; (ii) a strengthened awareness to stick to the Four Cardinal Principles and to implement the policy of reform, opening to the outside world and enlivening the economy; (iii) a better understanding of the Party's lines, guiding principles and policies in the new period; (iv) a comprehensive study of the basic theory and methods of management science which, in turn, leads to a better understanding of the importance of proper management and the realisation that without knowledge of modern management science, the modernisation of enterprise management would be impossible.

As far as many leading cadres are concerned, the training courses provided an aid in increasing their knowledge, broadening their horizon, adding to their work methods, seeking new approaches and bringing about a new prospect.

For example, an assistant director of the Yangzhou Wrist-Watch Plant applied what he had learned in the training course to market-forecast and analysis of consumer psychology. Based on the information that the sales of large-sized watches were stagnant while medium-sized ones were in great demand, and that there was a shortage of women's mini-watches, he promptly set out to adjust the product structure, made the decision to focus on the production of high-quality medium-sized and mini-watches with new designs and at competitive prices, and to seize the market in the rural areas and the remote border provinces and municipalities. This resulted in one million watches being turned out in 1986, a 25 per cent increase over the previous year. In one year alone, they succeeded in accumulating funds for the state which would be sufficient to build another plant of similar size.

To ensure the smooth implementation of the post/job-oriented training, corresponding policies and measures have been worked out, including:

(a) All leading cadres in large and medium-sized enterprises who have an educational level above vocational college must, during their tenure of office, receive post/job-oriented training and obtain the 'Post/job-oriented training certificate'. This will be deemed to be a necessary condition for reappointment as well as an essential basis on which appraisal, award and promotion will be built. The system of 'Training comes before coming into office' will be put into operation in the near future.

(b) To set up a committee for the direction of the teaching and training of the leading cadres in large and medium-sized enterprises, whose primary concern is to review and endorse training plans and syllabi and make assessment of the teaching standards.

(c) To conduct examinations of the credentials of the colleges and schools that are to undertake such training.

(d) To invite experts and professors with a high level of learning, teaching, and practical experience, from universities, colleges and research institutes, to compile 25 specific training textbooks adapted to the needs of post/job-oriented training.

(4) Placing stress on the training of the leading cadres so as to provide an impetus to cadres training in general

Over the years, we have always placed high priority on training of leading cadres, in conducting cadres' training, because they are the leaders and decision-makers of particular enterprises and departments. Their quality will have a direct bearing on the performance, success and survival of enterprises. If special attention is given to training these persons and continued effort is made to enhance their political as well as professional quality, this will play a decisive role in our efforts to stick to the Four Cardinal Principles and the policy of reform, opening to the outside world and enlivening the economy and in improving the operational management of the enterprises, raising economic benefits and ultimately accelerating the national economic development.

In these years, we have given high priority to enterprises in our work to train cadres. At the same time, attention shall be paid to training cadres in the economic administrative departments. Starting from 1979, in order to match the changes in the foundation of the administrative departments and to give more effective overall leadership to economic work, the central ministries and commissions in charge of industry, transport, commerce, finance and banking have made continued efforts to provide training to directors of the corresponding departments in various provinces and municipalities. The State Economic Commission is in charge of the training of directors and deputy directors of the local economic commissions at provincial, prefectural and municipal levels. They were rotated through training twice. Their training took the form of special courses and seminars combined with practical economic issues in their work. They also exchanged experience in how economic work was done in their respective regions and departments while taking training programmes.

It should be noted that the country's education still remains underdeveloped. Moreover, matters such as the development of education and the training of personnel have not received universal attention. In the light of the above situation, we took the lead in organising training courses for leading cadres and then urged them to go about the training of their subordinates in the same way as they went about economic work. Now that they had tasted the benefits of training, they would come to realise the strategic importance of education and be more determined to commit themselves to train their staff and managers. Furthermore, they would be more willing to invest in education and select qualified personnel to attend training courses. At the same time, by personally attending the training courses, they would exert a strong influence on the whole enterprise and provide an impetus to the training of the rank and file in the enterprise. As many facts have shown, where the leading cadres are involved in training, cadre training is effective and efficient. Paying continued attention to the training of the leading cadres in an attempt to increase their understanding of education will continue to be the key to the effectiveness of cadres' training.

(5) Sticking to reform in an attempt to develop a new model with Chinese characteristics for cadres' training

For a long time, the country's cadres' training was, to a considerable extent, under the influence of regular education, and used without discrimination the educational model of regular schools regarding teaching contents and teaching methods, and achieved less than great results. Ever since the restoration of cadres' training in 1979, its development has always been marked by painstaking probings and continued efforts at opening up new paths. Now it may well be said that an initial pattern of cadres' training has taken shape, with multi-types, multi-forms and multi-channels of education which match the requirements of training cadres at all levels and in all posts. With regard to the types of education, diploma education and the practice of updating and filling in the gaps in knowledge and post/job-oriented training are allowed to coexist and complement one another. As far as educational forms are concerned, short-term, on-the-job, in-service, and part-time training are given priority, while long-term, off-the-job training made available to only a small number of people selected on a planned basis comes as a supplement. As for educational channels, it is thought advisable to adopt the form of society running education which is characterised by a combination of dispersion and concentration in conducting training. Great effort should be made to develop radio broadcast education, television education and correspondence education while attention is paid to strengthening cadres and worker's schools. Modern teaching devices should be given full play. Attempts are encouraged to run training courses through concerted efforts by cadres' schools and regular schools, it is important to stick to the principle of 'Give instructions according to needs, study for the purpose of application and combine theory with practice'. It is equally important for training to be closely tied in with the economic development, enterprise management, the varying foundations of knowledge and different learning needs of cadres at all levels. Likewise, stress should be placed on having what is taught properly directed and its practical application as well as on developing the abilities of the trainees. In respect of teaching methods, it is important to break with the one-way communication approach and encourage elicitation and discussion methods. This educational form, tailored to the actual conditions of the country, is favourably received by the masses of cadres and has been proved by practice to be full of vitality.

(6) Stepping up the development of training bases and establishing a cadres' training system

Over the last eight years, in order to meet the needs for large-scale training, we have, while engaging in training work, made great efforts to develop training-bases. In 1979, when cadres' training was resumed in China, fixed training sites were not available in many regions and departments, training courses were conducted in borrowed places. At the same time, efforts were made to restore the number of cadres' schools. In 1983, after the State Council had endorsed the establishment of cadres' management institutes, ministries and commissions under the State Council in charge of industry, commerce, transport and finance, and the various provinces, municipalities and autonomous regions set up, one after another, a total of 93 economic management cadres' institutes, among which 48 institutes were run by the provinces and municipalities, and 45 institutes operated under the auspices of concerned ministries and commissions under the State Council. Furthermore, the State Economic Commission, in collaboration with concerned departments and some provinces and municipalities, established ten training centres. Now it is three or four years since most of these institutes and training centres came into being. They have come to be basically equipped for providing training in terms of teaching facilities, faculty, books and reference materials. A few years ago, these institutes and centres, then still under construction, managed to offer training courses. By now, they have turned out a total of more than one hundred thousand graduates, including 11,000 students of vocational college level.

Besides this various prefectures and municipalities, as well as departments directly under the provinces, have restored or newly founded more than 500 cadre-schools respectively related to industry, transport, finance and trade. More than 8,000 large and medium-sized enterprises have also set up cadre-schools of their own. Some medium-sized and small enterprises have joined forces in opening cadres or workers schools. All this has resulted in a three-level hierarchy of economic management cadres' training in juxtaposition to that of regular education.

(7) Fostering a teaching force, handling properly the compilation of teaching materials and making continued effort to improve training standards

Teachers and teaching materials constitute a primary condition for running schools and a key to ensuring training standards. Over the last eight years, the biggest problem we have encountered in developing economic cadres training is the shortage of qualified teachers and the lack of teaching materials. For a long time, we had to engage teachers from regular universities and colleges, as well as from industry, and adopt textbooks used in regular schools. Consequently, due to the lack of practical experience in enterprise management of the engaged teacher, and because of the outdated contents of the textbooks, the needs of in-service training were not fully met. To solve this problem, we never failed to take building of faculty and the compilation of teaching materials as the two major concerns of the training work and give them the greatest attention when we built cadre schools or institutes. Growing out of nothing and expanding gradually, an initial teaching force with a combination of full-time and part-time teachers has eventually emerged as the result of the few years' efforts. Moreover, the various regions and departments have organised manpower to compile a number of badly needed textbooks for cadres training. At present, there are more than 7,500 full-time and 2,000 part-time teachers in the above mentioned 93 economic management cadres' institutes: some of them come from regular universities and colleges, and many of them come from government economic departments or enterprises who have practical experience. In order to help the teachers raise their academic level and professional knowledge, we have asked some universities such as Qinghua University, the People's University, Fudan University, Xian Jiaotong University and Harbin Polytechnic University to lend us a helping hand. They have aided in conducting a great number of teachers' refresher courses and postgraduate courses for teachers of the cadres' management institutes and schools. Besides this, we have sent a number of young and middle-aged teachers abroad for advanced studies.

In the area of textbook compiling, we have (centring around the state unified examination of factory directors and the undergraduate courses offered to cadres) compiled some special textbooks to meet the needs of cadres' training, though they are still far from being perfect and have not yet formed a complete set. In addition to this, in cooperation with foreign countries, in running training programmes, we have compiled a set of textbooks, introducing Western management science, with more than one million copies published. On the whole, the problem of teachers and teaching materials still remains a weak link in cadres' training. Judging from the present conditions of teachers as a whole, several deficiencies seem apparent: (a) insufficiency in number; (b) inadequate teaching qualifications; (c) lack of specialised teachers; (d) irrational teachers' structure and a universal lack of academic leaders and key teachers in all cadres' training colleges and schools; and (e) the lack of practical management experience on the part of many teachers. In the area of textbooks and teaching materials, a systematic set of textbooks and teaching materials geared to the characteristics of adult education and meant for use by management trainees has yet to take shape. Therefore, taking an overall view, both teachers and teaching materials seriously fall short of the needs for the development of economic management cadre training.

(8) Conducting training through cooperative effort and systematically bringing in foreign management science

To meet the needs of the socialist modernisation drive and the open door policy, the State Economic Commission, starting from 1980, began to establish cooperative projects on management training, successively with the United States, Canada, Japan, the Federal Republic of Germany, and the EC. Apart from training management personnel, our purpose in cooperating with foreign countries is to introduce from abroad management science, managerial experience, and experience in management training. We have put forth a guiding principle to the effect: 'Take ourselves as the dominant factor, draw upon the experience from different quarters, blend the thoughts of different schools, refine them and create a style of our own'. By 'take ourselves as the dominant factor', we mean: The first thing to do is to attach great importance to, and sum up, our own experience of enterprise management. Then, proceeding from the actual conditions of China, study and examine the experience of other countries so as to achieve the aim of 'Make foreign things serve China'. 'Draw upon the experience coming from different quarters and blend the thoughts of different schools and refine them' can be construed as: It is necessary to collect widely, and get acquainted with, the experience, expertise and approaches of management of other countries, make a study of the theories of different management schools, select the essence, and incorporate the strong points of the different schools to serve our needs. 'Create a style of our own' means: Gradually develop a socialist economic management with Chinese characteristics by summing up our own experience and that of other countries.

The cooperative projects include a postgraduate programme leading to a master's degree in management, research courses for factory directors and enterprise managers, and seminars on special topics. Besides this, three special workshops involving senior leading cadres in government economic administrative departments have been run by one of the Centres. In all these programmes, the courses and curricula are jointly decided by Chinese teachers and their foreign partners through consultation. Within the first few years of the cooperation, the other side played a major role in teaching work while the Chinese side provided appropriate teaching personnel to assist the foreigners in carrying out their teaching responsibilities. Training materials were also provided by our partners. Teaching contents and methods were made to conform to the usual practice of the country with whom we cooperated. This approach has the advantage of enabling us to get an overall and systematic understanding of the characteristics that mark modern management science and management training in foreign countries. Over the last eight years, we have turned out, in cooperation with other countries, more than 250 master degree students in management, more than 3,000 plant directors, managers, and other economic management personnel. According to the reports of the trainees, the managerial expertise and experience of various countries have much for us to learn and use for reference. However, as management science is basically an applied subject, on no account can any country copy it from other countries without discrimination. It is necessary to combine it with the actual conditions at home. What is needed is a process of digestion and assimilation.

For foreign experience to be more effectively tied in with China's reality, the training task should shift to a new arrangement which allows the Chinese side to play the major role. Already, in some training courses, the greater part of the teaching work is undertaken by Chinese teachers. In their capacity as a 'window' to the outside world, these projects will continue to play their role in helping bring in advanced managerial experience from abroad.

C. DEVELOPMENT PROGRAMME OF ECONOMIC CADRES TRAINING FOR THE COMING EIGHT YEARS (FROM 1987 ONWARDS)

It was laid down at the 12th Party Congress that in order to achieve the objective of economic development before the end of the present century, it must be specified in the strategic plan that development should proceed by two steps. In the first ten years, the primary concern is to lay a sound foundation, accumulate strength and create necessary conditions. Science and education are regarded as the strategic focal points which will contribute to the achievements of the Party's overall objective. In the next ten years, the country is to enter upon a new period of economic takeoff. Success in turning out qualified economic management personnel itself will make an important foundation and preparation. During the latter three years of the Seventh Five-Year Plan and the whole of the Eighth Five-Year Plan period, prospective key leaders and thousands of young and middle-aged potential management personnel will be selected mainly from current cadres, to be properly trained up. This will constitute a strategic task of economic management cadres training for the coming eight years (. . . .)

The training of economic cadres for the coming period will pose an extremely challenging prospect. To ensure a smooth fulfillment of this objective, what matters most is to expand training capacity and improve training standards. To this end, it is necessary to adopt effective measures and formulate relevant policies.

(a) Strengthening leadership and adopting overall planning.
  Economic administrations at all levels should, in collaboration with the personnel and education departments, strive to give more effective leadership to economic cadres training. Proceeding from the actual conditions of the various regions and departments and in the light of the requirements of the economic development plans, it is necessary to work out appropriate training plans. Similarly, it is important to supervise and

check on the implementation of the plans and seek solutions to problems that may arise in the training process.

(b) It is necessary to further improve the system of economic cadres training and do a good job in the development of training schools and institutes. Cadre training institutes and schools at all levels should keep up the tradition of being thrifty and industrious in running schools, and take the initiative to make reconnaisance of the training needs in their own regions and departments. It is equally important to adopt a variety of forms to meet these training needs to the maximum extent. Furthermore, it is important to establish the concept of catering to, and serving, the enterprises and strengthen the horizontal connections with them and turn out high-quality management personnel needed by enterprises and economic administrations by actively engaging in reforming teaching contents as well as teaching methods, and by making continued efforts to improve training services.

(c) Great effort should be made to foster a teaching force and properly handle the compilation of teaching materials.

The development of cadres' training is determined by the development of teachers as a whole. We should do whatever we can to create a teaching force by 1990, which [is appropriate] in terms of [both] quality and quantity. The teachers in our cadres' institutes, besides teaching, should also be qualified to undertake scientific research, information services and consultation. This teaching force has as its mainstay full-time teachers but also includes part-time teachers. We should strengthen teachers' training and appraisal and encourage them to go deep into the realities of the enterprise's management, and make investigations. We should also make constant efforts to update their knowledge, enrich teaching contents and improve training services.

Besides this, we should organise manpower to compile a variety of teaching materials which will fit in with the training tasks and are marked by an integration of theory and practice, and which meets the needs for training different types of personnel. There should be an increased exchange of teaching materials between different schools. Sufficient attention should be given to the compilation and accumulation of teaching cases.

(d) It is necessary to stick to the principle of 'Learn what you need to do and make up what is missed' and integrate learning with application. We should do away with the practice of concerning oneself exclusively with seeking schooling and diplomas without caring about practical results. We should combine a cadre's academic achievements with his appraisal and appointment, and gradually establish the system of 'Training comes before going into office'.

Appendix 2 Regulations Concerning Academic Degrees in the People's Republic of China

Source: State Education Commission, Beijing (1986). (edited version).

GENERAL

Article 1

The Regulations are laid down to promote the growth of special talents in science, raise the academic level of various branches of learning and forward the development of education and science so as to meet the needs of socialist modernisation.

Article 2

All citizens who support the leadership of the Communist Party of China and the socialist system and who attain a certain academic level may apply for appropriate academic degrees in accordance with the requirements stipulated by the Regulations.

Article 3

Academic degrees are of three grades: the bachelor's degree, the master's degree and the doctor's degree.

Article 4

The bachelor's degree shall be conferred on graduates from institutions of higher learning who excel in their studies and attain the following level:

(1) a good command of basic theories, specialised knowledge, and basic skills in the branch of learning concerned;
(2) some ability to undertake scientific research or to engage in technical work.

Article 5

The master's degree shall be conferred on postgraduates from institutions of higher learning or scientific research institutes, or on those with equivalent qualifications who have passed written examinations in the prescribed courses and an oral examination on the thesis leading to the master's degree, and who attain the following academic level:

(1) a firm grasp of basic theories and systematic knowledge in the branch of learning concerned;
(2) an ability to undertake scientific research or to engage in independent technical work.

Article 6

The doctor's degree shall be conferred on postgraduates from institutions of higher learning or scientific research institutes, or on those with equivalent qualifications, who have passed written examinations in the prescribed courses and an oral examination on the dissertation leading to the doctor's degree, and who attain the following academic level:

(1) a firm and comprehensive grasp of basic theories and systematic, profound and specialised knowledge in the branch of learning concerned;
(2) an ability to undertake independent scientific research;
(3) an indication of ability for creative achievements in science or technology.

Article 7

Under the State Council, a Committee on Academic Degrees is established; its function is to supervise the conferring of academic degrees. The Committee on Academic Degrees is to have a chairman, a certain number of vice-chairmen and members. The chairman, vice-chairmen and members are appointed and removed by the State Council.

Article 8

The bachelor's degree shall be conferred by those institutions that have been authorised by the State Council. The master's and doctor's degrees shall be conferred by those institutions of higher learning or scientific research institutes that have been authorised by the State Council.

A list of institutions of higher learning and scientific research institutes authorised to confer academic degrees (abbreviated to 'academic degree conferring units' below) and a list of the branches of learning in which academic degrees of State Council, and shall be approved and promulgated by the State Council.

Article 9

An academic degree conferring unit shall set up an academic degree evaluation committee and form an oral examination board on the thesis leading to an academic degree in the branch of learning concerned.

The oral examination board shall include specialists from other units. Its members are to be selected and decided by the academic degree conferring unit. A list of the members of the academic degree evaluation committee is to be drawn up by the academic degree conferring unit and submitted for approval by the department in charge. The department in charge, in turn, shall submit the approved list to the Committee on Academic Degrees of the State Council, where it shall be kept on record.

Article 10

The oral examination board shall examine the thesis or dissertation leading to the master's or doctor's degree, conduct an oral examination and decide whether or not to confer the master's or doctor's degree. The decision is to be reached by secret ballot and requires a two-thirds majority of all the members. The decision is then to be submitted to the academic degree evaluation committee.

The academic degree evaluation committee shall examine and approve the list of candidates for the bachelor's degree. It shall decide whether or not to approve the list of candidates for the master's or doctor's degree submitted by the oral examination board. The decision, which is to be reached by secret ballot, shall require a simple majority of all the members. The list is to be submitted to, and kept on record by, the Committee on Academic Degrees of the State Council.

Article 11

After the decision to confer academic degrees has been reached by the academic degree evaluation committee, the academic degree conferring unit is to grant to the academic degree candidates certificates of their respective degrees.

Article 12

Upon the recommendation of their own units, postgraduates who have completed their course of study in other units than the academic degree conferring units may apply to an academic degree conferring unit in their vicinity for academic degrees. Upon approval after examination by the academic degree conferring unit, the applicants who have passed the oral examination and attain the academic level stipulated by the Regulations are to be granted the appropriate degrees.

Article 13

Those who have published important works, or who have made important inventions or discoveries, or who have contributed to the development of science and technology, may, upon the recommendation of specialists and upon the approval of an academic degree conferring unit, be exempt from written examinations and take directly the oral examination on the dissertation leading to the doctor's degree. The doctor's degree is to be conferred on those who have passed the oral examination.

Article 14

Outstanding scholars and noted public figures, both Chinese and alien, may, upon the nomination of an academic degree conferring unit and upon approval by the Committee on Academic Degrees of the State Council, be granted an honorary doctor's degree.

Article 15

Foreign students who are studying in China and foreign scholars who are engaged in research work in China may apply to an academic degree conferring unit for academic degrees. Those who attain the academic level stipulated by the Regulations may be granted the appropriate academic degrees.

Article 16

If a unit other than the academic degree conferring units or an academic body does not concur in the resolutions and decisions concerning the conferring of academic degrees of an academic degree conferring unit, it may make its views known to the academic degree conferring unit or to the Committee on Academic Degrees of the State Council. The academic degree conferring unit and the Committee on Academic Degrees of the State Council shall make a study of these views and deal with them accordingly.

Article 17

If any irregularities or fraudulent practices are found in flagrant violation of the stipulations of the Regulations, the academic degree conferring unit concerned may annul the academic degrees conferred, after the case has been reviewed by the academic degree evaluation committee.

Article 18

The State Council may suspend or revoke the right to confer academic degrees of approved units if it is definitely established that these units have been unable to maintain the proper level of the academic degrees conferred.

Article 19

The measures for the implementation of the Regulations are to be drafted by the Committee on Academic Degrees of the State Council and submitted to the State Council for approval.

Article 20

Approved for the implementation by the State Council on 20 May 1981.

ACADEMIC DEGREES

Article 1

These provisional measures are laid down according to the Regulations Concerning Academic Degrees in the People's Republic of China.

Article 2

Academic degrees are to be conferred in the following branches of learning: philosophy, economics, law, education, literature, history, the natural sciences, engineering, agriculture and medicine.

THE BACHELOR'S DEGREE

Article 3

The bachelor's degree shall be conferred by those institutions of higher learning which have been authorised by the State Council.

The bachelor's degree shall be conferred on those graduates from institutions of higher learning who have fulfilled all the requirements of the teaching programme and have been approved for graduation, provided that the results of the courses they have taken and the grade of their graduation thesis (or graduation design or other forms of graduation practice) clearly indicate that they have acquired a fairly good command of the basic theories, specialised knowledge and basic skills in the branch of learning concerned, and that they have shown an initial ability to undertake scientific research or to engage in technical work.

Article 4

Institutions of higher learning authorised to confer the bachelor's degree shall evaluate the results of each graduate's studies and examine his or her graduation appraisals through the various departments in charge. Students conforming to Article 3 of the present document and other related stipulations shall be recommended to the Academic Degree Evaluation Committee of their institution and their names shall be entered in the list of candidates for the bachelor's degree.

Undergraduates who have completed their courses of study in institutions other than the academic degree conferring ones and who have reached the required level for the bachelor's degree are to be recommended by their departments to their institution for approval, so that they may be recommended by their institution for the bachelor's degree to a nearby academic degree conferring institution of their own educational system and in their own district. The related department in the academic degree conferring institution shall examine the case of the recommended graduate from the non-academic degree conferring institution. In conformity with Article 3 of the present document and other related stipulations, the graduate shall then be recommended to the academic Degree Evaluation Committee of the academic degree conferring institution and be listed among the candidates for the bachelor's degree.

Article 5

The list of candidates for the bachelor's degree shall be examined and approved by the Academic Degree Evaluation Committee of the academic degree conferring institution and the bachelor's degree shall be conferred by that institution.

THE MASTER'S DEGREE

Article 6

The master's degree shall be conferred by those institutions of higher learning and scientific research institutes which have been authorised by the State Council.

Applicants for the master's degree shall submit their application, their thesis leading to the master's degree and other material to an academic degree conferring unit before the time limit prescribed by that unit. The same unit shall examine the applicant's case within two months of the deadline, make a decision of yes or no and notify the applicant and his unit of the result. Postgraduates from non-academic degree conferring units applying for the master's degree shall submit a letter of recommendation from their own unit to support the application.

Applicants with equivalent qualifications shall submit two letters of recommendation from associate professors, full professors or specialists with corresponding titles. The academic degree conferring unit may examine the applicant without a university graduate status on some university courses in an appropriate way before accepting his application.

Applicants should not submit applications to two academic degree conferring units at the same time.

Article 7

The courses to be examined on and the requirements to be fulfilled for the master's degree:

(1) *Marxist theory*. It is required to grasp the fundamental theories of Marxism.
(2) *Usually 3 to 4 courses on basic theories and specialised subjects*. It is required to have a firm grasp of basic theories and systematic specialised knowledge in the branch of learning concerned.
(3) *One foreign language*. It is required to have proficiency in reading reference materials in a foreign language.

The examinations for graduate students of non-academic degree conferring units on the required courses leading to the master's degree shall be arranged by academic degree conferring units. After studying the contents of the courses taken and the results achieved in the applicants' own units, the academic degree conferring units may exempt the applicants from part or all of the course examinations.

The examinations for applicants with equivalent qualifications on the required courses leading to the master's degree shall be arranged by academic degree conferring units.

Applicants for the master's degree must pass the examinations on the required courses before they can take the oral examination on the thesis leading to the master's degree. In case of failure in one course examination, a make-up examination may be conducted within half a year. Applicants who fail in a make-up course examination shall not be allowed to take the oral examination on the master's degree thesis.

Those academic degree conferring units which are trying out the credit system shall set the credits of the course leading to the master's degree according to the above-mentioned course requirements. Applicants for this degree shall not take the oral examination on the master's degree thesis until they have made the required number of credits.

Article 8

There should be some ideas about the subject studied in the thesis leading to the master's degree to show that the author of the thesis has an ability to undertake scientific research or to engage in independent technical work.

The academic degree conferring units should ask one or two specialists in the branch of learning concerned with the thesis to read and appraise the thesis. Then the specialists should make detailed academic comments on the thesis for the reference of the oral examination board.

The oral examination board on the thesis leading to master's degree shall include three to five members, among whom there should generally be specialists from other units. The chairman of the board should be an associate professor, a full professor or a specialist with a corresponding title.

The oral examination board shall decide, according to the results of the examination, whether or not to confer the master's degree. The decision shall be reached by secret ballot and shall require a two-thirds majority of all the members. The decision shall then be submitted to the Academic Degree Evaluation Committee after the chairman of the board has signed it.

An applicant who has failed in the oral examination on the thesis leading to the master's degree may, with the consent of the oral examination board, revise his or her thesis and take another oral examination within one year.

Article 9

If the majority of the board for the master's degree opine that the applicant's thesis has reached the academic level of the doctor's degree they, in addition to making a decision to confer the master's degree on the applicant, may make a proposal to a doctor's degree conferring unit which shall handle the case according to the related regulations concerning the doctor's degree in the present document.

THE DOCTOR'S DEGREE

Article 10

The doctor's degree shall be conferred by those institutions of higher learning or scientific research institutes which have been authorised by the State Council.

An applicant for the doctor's degree should submit his application, a dissertation leading to the doctor's degree and other material to academic degree conferring unit within the time limit set by that unit. The same unit should examine them within two months of the application deadline, decide whether or not to accept the application and notify the applicant and his unit of the result.

Applicants with equivalent qualifications should submit letters of recommendation from two professors or specialists with a corresponding title. In the case of applicants without the master's degree, an academic degree conferring unit may, before accepting their applications, arrange, in an appropriate way, examinations on some courses on basic theory and specialised knowledge leading to the master's degree.

Applicants should not submit applications to two academic degree conferring units at the same time.

Article 11

The courses to be examined on and the requirements to be fulfilled for the doctor's degree:

(1) *Marxist theory*. A better command of the basic theories of Marxism is required.

(2) *Basic theories and specialised knowledge.* A firm and comprehensive grasp of basic theories and systematic, profound and specialised knowledge in the branch of learning concerned is required. The range of examinations shall be decided by the Academic Degree Evaluation Committee of the academic degree conferring unit and the examinations on courses on basic theories and specialised knowledge shall be conducted by an examination committee made up of three specialists appointed by the Academic Degree Evaluation Committee [any member of the former] must be a professor, an associate professor or a specialist with a corresponding title.

(3) *Two foreign languages.* For the first foreign language, proficiency is required in reading reference materials in the specialised field concerned and some ability to write. For the second foreign language, an initial ability is required to read reference materials in the specialised field concerned. For applicants in certain fields or specialities, only the first foreign language is required with the approval of the Academic Degree Evaluation Committee of the academic degree conferring unit.

The examinations for graduate students working for the doctor's degree on the courses leading to that degree may be arranged according to the above-mentioned course requirements and their respective training programmes.

Article 12

Applicants for the doctor's degree must pass the examinations on the courses leading to that degree before they can take the oral examination on the dissertation leading to that degree.

Applicants for the doctor's degree who have published important works, made important inventions or discoveries in science and technology, or who have made important contributions to their development should submit their publications, appraisals or certificates of their inventions or discoveries to an academic degree conferring unit. Upon recommendation by two professors or specialists with a corresponding title, the unit may examine and approve these materials according to Article 11 of the present document and exempt the applications from part or all of the course examinations.

Article 13

The dissertation leading to the doctor's degree should indicate that its author has an ability to undertake independent scientific research and has made creative achievements in science or technology. The dissertation or its abstract should be sent to the related units three months before the oral examination on the dissertation takes place to be commented by colleagues working in the same field.

The academic degree conferring unit should engage two specialists in the branch of learning concerned with the dissertation to read and appraise the dissertation and one of them should be from another unit. These specialists should make detailed academic comments on the dissertation for the reference of the oral examination board on the dissertation leading to the doctor's degree.

Article 14

The oral examination board on the dissertation leading to the doctor's degree shall be made up of five to seven members, more than half of whom should be professors or specialists with a corresponding title. Two or three professors or specialists among the members on the board must be from other units. The chairman of the board should generally be a professor or a specialist with a corresponding title.

According to the result of the oral examination, the oral examination board shall decide whether or not to confer the doctor's degree. The decision shall be made by secret ballot and shall require a two-thirds majority of all the members for its adoption. The decision shall be signed by the chairman of the board and submitted to the Academic Degree Evaluation Committee. The minutes of the meeting should be kept.

Generally the oral examination should be conducted in public. The dissertation or its abstract, after it has been passed, should be published (classified specialities being excepted).

Article 15

When the oral examination board opines that the applicant's dissertation, though not attaining the academic level of the doctor's degree, has nevertheless reached that of the master's degree, the board may decide to confer the master's degree on the applicant, if the latter has not yet taken that degree in the subject concerned and may submit the decision to the Academic Degree Evaluation Committee.

THE HONORARY DOCTOR'S DEGREE

Article 16

The honorary doctor's degree shall be conferred by those units which have been authorised by the State Council to confer the doctor's degree.

Article 17

The conferring of an honorary doctor's degree must be discussed and approved by the Academic Degree Evaluation Committee of the academic degree conferring units, which submit the case to the Academic Degree Committee of the State Council for approval.

THE ACADEMIC DEGREE EVALUATION COMMITTEE

Article 18

The Academic Degree Evaluation Committee of an academic degree conferring unit assumes the following responsibilities within the scope of authority as prescribed by the State Council:

(1) To examine, pass and accept the list of applicants for the master's degree and the doctor's degree.
(2) To decide on the subjects of the course examinations and the number of courses to be examined on that will lead to the master's degree, to define the range of examinations on the courses on basic theories and specialised knowledge that will lead to the doctor's degree, and to examine and approve the list of names of the chief examiner and the members on the oral examination board on the thesis or dissertation.
(3) To approve the list of candidates for the bachelor's degree.
(4) To make decisions on the conferring of the master's degree.
(5) To examine and approve the list of applicants for the doctor's degree who apply for the exemption of part or all of the course examinations.
(6) To make decisions on the conferring of the doctor's degree.
(7) To approve the list of candidates for the honorary doctor's degree.
(8) To make decisions on cancellation of degrees conferred in violation of the regulation.
(9) To study and handle controversies on the conferring of academic degrees and other matters.

Article 19

The Academic Degree Evaluation Committee of an academic degree conferring unit shall include nine to twenty-five members, for a term of two to three years. The members should include the leading cadres of that unit as well as teaching and research personnel.

In a bachelor's degree conferring institution of higher learning, representatives of the teaching personnel on the Academic Degree Evaluation Committee should be chosen from among those above the lecturer's rank. In a unit conferring the bachelor's, master's and doctor's degrees, teachers and researchers sitting on the Academic Degree Evaluation Committee should be selected mainly from its own associate professors, professors or specialists with corresponding titles. In a doctor's degree conferring unit, there should be at least over half of the members on the Academic Degree Evaluation Committee who are professors or specialists with a corresponding title.

The chairman of the Academic Degree Evaluation Committee should be leading cadre of the unit who is a holder of a professorial or an associate professorial rank or has a corresponding title (e.g. the president of a university, the vice-president of a university in charge of teaching, scientific research and graduate studies or someone with corresponding titles in a scientific research institute).

The Academic Degree Evaluation Committee may set up subcommittees for different branches of learning. Each subcommittee shall be composed of seven to fifteen members and function for a term of two to three years. The chairman of a subcommittee must be a member of the Academic Degree Evaluation Committee. The function of the subcommittees is to assist in the work of the Academic Degree Evaluation Committee.

The list of the members of the Academic Degree Evaluation Committee should be submitted to the governmental department in charge for approval and this department, in turn, should submit the list to the State Council, where it shall be kept on record.

The Academic Degree Evaluation Committee may be provided, according to needs, with necessary assistants (full-time or part-time) to take care of the daily routine.

Article 20

The academic degree conferring unit should each year submit the number of winners of the bachelor's degree, the lists of winners of the master's degree and the doctor's degree respectively, and other related master's, to both the governmental department in charge and the Academic Degree Committee of the State Council, where they shall be kept on record.

OTHER STIPULATIONS

Article 21

Foreign students applying for the bachelor's degree in our country should be treated according to Article 3 of the present document and related regulations. Foreign students who are studying in China and foreign scholars who are teaching or engaged in research work in China should be treated according to the related regulations of the present document, if they should apply for the master's degree or the doctor's degree.

Article 22

The form of the certificate for the bachelor's degree shall be designed by the Ministry of Education. That for the master's degree and the doctor's degree respectively shall be designed by the Academic Degree Committee of the State Council. These academic degree certificates shall be issued by the academic degree conferring units.

Article 23

One copy of the approved thesis for the master's degree and of the dissertation for the doctor's degree should be kept in the library of the academic degree conferring unit; one copy of the approved dissertation for the doctor's degree should also be kept respectively in the National Library of China and other related specialised libraries.

Article 24

People at their posts applying for the master's degree or the doctor's degree, after being approved by the academic degree conferring unit to take the course examinations and the oral examination on the thesis or dissertation, may be granted a leave of not more than two months to prepare for the examinations.

Article 25

The academic degree conferring units may work out, according to the present document, detailed rules on conferring academic degree.

Appendix 3
China–EC Joint MBA Programme

Source: Chinese–European Community
Management Institute (CEMI) (1990).

COURSE STRUCTURE

The MBA programme by the end of the 1980s consists of 24 courses, each of which involves 36 hours of teaching (exclusive of time for project preparation, revision and examination). Four courses are taught in each eight-week module, and each course occupies two half-day sessions each week. An exception to this arrangement is the fifth week of the module. In that week there are no classes as students prepare and pilot, with faculty assistance, their project assignment inside an industrial enterprise.

English is used throughout the course. Students are selected partly for their linguistic aptitude. A special effort is to make sure that all teaching material presented to students, whether in a written or a verbal form, is expressed in simple and clear English.

The programme is structured in such a way that most classroom teaching takes place between 8.00 a.m. and 11.30 a.m., and that most afternoons are devoted to library work, project work or project team tutorials. The courses offered in the first year of the programme are shown in Table A3.1. The courses offered in the second year are shown in Table A3.2.

Students must attend each course in order to obtain an MBA degree. Detailed attainment and examination requirements are set out in the *MBA Students Handbook*.

The MBA course is project based. Students working in teams of four are expected to carry out series of projects within industrial enterprises over a period of two years.

In addition to the enterprise project students are assessed on the basis of their performance in examinations and/or assignments given in each of the courses.

A general guide to the weekly workload associated with each course is that, in addition to the six hours of classwork required for each course, students will have approximately ten hours of library work and some project-related course assignments – a total of approximately 16 hours of

Table A3.1   Outline of MBA programme – year 1

Pre-MBA Module (March–April)
- Commercial English
- The Effective Manager
- Introduction to Project Work Methods
- Introduction to Computing (including Wordprocessing and Lotus 123)
- Remedial Mathematics

First Module (May–June)
- Introductory Accounting and Finance
- Statistics
- Macroeconomics
- Organisational Behaviour

Enterprise Projects (July and August)

Second Module (September–October)
- Production and Operations Management
- Microeconomics
- Decision Sciences
- Management Accounting

Third Module (November–December)
- Marketing and Market Research
- Financial Management
- Management Information Systems
- Business Game and Simulation

Enterprise Projects relating to Modules 2 and 3 (January–April)

Table A3.2   Outline of MBA programme – year 2

Fourth Module – The Management Process (May–June)
- Human Resource Management
- Management Skills (communication, interviewing, conducting meetings, negotiation, managing teams, decision skills)
- Management of Organisational Change
- Management of Innovation

Consultancy Project Reports and Preparation of First Drafts of Company Case Studies (July–September)

Fifth Module – Key Areas of Policy (September–October)
- Strategic Management
- Operations Policy, Design and Work Organisation
- Industrial Marketing and Technology Transfer

Table A3.2   *continued*

- Forecasting and Information Analysis (including modelling and decision support systems)

Sixth Module – International Management (October–December)
- International Economics and Marketing (including economic geography)
- International Commercial and Contract Law
- International and Multinational Business Organisation
- External Relations in the International Environment

During the period September–December in the second year, students will be completing their company case studies

---

work a week per course, or 64 hours for all four courses taken together. This time estimate assures a very high proficiency in English and some students may find themselves working longer hours in the week.

PROJECT WORK

The enterprise projects are the backbone of the programme and are designed to provide the experience of applying classroom concepts and methods to the Chinese situation and, in the second year, to use this accumulated experience to conduct a consultancy project and to write a teaching case study.

The skills developed through project work include:

Descriptive skills: How does one describe something as complex as an enterprise in a way that helps one understand its inner workings?

Diagnostic skills: How does the description of an enterprise help one to assess its strengths and its weaknesses?

Prescriptive skills: How does one identify and implement a course of action that will improve the performance of an enterprise?

The enterprise projects are divided into three phases (see Figure A3.1):

- An audit phase in which the student will undertake a selective description and accompanying analysis of an enterprise or its environment, covering its marketing, finance, accounting, technology, and organisational activities. The audit will last ten months.
- A consultancy phase in which, in consultation with the management of the enterprise, a critical problem is selected for an in-depth examination and recommendations made for its solution. Enterprise managers and students will attempt to use the audit data and their newly acquired

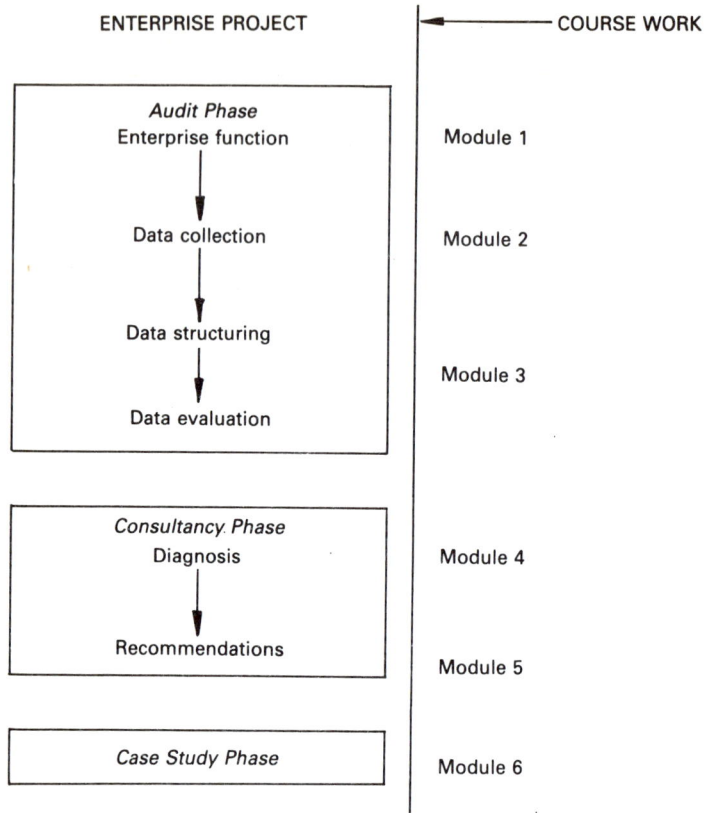

Figure A3.1   China–EC Joint MBA Programme: phases of the enterprise project.
Source: CEMI (1990).

management skills to identify a key problem of the enterprise upon which the student will present his recommendations to the enterprise managers and suggest ways of implementing them.

• A case study phase in which, using the data accumulated in the first two phases, each student working in collaboration with his/her team produces a teaching case study with a teaching note in which he or she demonstrates a both theoretical and practical grasp of the project experience. The case study will form part of the students' group work even though the contribution of individual students will be identified.

A report typed in English will be required from each project team at the end of each project. The report will be examined and graded by the Faculty and monitored by the Dean and Academic Council.

The enterprise project calls for three different types of involvement by the Faculty:

- Adaptation of course material, and in particular assignments, to project requirements. The more the students see a direct connection between their classroom work and their fieldwork, the better.
- Advice to project teams on an *ad hoc* basis wherever a Faculty member's specialist knowledge might be needed.
- Grading of projects.

EUROPEAN IN-COMPANY TRAINING

Following the completion of their MBA courses, students are sent to Europe for a six-month period of in-company training.

The purpose of this training period is twofold:

1. To give students a broad exposure to the European corporate environment.
2. To give students an opportunity to apply some of the management concepts they acquired in their courses in a European corporate context.

Each student is therefore asked to carry out a case study on some aspect of his host company's operations under the joint supervision of the Institute and a member of the firm.

Plans are being made to encourage Faculty members to act as mentors to MBA graduates during their internship with companies located within the Faculty's own countries.

STUDENT ASSESSMENT

To obtain an MBA degree, a grade minimum of 35 per cent must be obtained in every course.

Students obtain their degree by accumulating two types of credit. First, 20 course credits must be obtained. Course grades are awarded, following course examination on an individual basis. Students' classroom work is graded by individual professors and for each course that the student passes in, he will be awarded a credit. The minimum examination grade for obtaining a credit in a given course is 50 per cent, and the student is required to maintain a grade average of 60 per cent on all 24 courses in order to obtain the degree, as well as passing all 24 courses with no less than a grade of 35 per cent. There is no provision for re-sitting examinations where a mark of less than 35 per cent has been awarded.

Second, by obtaining 24 project credits out of 40 available. These are assigned in the following way:

- 20 of them are for project assignments given in the first four modules of the course. Five credits are available for each module and these are awarded to teams rather than individuals.

- 20 are for individual case studies carried out during modules 5 and 6, based on the project work that was carried out in the first four modules by an individual and his team. A minimum of 12 credit points must be obtained by an individual on his case study before they can count toward his total credit score. Case studies are graded by the relevant Faculty members and monitored by the Dean and Academic Council.

EXAMINATION GRADES

The minimum acceptable grade is 35 per cent for each course, the pass mark is 50 per cent and 80 per cent is considered to be excellent.

Appendix 4
China–EC Management Programme: MBA Students 1987–88

Source: CEMP (now CEMI) (1987).
(edited version).

Names	Sex	Birth	Graduated from	Unit (positions)
CHANG Bo	M	1961	North China University (Beijing) (1983)	Taiyuan Locomotive Factory, Shanxi Province (Engineer Assistant)
CHEN Dajun	M	1954	Beijing Forestry University (1982)	Beijing Forestry Cadre Management College (Teacher)
CHEN Dalong	M	1955	Beijing Finance and Trade University (1982)	Beijing Huaguang Industrial Co. (Senior Staff)
CHEN Huanming	M	1956	Shejiazhuang Railway Institute, Hebei Province (1982)	Shejiazhuang Railway Institute, Hebei Province (Teacher)
CHEN Xiaoguang	M	1961	Shenyang Metallurgical Machine College, Liaoning Province (1982)	Shenyang Cement Machinery Manufacturing Plant
FAN Jingming	M	1964	Beijing Commercial College (1984)	Beijing Second Foreign Language Institute (Teacher)
GAO Jun	F	1950	China People's University (1982)	Beijing Second Foreign Language Institute (Teacher)
GAO Qi	M	1959	Shenyang Polytechnic University, Liaoning Province (1981)	Shenyang Polytechnic University (Teacher)

197

Appendix 4 *continued*

Names	Sex	Birth	Graduated from	Unit (positions)
GAO Weijia	M	1958	Xi'an Junior College, Shaanxi Province (1983)	Xi'an Junior College (Assistant Junior)
GAO Yuan	F	1959	China University of Science and Technology (1983)	Northern Jiaotong University, Beijing (Teacher)
GU Chengyuan	M	1958	Qinghua University, Beijing (1982)	China Merchants Steam Navigation Group, Training Centre, Shekou SEZ (Trainer)
GU Yongzhong	M	1962	Wuxi Staff and Workers College, Jiangsu Province (1981)	Fourth Electric Capacity Factory, Wuxi (Officer)
GUO Hong	M	1961	Northern Jiaotong University, Beijing (1983)	Northern Jiaotong University (Lecturer)
GUO Jingtian	M	1952	Beijing Economics Institute (1983)	Beijing Economics Institute (Editor and Teacher)
GUO Yijun	M	1955	Luoyang University of Technology, Henan Province (1982)	Luoyang University of Technology (Teacher)
HENG Heng	M	1956	North Industrial University (Beijing) (1982)	Kunming Institute of Technology, Yunnan Province (Teacher)
HU Guozhang	M	1955	Worker College of Chongqing Special Steel Works, Sichuan Province (1982)	Worker College of Chongqing Special Steel Works (Teacher)
HU Xiaoshang	M	1960	Northern Jiaotong University, Beijing (1983)	Northern Jiaotong University (Teacher)
HU Zuoning	M	1958	Xiamen University, Fujian Province (1983)	Cadre College of the Ministry of Machinery and Equipment, Fujian Province (Teacher)

Appendix 4 *continued*

Names	Sex	Birth	Graduated from	Unit (positions)
JIA Xianfeng	M	1962	Beijing University of Iron and Steel Technology (1984)	Beijing University of Iron and Steel Technology (Teacher Assistant)
JIANG Bing	M	1953	The Secondary Branch School of Beijing Industrial College (1983)	The Northern Industrial University, Beijing (Teacher)
JING Jian	M	1957	Wuhan Industrial University, Hubei Province (1982)	State Bureau for Building Material Industry, Beijing (Researcher)
KAN Deyu	M	1955	Shenyang Industrial University, Liaoning Province (1982)	Beijing Precision Machine Tool Maintenance Centre (Responsible for quality control)
LEI Lei	F	1955	Shaanxi Mechanical Engineering Institute (1982)	Shaanxi Mechanical Engineering Institute (Teacher)
LI Fanyuan	F	1960	Northwest Electronic Communication Polytechnic, Xi'an, Shaanxi Province (1983)	Shenzhen City, Shekou Industrial Party Commission (Secretary)
LI Guanghui	M	1962	Shanghai Jiaotong University (1982)	Guangzhou Shipyard (Vice-Director of a workshop)
LI Jiansheng	M	1951	Beijing Airplane Engineering Institute (1982)	Beijing First Light Industry Bureau (Clerk)
LI Yongling	M	1963	Beijing Civil Engineering College (1984)	Beijing Second Foreign Language Institute (Teacher)
LI Zhao	M	1960	Liaoning University, Liaoning Province (1983)	Shenyang Economic Cadre College, Liaoning Province (Teacher)
LIANG Mingying	F	1963	Beijing College of Economics (1984)	Beijing Second Foreign Language Institute (Teacher)

Appendix 4 *continued*

Names	Sex	Birth	Graduated from	Unit (positions)
LIAO Xinchun	M	1959	Changsha Traffic Institute, Hunan Province (1982)	Hengyang Industrial Institute, Hunan Province (Teacher)
LIN Jianping	M	1962	Nanjing Institute of Technology, Jiangsu Province (1983)	Wuxi Television Factory, Jiangsu Province (Technician)
LIN Wei	M	1958	Hunan University (1982)	Guangdong Provincial Cadre Institute of Economic and Management (Teacher)
LIU Hong	F	1962	The Provincial Architectural Engineering College of Guangdong (1982)	The Municipal Economic Administration Cadre College of Guangzhou, Guangdong Province
LIU Jie	M	1953	Beijing Labour Spare Time University (1985)	Beijing Power Institute (Office staff)
LIU Ximing	M	1958	Jilin Industry University, Jilin Province (1982)	Shaanxi Mechanical Institute (Teacher)
LIU Yuejin	M	1958	Nanjing Communication Institute, Jiangsu Province (1982)	Chengde Telecommunications Bureau, Hebei Province (Engineer)
LIU Zhiyao	M	1959	Xi'an Junior College, Shaanxi Province (1983)	Shaanxi Highway Transportation School, Shaanxi Province (Teacher Assistant)
LONG Long	M	1958	Northeast China University of Technology, Shenyang, Liaoning Province (1983)	North China University of Technology (Teacher)
LUO Xiaofeng	M	1955	Beijing University of Iron and Steel Technology (1982)	Beijing University of Iron and Steel Technology (Librarian)
MA Zhifang	M	1951	Television University, Beijing (1982)	Metallurgical Management College (Teacher)
NIE Axin	M	1955	Lanzhou Railway College, Gansu	The Car and Locomotive Co., Tanshan, Hubei

Appendix 4 *continued*

Names	Sex	Birth	Graduated from	Unit (positions)
			Province (1982)	Province (Production Manager)
PENG Xiaoguang	F	1960	Beijing University (1984)	State Economic Commission (Teacher Assistant)
QIN Yuanjin	M	1959	Wuhan Institute of Technology, Hubei Province (1982)	Wuhan Institute of Technology, Hubei Province (Instructor)
SHEN Guofeng	M	1959	Taiyuan Machinery Institute, Shanxi Province (1982)	Liaoning Ship Breaking and Steel Rolling Company, Liaoning Province (Assistant Manager)
SU Xinghua	M	1956	Beijing Finance and Trade College (1983)	Beijing Tourist Company (Businessman)
TANG Xudong	M	1963	Hubei Industrial College in Wuhan, Hubei Province (1982)	Chongqing Paper Mill, Sichuan Province (Engineer)
TIAN Ming	M	1957	Zhenjing Shipbuilding Institute, Jiangsu Province (1982)	Shanghai Hongdong Shipyard (Engineer)
WANG Shiyan	M	1951	Beijing Industrial University (1978)	Beijing Valve Factory, Since one week before MBA Programme: Beijing Economic Commission
WANG Tingru	M	1956	Northeast Heavy Machine Building College, Heilongjiang Province (1982)	Beijing Institute of Management Engineering (Teacher)
WANG Xiaodong	M	1961	Shandong University, Shandong Province (1982)	China Merchants Shekou Indust. Zone, Telecom. Co. Guangdong Province (Project Manager)
XIA Ze	F	1956	Jilin Polytechnic University, Jilin Province (1986)	Beijing Machinery Industry Management Institute (Assistant)
XU Dian	M	1955	Beijing Post and Telecommunications Institute (1983)	The Space Industry Ministry (Officer)
YANG Sen	M	1956	North Jiaotong University, Beijing	The Planning and Statistics Bureau of Railway Ministry

Appendix 4 *continued*

Names	Sex	Birth	Graduated from	Unit (positions)
			(1982)	(Engineer)
YANG Weiping	M	1960	The Institute of International Relations (1984)	China Petrochemical Corporation, SINOPEC Int. (Marketing Manager)
YANG Yongtai	M	1963	North West Teacher's College, Lanzhou, Gansu Province (1983)	Gansu Province Economic Commission (Cadre)
YIN Xueming	M	1961	Shanghai Jiaotong University (1982)	Guangzhou Shipyard, Guangzhou Province (Manager)
YU Tian	M	1959	Shanghai Worker's College (1984)	Pengpu Machine Building Plant, Shanghai (Engineer)
ZENG Yixin	M	1960	Tianjin Northern Ocean University (1983)	Guangzhou Shipyard, Guangzhou Province (Supervisor)
ZHANG Falin	M	1952	Southwest Petroleum College, Sichuan Province (1977)	Planning Department of Bohai Oil Corporation, Tianjin (Project Evaluator)
ZHANG Fengkai	F	1954	Beijing Polytechnic University (1982)	Beijing Public Transportation Institute (Engineer)
ZHANG Jiwen	M	1951	Shanghai Television University (1982)	Shanghai Number Two Radio Factory (Personnel Manager)
ZHANG Keping	M	1950	Beijing University (1982)	Northern Jiaotong University, Beijing (Teacher)
ZHANG Yuan	M	1956	Harbin Shipbuilding Institute, Heilongjiang Province (1982)	Guangzhou Shipyard, Guangdong Province (Engineer Assistant)
ZHI Hong	M	1961	Beijing People's University of China (1983)	Northern Jiaotong University of China, Beijing (Lecturer)
ZHOU Hongjun	M	1960	Jilin Industry University, Jilin Province (1982)	Wuhan Technology Institute, Hubei Province (Teacher)

References

Bain, G., 'Heads for business', *Times Higher Educational Supplement*, 12 January 1990, p. 10.

Boisot, M., 'Industrial feudalism and enterprise reform – could the Chinese use some more bureaucracy?', in Warner, M. (ed.), *Management Reforms in China* (London: Pinter, 1987), pp. 232–3.

Boltanski, L., *The Making of a Class: Cadres in French Society* (Cambridge: CUP, 1987).

CEDEFOP, *Vocational Training in the PRC*, (Berlin, 1987), 119 pp.

CEMA, *Chinese Enterprise Management Association* (Beijing, 1983) 24pp.

Chan, L. and Guan, Z., 'Management education in the PRC: with special reference to recent support programs by foreign countries', *Management Education and Development*, Vol. 17, No. 3, 1986, pp. 181–90.

Chandler, A. D., *The Visible Hand* (Cambridge, Mass.: Harvard University Press, 1977).

Chen, D., 'Chinese models of economic development and their implications for management training', *China Information*, Vol. 3, No. 2, Autumn 1988, pp. 38–50.

Child, J. and Xu, X., *The Communist Party's Role in the Enterprise Leadership at the High-Water of China's Economic Reform*, Working Paper mimeo (Beijing: China–EC Management Institute (CEMI), 1989), 50pp.

China Quarterly, Special Issue: 'The readjustment in the Chinese economy', No. 100, 1984.

Confucius, *The Analects* (trans. D. C. Lau) (Harmondsworth: Penguin, 1979).

Constable, J., 'Managing the USSR', *Management Today*, September 1984, pp. 78–82.

Cornwall-Jones, A. T., *Education for Leadership: The International Administrative Staff College, 1948–1984* (London: Routledge and Kegan Paul, 1985).

Crawford, S., *Technical Workers in Advanced Society: The Work, Careers and Politics of French Engineers* (Cambridge: CUP, 1989).

Davis, D., 'Unequal changes, unequal outcomes: pension reform and urban inequality, *China Quarterly*, No. 114, 1988, pp. 223–42.

Doeringer, P. B., 'Occupational education and training for the 1980s', in Doeringer, P. B. and Vermeulen, B. (eds), *Jobs and Training in the 1980s* (Boston: Nijhoff, 1981), pp. 1–8.

Dore, R. P., *British Factory – Japanese Factory* (London: Allen & Unwin, 1973).

Dore, R. P. and Sako, M., *How the Japanese Learn to Work* (London: Routledge, 1989).

Easterby-Smith, M., *Evaluation of Management Education Training and Development* (Aldershot: Gower, 1986).

The Economist, 'Special Survey of China's Economy: A World Turned Upside Down', 1 August 1987, 22pp.

Fairbank, J. K., 'Why China's rulers fear democracy', *New York Review of Books*, Vol. 36, No. 24, 1989, pp. 32–3.

Gittings, J., *China Changes Face: The Road from Revolution 1949–1989* (Oxford: OUP, 1989).

Gow, I., 'Japan', in Handy, C., Gordon, C., Gow, I. and Randlesome, C., *Making Managers* (London: Pitman, 1988), pp. 16–50.

Granick, D., *The Red Executive: A Study of the Organisation Man in Russian Industry* (New York: Doubleday, 1961).

Griffiths, B. and Murray, H., *Whose Business?* (London: Institute of Economic Affairs, 1985).

Harris, R. G., 'The values of economic theory in manpower education', *American Economic Review*, Vol. 74, No. 2, 1984, pp. 122–6.

Hayhoe, R., *China's Universities and the Open Door* (London: M. E. Sharpe, 1989).

Henley, J. S., 'The managerial environment', in Child, J. and Lockett, M. (eds), *Advances in Chinese Industrial Studies, Vol. 1, Part A: Reform Policy and the Chinese Enterprise* (Greenwich, Conn.: JAI Press, 1990), pp. 3–20.

Henley, J. S. and Nyaw, M. K., 'Introducing market forces into managerial decision making in Chinese industrial enterprises', *Journal of Management Studies*, Vol. 23, No. 6, 1986, pp. 635–56.

Henley, J. S. and Nyaw, M. K., 'The system of management and performance of joint ventures in China', in Child, J. and Lockett, M. (eds), *Advances in Chinese Industrial Studies, Vol. 1, Part A: Reform Policy and the Chinese Enterprise* (Greenwich, Conn.: JAI Press, 1990), pp. 277–94.

Hobsbawm, E. J., *Industry and Empire* (Harmondsworth: Penguin, 1969).

Jin, L., 'China's economic challenge: recentralisation or a free market', *Britain–China*, Newsletter of the Great Britain–China Centre, No. 41, Summer 1989, pp. 17–20.

Karsh, B., 'Human resources management in Japanese large-scale industry', *Journal of Industrial relations*, Vol. 26, June 1984, pp. 226–45.

Khanna, A., *Issues in the Technological Development of China's Electronics Sector*, World Bank Staff Working Paper No. 762 (Washington DC: The World Bank, 1986).

Kueh, Y. Y., 'The Maoist legacy and China's new industrialisation strategy', *China Quarterly*, No. 119, 1989, pp. 420–47.

Laaksonen, O., *Management in China During and After Mao* (Berlin: De Gruyter, 1988).

Lane, C., *Management and Labour in Europe* (London: Edward Elgar, 1989).

Lee, P., 'Enterprise autonomy policy in post-Mao China: a case study of policy-making, 1978–1983', *China Quarterly*, No. 105, 1986, pp. 59 ff.

Lee, P., *Industrial Management and Economic Reform in China 1949–1984* (Oxford: OUP, 1988).

Levine, S. B. and Kawada, H., *Human Resources in Japanese Industrial Development* (Princeton, NJ: Princeton University Press, 1980).

Lindsay, C. P. and Dempster, B. L., 'Ten painfully learned lessons about working in China: the insights of two American behavioural scientists', *Journal of Applied Behavioural Science*, Vol. 19, No. 3, 1983, pp. 265–76.

Locke, R., *The End of the Practical Man: Entrepreneurship and Higher Education in Germany, France and Great Britain, 1880–1940* (Greenwich, Conn.: JAI Press, 1984).

Locke, R., *Management and Higher Education Since 1940: The Influence of America and Japan on West Germany, Great Britain and France* (Cambridge: CUP, 1989).

Lockett, M., 'China's Special Economic Zones: the cultural and managerial challenges', *Journal of General Management*, Vol. 12, No. 2, 1987, pp. 21–31.

Lockett, M., 'Culture and the problems of Chinese management', *Organization Studies*, Vol. 9, No. 4, 1988, pp. 475–96.

Lockett, M., 'The urban economy', in Benewick, R. and Wingrove, P., *Reforming the Revolution: China in Transition* (London: Macmillan, 1988), pp. 108–26.

Ma, H., *New Strategy for China's Economy* (Beijing: New Worl Press, 1983).

McCormick, K. J., 'Professionalism and work organization', *Sociology*, Vol. 19, No. 2, 1985, pp. 284–94.

McCormick, R., 'The Radio and Television Universities and the development of higher education in China', *China Quarterly*, No. 105, 1986, pp. 72–94.

McMillan, C. J., *The Japanese Industrial System* (Berlin: De Gruyter, 1984).

Marceau, J., *A Family Business? The Making of an International Business Elite* (Cambridge: CUP, 1989).

Maurice, M., Sorge, A. and Warner, M., 'Societal differences in organising manufacturing units: a comparison of France, West Germany and Great Britain', *Organization Studies*, Vol. 1, No. 1, 1980, pp. 1–21.

Mintzberg, H., *Mintzberg on Management: Inside Our Strange World of Organizations* (New York: Free Press, 1989).

NEDO/MSC, *Competence and Competition* (London: National Economic Development Office and Manpower Services Commission, 1984).

Orleans, L. A., 'Graduates of Chinese universities: adjusting the total', *China Quarterly*, No. 111, September 1987, pp. 444–9.

Pan, C. L., 'Management thought in Ancient China' (Beijing: Unpublished ms, 1988)

Parkinson, G., 'Skills at a premium in China', *Times Higher Education Supplement*, 4 December 1987, p. 7.

Perkins, D. H., 'Reforming China's economic system', *Journal of Economic Literature*, Vol. 26, No. 2, June 1988, pp. 601–45.

Pollard, S., *The Genesis of Modern Management* (Harmondsworth: Penguin, 1965).

Porter, M. E., *The Competitive Advantage of Nations* (London: MacMillan, 1990).

Prybyla, J. S., 'Economic reform of socialism: the Dengist course in China', in Prybyla, J. S. (ed.), *Special Issue on Privatising and Marketising Socialism: The Annals of the American Academy of Political and Social Science*, Vol. 507, January 1990, pp. 113–22.

Qiu, X. Y., Yu, K. C. and Xu, C. M., 'An evolutionary account of management and the role of management development in China', in Davies, J., Easterby-Smith, M., Mann, S. and Tanton, M. (eds), *The Challenge to Western Management Development: International Alternatives* (London: Routledge, 1989).

Qinghua University, *Qinghua University Catalogue* (Beijing, 1986–1987), p. 3.

Redding, G. and Wong, Y. Y., 'The psychology of Chinese organizational behaviour', in Bond, M. H. (ed.), *The Psychology of the Chinese People* (Hong Kong and Oxford: OUP, 1986), pp. 267–95.

Riskin, C., *China's Political Economy: The Quest for Development Since 1949* (Oxford: OUP, 1987).

Rose, H. B., *Management Education in the 1970s* (London: HMSO, 1970).

St John Hunter, C. and McKee Keehn, M. (eds), *Adult Education in China* (Beckenham: Croom Helm, 1985).

Schram, S., 'China after the 13th Congress', *China Quarterly*, No. 114, 1988, pp. 177–97.

Shenkar, O. and Chow, I. H. S., 'From political praise to stock options: reforming compensation systems in the PRC', *Human Resource Management*, Vol. 28, 1989, No. 1, pp. 65–85.

Simon, D. F., 'Managing technology in China: is the development and application of computers the answer?', in Warner, M. (ed.), *Management Reforms in China* (London: Pinter, 1987), pp. 198–216.

Sorge, A., *The Management Tradition: A Continental View*, in Fores, M. and Glover, I. (eds), *Manufacturing and Management* (London: HMSO, 1978), 87–104.

Sorge, A. and Warner, M., *Comparative Factory Organization* (Aldershot: Gower, 1986).

Spence, J., *To Change China: Western Advisors in China, 1620–1960* (Harmondsworth: Penguin, 1980).

State Economic Commission, Higher Education Bureau, *Courses and Disciplines Related to Management in Chinese Universities and Institutes*, Paper for International Seminar on Management Education, Beijing, October 1987, p. 12.

State Education Commission, Department of Higher Education, *Courses and Disciplines Related to Management in Chinese Universities and Institutes*, mimeo, Beijing, October 1987, p. 11.

Statistical Outline of China (*Zhongguo tongji zhaiyao* Beijing: Zhongguo tongji chubanshe, various editions).

SWB (*Summary of World Broadcasts*) (London: British Broadcasting Corporation, various – see text).

Tanton, M. and Easterby-Smith, M., 'Is the Western view inevitable? A model of the development of management education', in Davies, J., Easterby-Smith, M., Mann, S. and Tanton, M. (eds), *The Challenge to Western Management Development* (London: Routledge, 1986), pp. 11–28.

Terrill, R., 'Sichuan: China changes course', *National Geographical Magazine*, Vol. 168, No. 3, 1985, pp. 280–317.

Tesar, G. and Suzuki, N., 'Management training programmes in Japan', *The Business Graduate*, January 1984, pp. 23–4.

Thomas, T., 'High degrees a passport to more lucrative careers', *The European*, 8–10 June 1990, p. 21.

Tidrick, G., and Chen, J., (eds), *China's Industrial Reform* (Oxford: OUP and World Bank, 1987).

Vermeer, E. B., 'Chinese management training programmes', *China Information*, Vol. 3, No. 2, Autumn 1988, pp. 51–62.

Walder, A. G., *Communist Neo-Traditionalism: Work and Authority in Chinese Industry* (Berkeley: University of California Press, 1986).

Walder, A. G., 'Factory and manager in an era of reform', *China Quarterly*, No. 118, June 1989, pp. 242–64.

Wallace, J., 'The promotion of effective management development' in Davies, J., Easterby-Smith, M., Mann, S. and Tanton, M. (eds), *The Challenge to Western Management Development* (London: Routledge, 1986), pp. 167–89.

Warner, M., *Organizations and Experiments: Designing New Ways of Managing Work* (Chichester: Wiley, 1984).

Warner, M., 'The long march of Chinese management education', *China Quarterly*, No. 106, 1986a, pp. 362–42.

Warner, M., 'Managing human resources in China', *Organization Studies*, Vol. 7, No. 4, 1986b, pp. 353–66.

Warner, M., 'Training China's managers', *Journal of General Management*, Vol. 11, No. 2, 1986c, pp. 12–26.

Warner, M., 'Human resources implications of new technology', *Human Systems Management*, Vol. 6, No. 4, 1986d, pp. 279–88.

Warner, M. (ed), *Management Reforms in China* (London: Pinter, 1987a).

Warner M., 'Industrialisation, management education and training systems: a comparative analysis', *Journal of Management Studies*, vol. 24, No. 1, 1987b, pp. 91–111.

Warner, M., 'Industrial relations in the Chinese factory', *Journal of Industrial Relations*, Vol. 23, No. 2, 1987c, 217–32.

Warner, M., 'Microelectronics and manpower in China', *New Technology, Work and Employment*, Vol. 4, No. 1, 1989, pp. 20–8.

Warner, M. 'Developing key human resources in China', *International Journal of Human Resource Management*, Vol. 1, No. 1, June 1990, pp. 87–106.

White, G., 'The politics of economic reform in Chinese industry: the introduction of the labour contract system', *China Quarterly*, No. 111, September 1987, pp. 365–89.

Whitley, R., Thomas, A. and Marceau, J., *Masters of Business? Business Schools and Graduates in Britain and France* (London: Tavistock, 1981).

Whyte, M. K., 'Bureaucracy and modernization in China: the Maoist critique', *American Sociological Review*, Vol. 38, No. 2, 1973, pp. 149–63.

World Bank, *China: Issues and Prospects in Education* (Washington DC: World Bank, 1985).

Xinhua News Agency – see *SWB*.

Yue, H., 'How to hire and dismiss employees', *Beijing Review*, Vol. 30, No. 41, 12 October 1987, pp. 24–5.

Zhao, Z., 'Report to the Party Congresses', *Beijing Review*, Vol. 30, No. 45, 9–15 November 1987, pp. vii–viii.

Index